Rome of the XII Tables

Rome of the XII Tables

Persons and Property

By Alan Watson

Princeton University Press, New Jersey

Library of Congress Cataloging in Publication Data will
be found on the last printed page of this book

Publication has been supported by a grant from
The Andrew W. Mellon Foundation

This book has been in composed in Linotype Janson

Printed in the United States of America
by Princeton University Press, Princeton, New Jersey

For the Virginia Law School

Contents

vii

Contents

Preface

This book is concerned with those legal topics of greatest importance in early social life; persons, succession, and property. Within its limits of time and place—the mid-fifth century B.C. at Rome—and subject matter, it attempts to be comprehensive. The aim is to explain the meaning of the relevant clauses of the XII Tables, to show which subjects were not dealt with in that code and yet elucidate the law. In the process the extent to which provisions of the XII Tables have been lost to us should become clearer. To achieve this stated aim it is necessary to learn as much as possible about the archaeological evidence for early Rome, about early religion and the historical tradition. This I have tried to do, yet in this volume these subjects are kept in the background. The XII Tables are fundamental for our knowledge of early Rome and its society, and, as a matter of method, it seems preferable for a lawyer to start by deciding which interpretation best fits the evidence for legal rules, then checking to ensure that this is in harmony with other evidence. The converse method of starting with the archaeological, religious, and historical evidence and interpreting the legal rules in accordance with it carries the danger of blunting one's perception of what the legal texts actually say. Throughout this book I have tried to base my arguments firmly on existing positive evidence rather than frame hypothetical constructs.

My list of debts for personal help is long. Mr. John A. Crook, Dr. Alan Rodger, Professor F. Wieacker, and Professor Reuven Yaron all read the typescript at one stage or another, and with the first two named I had the opportunity of prolonged discussion of difficulties. Professor H. H. Scullard dealt with a long list of archaeological questions and Professor Robert M. Ogilvie gave me much needed help with historical problems. Professor Giuliano Crifò accompanied me to sites in Tarquinia, Cerveteri, Rome and nearby, imparted his own knowledge, and introduced me to archaeologists and historians. Many other scholars, too many to mention here, gave help with individual points. Drafts of particular sections of the book formed the subject matter of lectures or seminars given at the Universities of Leiden, Amsterdam, Rotterdam, and Freiburg-im-Breisgau between 1971 and 1974; I learned much from the searching questions and criticisms of participants. The award of a generous research grant by the Leverhulme Trust enabled me to work in libraries in Europe and conveniently meet continental scholars, and to examine Roman and Etruscan sites on the ground. Finally, I should add that, as in the past, Mrs. Mary Schofield coped admirably with a very untidy manuscript. To all I am grateful.

ALAN WATSON

Edinburgh.
August 1974.

Abbreviations

Bruns	C. G. Bruns, *Fontes Iuris Romani*, 7th ed. by O. Gradenwitz (Tübingen, I.C.B. Mohr, 1909)
Buckland, *Textbook*	W. W. Buckland, *A Textbook of Roman Law*, 3rd ed. revised by P. Stein (Cambridge, Cambridge University Press, 1963)
Corbett, *Marriage*	P. E. Corbett, *The Roman Law of Marriage* (Oxford, Clarendon Press, 1930)
Diósdi, *Ownership*	D. Diósdi, *Ownership in Ancient and Preclassical Roman Law* (Budapest, Akadémiai Kiadó, 1970)
Ernout & Meillet, *Dictionnaire*	A. Ernout & A. Meillet, *Dictionnaire étymologique de la langue latine*, 4th ed. (Paris, C. Klincksieck, 1956-60)
FIRA I	*Fontes Iuris Romani Antejustiniani*, vol. 1, 2nd ed. (Florence G. Barbèra, 1941)
Gjerstad, *Early Rome* 4, 5, 6	E. Gjerstad, *Early Rome*, vol. 4, part ii: *Synthesis of Archeological Evidence* (Skrifter Utgima av Svenska Institutet i Rom, Lund, 1966); vol. 5: *The Written Sources* (Lund, 1973); vol. 6: *Historical Survey* (Lund, 1973)
Jolowicz-Nicholas, *Introduction*	H. F. Jolowicz and B. Nicholas, *Historical Introduction to the Study of Roman Law*, 3rd ed. (Cambridge, Cambridge University Press, 1973)

Abbreviations

JRS	*Journal of Roman Studies*
Kaser	M. Kaser
Eigentum	*Eigentum und Besitz im älteren römischen Recht*, 2nd ed. (Cologne, Graz, H. Böhlau, 1956)
Ius	*Das altrömische Ius* (Göttingen, Vandenhoek & Ruprecht, 1949)
RPR 1	*Das römische Privatrecht*, vol. 1, 2nd ed. (Munich, C. H. Beck, 1971)
ZPR	*Das römische Zivilprozessrecht* (Munich, C. H. Beck, 1966)
Marquardt, *Privatleben* 1	J. Marquardt, *Das Privatleben der Römer*, vol. 1 (Leipzig, S. Hirzel, 1886)
Mommsen, *Staatsrecht* 1, 2, 3	T. Mommsen, *Romisches Staatsrecht*, vols. 1 and 2, 3rd ed. (Leipzig, S. Hirzel, 1887); vol. 3, 1st ed. (Leipzig, S. Hirzel, 1888)
Ogilvie, *Commentary*	R. M. Ogilvie, *A Commentary on Livy, Books 1-5* (Oxford, Clarendon Press, 1965)
RE	*Paulys Real-Encyclopadie der klassischen Altertumswissenschaft*, rev. G. Wissowa et al. (Stuttgart, J. B. Metzler, 1873—)
RHD	*Revue historique de droit français et étranger*
RIDA	*Revue internationale des droits de l'antiquité*
RISG	*Rivista italiana per le scienze giuridiche*
TLL	*Thesaurus Linguae Latinae* (Leipzig, Teubner, 1900—)
T.v.R.	*Tijdschrift voor Rechtsgeschiedenis*
Watson	A. Watson
Law Making	*Law Making in the Later Roman Republic* (Oxford, Clarendon Press, 1974)

"Leges Regiae"	"Roman Private Law and the *'Leges Regiae*,'" *JRS* 42 (1972), 100ff
Obligations	*The Law of Obligations in the Later Roman Republic* (Oxford, Clarendon Press, 1965)
Persons	*The Law of Persons in the Later Roman Republic* (Oxford, Clarendon Press, 1967)
Private Law	*Roman Private Law around 200 B.C.* (Edinburgh, Edinburgh University Press, 1971)
Property	*The Law of Property in the Later Roman Republic* (Oxford, Clarendon Press, 1968)
Succession	*The Law of Succession in the Later Roman Republic* (Oxford, Clarendon Press, 1971)
Wieacker "XII Tafeln"	F. Wieacker, "Die XII Tafeln in ihrem Jahrhundert," in *Fondation Hardt, Entretiens sur l'Antiquité classique, 13, Les Origines de la République romaine* (Vandoeuvres-Genève, 1967)
Wissowa, *Religion*	G. Wissowa, *Religion und Kultus der Römer*, 2nd ed. (Munich, C. H. Beck, 1912)
ZSS	*Zeitschrift der Savigny-Stiftung* (romanistische Abteilung)

Rome of the XII Tables

Introduction

This book is written in the belief that the available evidence can provide us with a reasonably clear and precise picture of the law of persons and property in the XII Tables and of the legal rules which existed at Rome in the mid-fifth century B.C. but were not contained in the codification, and that this early Roman law is of great importance in the history of mankind. It is the foundation stone of modern Western jurisprudence. Moreover, the XII Tables are the best evidence we have for life, and for moral and social values, in early Rome. If it is the case, as I believe, that we can go a long way toward the reconstruction of this early law, then we shall have a better understanding of social life and hence a tool to help us evaluate the general accuracy of the later historical tradition about early Rome.

One aspect of this tradition will be accepted without further investigation, namely, that the XII Tables were a Roman codification of law, of around 450 B.C. Methodologically it was right for modern scholars to question the accuracy of this belief, but the result of the probing has been to uncover elements in the provisions themselves which confirm the tradition.[1] It will also be accepted that the period of Etruscan domination was over, that Rome was a Republic and had been so for a considerable number of years even

---

[1] See now above all F. Wieacker, "XII Tafeln," pp. 293ff. For a historian's viewpoint see J. Heurgon, *The Rise of Rome to 264 B.C.* (Berkeley, University of California Press, 1973), pp. 169ff; see also Gjerstad, *Early Rome 5*, pp. 308f.

if the expulsion of the kings is not to be dated precisely to
509,[2] that Rome was still a very small city-state whose economic and social basis was farming,[3] and that the period of
expansion was still in the future.[4]

Two factors which play a part in our knowledge and understanding of the xii Tables require special mention. The
first is that Roman tradition relates the coming into existence of a number of legal rules during the regal period; for
private law these concern above all the relationship of
patron and client and *patria potestas*. The rules as stated in
the sources have a recognizable pattern which is explicable
only on the basis that they do, in fact, give very early Roman law.[5] These *leges regiae* provide a yardstick for the
xii Tables. We are, to begin with, in a fair position to know
whether individual provisions of that code represent innovations, reversals of previously accepted doctrines, or mere-

[2] Gjerstad would date the beginning of the Republic to around 450
B.C., just before the xii Tables; now in *Early Rome* 5, pp. 365ff. This
dating, if correct, would have little effect on the arguments in this
book but against it see e.g. A. Momigliano, "An Interim Report on
the Origins of Rome," *JRS* 53 (1963), 95ff, especially at 103ff; M. Pal-
lottino, "Fatti e leggende (moderne) sulla più antica storia di Roma,"
Studi Etruschi 31 (1963), 3ff; A. Alföldi, *Early Rome and the Latins*
(Ann Arbor, Michigan University Press, n.d.), pp. 56ff, especially
at pp. 72ff; J. Heurgon, *Rise of Rome*, pp. 158f. Other scholars prefer
a date intermediate between 509 and 450; e.g. R. Bloch, *Tite-Live et
les premiers siècles de Rome* (Paris, Belles Lettres, 1965), pp. 62ff.

[3] The importance of farming is to be observed in many of the
provisions of the xii Tables. There is no indication there of trade
unless it is implicit in Tab. ii.2, which shows that a foreigner might
be a party to a lawsuit, or Tab. iii.7 is used to argue that certain
rights of acquisition of ownership by foreigners were recognized.

[4] Veii, the southernmost of the main Etruscan cities and only 10
miles north of Rome, was taken only at the beginning of the 4th
century.

[5] It should be emphasized that the existence of the pattern may
lend credence to the general accuracy of the tradition but does not
in itself justify belief in the accuracy of individual details. For the
detailed argument see Watson, "*Leges Regiae*." The picture given
there of the mid-5th century law on *patria potestas* should be modified in the light of this book.

4

ly restate the existing law. We can also see the kind of law which the Romans were interested in having in writing, and the matters which they left unwritten. It is not a coincidence that the range of recorded contents of the *leges regiae* on private law matters and the scope of this book, mainly family law including the order of succession, overlap so greatly. Partly this is because of the *leges regiae* themselves and the help they give in understanding the XII Tables. Much more, however, it is because the reported rules of the laws of the kings reflect the interests of later Romans. We know about the law of personal relations because non-legal writers thought it worthy of the attention of their readers. This is true of the *leges regiae*; it is also true for the law of the time of the XII Tables. There is much incidental information in the historians, especially Livy, about personal relations and early law, but nothing about the law of property or obligations. What we know about these other matters is little more than what is reported by legal writers, grammarians, and antiquarians about the wording (and meaning) of provisions of the XII Tables. Where there was no provision, or no recorded provision, we know virtually nothing about the law. Where there was a recorded provision we have scarcely any surrounding information to help with its understanding. The outstanding instance must be the three provisions on physical injuries to humans. What is meant by *os fractum, membrum ruptum*, and *iniuria*? What are the dividing lines between them? Is *os fractum* or *membrum ruptum* the more serious injury? Why is the method of assault expressed for *os fractum*, but not for the others? No convincing answer to any of these questions has been given. Further but less extreme examples can even be given from property law which is discussed in this book. Thus, we know that the XII Tables contained provisions for the protection of neighbors. But we cannot even make responsible conjectures as to the existence of neighbors' rights which are not expressly recorded for us. Again we know of a provision "Si aqua pluvia nocet,"[6] but for its scope can only argue—rather ineffectually—from the function of the *actio aquae pluviae arcendae* in much later times. It was to keep the focus as sharp as possible that I preferred to restrict this book to those subjects for which we seem able to write a cohesive and comprehensive account. Hence obligations are omitted.[7]

The other factor which must be mentioned for the part it plays in our understanding of the XII Tables is the *tripertita* of Sextus Aelius Paetus Catus which saved for the Romans all that was still known of the XII Tables around 200 B.C. The general accuracy of the tradition of the contents of the XII Tables seems well established,[8] and the trustworthiness of detail relevant to us will be discussed in the appropriate places; here it is enough to say that the tradition is due to Sextus Aelius. His *tripertita* set out each clause of the XII Tables, its interpretation, and the apposite form of action. He reported and discussed provisions which were obsolete and no longer understood.[9] Traces of the great majority of the provisions known to Sextus Aelius will have survived in one form or another. But what was lost by then was lost forever. And what would be lost were above all these rules which were replaced by later statutory enactments. The importance of statute for the early conception of *ius civile* is already shown by Quintus Mucius Scaevola's famous work of the same name. That commentary, whose contents can very largely be reconstructed,[10] is noteworthy for its limited and historically dated scope. So far as we can tell, no topic of lesser antiquity than the *lex Aquilia* (of 287 B.C.) was discussed. But the *lex Aquilia*, precisely because it was so important, superseded much of the earlier law on

[6] D.40.7.21pr (Pomponius 7 *ex Plautio*).

[7] I do not mean to imply that I find progress on individual topics in obligations impossible.

[8] See above all Wieacker, "XII Tafeln."

[9] See Watson, *Law Making*, pp. 134ff.

[10] See Watson, *Law Making*, pp. 143ff.

damage to property which cannot now be reconstructed. Fortunately, though, early statutes which had much effect on private law were very few in number.

Some readers will be surprised and even shocked that so little use is apparently made of our knowledge of other early systems of law. The absence of comparisons is deliberate and need not be considered proof of ignorance. It is my firm belief that too often the picture of early Roman law is obscured by arguments adduced from evidence for other systems. It has never been shown that early law everywhere develops in the same way,[11] nor can we fill gaps in our knowledge of Roman law from the customs, practices, and legal rules of the Babylonians, Jews, Greeks, and Germans.[12] Even where similarities are observable for a legal institution in two societies, the institutions cannot be presumed also to be similar in those parts for which we lack evidence.[13] But a knowledge of other early and unrelated systems is valuable in three ways. First, it can prevent rash statements as to what is primitive or advanced in Roman law and it can enable us to estimate more clearly the contribution made by Roman law. Secondly, it can provide us with hypotheses. A modern scholar, faced with a problem of early law, may not see all the possible solutions since he is inevitably limited by his own experience. A knowledge of other early systems can show the existence of further alternatives.[14] Thirdly, where the Roman evidence points to

[11] See A. Watson, *Legal Transplants: an Approach to Comparative Law* (Edinburgh, Scottish Academic Press; Charlottesville, University Press of Virginia, 1974), pp. 12ff.

[12] For particular attempts to do so, see infra, pp. 129, 159, n. 16. Often the law in the system adduced as evidence is in reality as obscure as the point of law in the system for which it is adduced.

[13] See the instructive example adduced by A. Momigliano, "Osservazioni sulla distinzione fra patrizi e plebei," in *Les Origines de la République romaine* (Fondation Hardt, entretiens 13, Vandoeuvres-Genève, 1967), pp. 199ff, at pp. 202f.

[14] See F. W. Maitland, "Explorations in foreign climes may often tell us what to look for, but never what to find" in *Township and*

a conclusion which seems impossible or difficult for us to accept, then knowledge that a different system had something similar may persuade us to accept the Roman evidence as plausible.

When the direct evidence for archaic Roman law is inconclusive we often have a safer guide than that provided by unconnected systems, namely, developed Roman law. There is really very little connection between early Roman law and, say, the law of Babylon, but the law of the later Roman Republic and of the classical period is the immediate descendant of the law of the early Republic and the XII Tables. When, for example, it is disputed whether the onus of proof was on the plaintiff or the defendant in the *legis actio sacramento in rem* it is surely more reasonable to take the line that probably it was on the plaintiff as in the classical *vindicatio*, rather than on the defendant as it is said to have been in some similar action in early Greek, Germanic, Babylonian, and Egyptian law. Happily, however, we have in that instance evidence which is neglected but points conclusively to the former solution.[15]

Borough (Cambridge, Cambridge University Press, 1898), p. 24; and J. P. Reid, "Comparative anthropological jurisprudence is a perilous discipline when employed to provide answers, not merely to frame questions" in *A Law of Blood: The Primitive Law of the Cherokee Nation* (New York, New York University Press, 1970), p. 20.

[15] On this topic see infra, pp. 125ff. It is impossible to put flesh on the bones of early Roman law with any authority. But one can find modern societies where, conceivably, aspects of social life and attitudes are sufficiently similar to early Rome to enable us to envisage how the legal rules might have fitted into the scheme of things. I have found illuminating C. G. Chapman, *Milocca: A Sicilian Village* (London, Allen & Unwin, 1973).

ONE

The Creation of *Manus* and Marriage

The family was the most important social unit of the time and it was very much under the control of its head, the *paterfamilias*, who was the oldest living direct male ascendant. In most cases, a wife entered the family of her husband and so became subject to the authority of its head (whether her husband himself or his ascendant),[1] though it was equally possible for her to remain instead a member of her old family.[2]

This authority over a wife is known as *manus*[3] and, although we have no text which expressly says so, there was, I submit, a clause in the XII Tables which listed the three ways in which it was created. The argument for this proposition is straightforward. The three ways of creating *manus* are listed in only four texts, none earlier than the second century A.D., and these four texts—or at least three of them —are of widely differing provenance. Gaius 1.110 and Boethius *II ad Top. Cic.* 3.14 say "usu, farreo, coemptione," while Arnobius *Adv. gent.* 4.20, and Servius *in Verg. Georg.* 1.31, record "usu, farre, coemptione."[4] The lists in the four

---

[1] In classical law a wife married *cum manu* to a *filiusfamilias* was regarded juristically as being in the *manus* of the *filius*, but this was not the case in early law. For the argument see A. Watson, "Two Notes on *Manus*' to appear in *Études Dumont*" (Paris, Geuthner, 1975).

[2] G.1.111.

[3] Whether *manus* at this time was technically used of this power, whether this term alone was used to designate the power over a wife, and whether it was also used to denote other kinds of power will be discussed infra, pp. 42ff.

[4] Boethius, who is concerned with the term *materfamilias*, goes on to describe the formalities of *coemptio* after he lists the ways in which *manus* is acquired and says, "Quam solemnitatem in suis Insti-

texts correspond to a remarkable degree. To begin with, the order is always the same—*usus, confarreatio, coemptio*. It is difficult to imagine this as the historical order of emergence of the ways of obtaining *manus*[5] and, moreover, it is hard to think of any logical justification for the arrangement. Then, the ways are always listed in the ablative. Other constructions, for instance where *usus*, etc., were the subject of the sentence, would have been just as appropriate. Finally, there is the use of *far*, spelt, or *farreum*, a spelt cake, instead of *confarreatio*. Indeed, the ablative of the instrument here is rather striking. These similarities in the four texts must be significant and they cannot be explained away on the hypothesis that one of the texts derives from another or that one source, perhaps Varro, was common to more than one writer. And the presence of "farre" in two, of "farreo" in the other two is a slight but definite argument against more than two coming from the same immediate source. Not even a common tradition of the exposition of *manus* would be a sufficient explanation of the common factors in the texts—that could account for the appearance of the same order in all of them but not for the other similarities. Yet clearly all the texts must derive from the same ultimate source, which must have had two qualities. First, it must have been of very considerable authority—the retention of "farre" or "farreo" in all four, instead of a switch to "confarreatione," points to a reluctance to alter the wording. Whether "farre" or "farreo" is the original is not greatly

---

tutis Ulpianus exponit." Although in this he is specifically referring to the solemnity of *coemptio* it may be that his order "usu, farreo, coemptione" also derives from Ulpian's *Institutes*, in which case Boethius would not be providing us with independent evidence since Ulpian's *Institutes* derive from those of Gaius. The question of the authorship of the *Institutes* of Ulpian does not concern us. They have not survived, but there is an epitome in existence which at the relevant point (§9) does not list the ways in which *manus* is acquired.

[5] G. Dumézil considers there is no reason for imagining a chronological order of emergence: *Archaic Roman Religion* 2 (Chicago, University of Chicago Press, 1970), 615.

important since the other could easily be introduced accidentally in transmission. Secondly, the source must have been very widely known. It is hard to believe, I think, that these qualities could have been combined in a writer, lay or legal, or, indeed, found in an edict. It seems much more likely that the words derive from a statute and, moreover, from a statute of wide importance. That statute can only have been the XII Tables since no other piece of legislation known to us (and one unknown to us could hardly have had the necessary importance) fits the requirements except Augustus' marriage laws and they can be excluded. There is no place in Augustus' legislation for a list of the ways of creating *manus* marriage unless by way of introduction to changes in the law, and introductions of this kind would not seem to have occurred. Moreover, *confarreatio* would have been much more likely to have been the term used at this late period rather than *far* or *farreum*. Indeed, it is reasonable to think the listing dates back originally to a time before *confarreatio* became a common (or technical?) term.

If the above argument is correct and there was in the XII Tables a list, "usu farre(o) coemptione," this can only have been of the ways in which *manus* was created, not of the ways by which a marriage came into being. As we shall see, a marriage which did not involve *manus* was already perfectly possible.

Confarreatio is the only one of the three which was a religious ceremony;[6] like *coemptio* it not only created *manus* but was at the same time the actual marriage. Its formalities are described in a number of sources.[7] The central part of the ceremony consisted of a sacrifice to Juppiter Farreus of, above all, bread of spelt, but also fruits of the earth and salt cake (*mola salsa*), with the assistance of the *flamen Dialis* and the *pontifex maximus* and in the presence of ten wit-

---

[6] Of course, all marriages were marked by religious observances: see Varro *Rust.* 2.4.9; Servius *in Aen.* 3.136; 4.346.

[7] G.1.112; *Epit.Ulp.* 9.1; Servius *in Verg. Georg.* 1.31; *in Aen.* 4.103, 339, 374.

nesses. Formal words were spoken, we are not told by whom. The bridal pair, with covered heads, sat on two stools which had been joined together and over which was placed the skin of a sacrificed sheep.

The antiquity of *confarreatio*—according to Dionysius of Halicarnassus 2.25.1, it was established by Romulus—has been doubted[8] but, to my knowledge, it has not been argued that it did not exist at the time of the XII Tables. Kaser[9] suggests that *confarreatio* is very old in its elements[10] but did not originally create *manus*. He decides this above all from the absence here of a demand for payment of a price which, in early times, apart from comitial acts was, in his view, essential for all acts which transferred authority (of whatever sort); and he also observes that nothing is said about the cooperation of the woman's *paterfamilias* although he is (apparently) losing his *potestas* over her. But against this, in early law reference to payment in an act is confined to *mancipatio* (and its numerous offshoots) and *nexum* (if this differs from *mancipatio*) where its presence is easily explained by the nature of the transaction.[11] There seems no reason to force all legal acts into the same mold; indeed, the comitial acts show that this cannot be done. Moreover, even in *mancipatio*, the transferor—like the bride's *paterfamilias*—says nothing to indicate he is giving up his rights. Again, the list "usu farre(o) coemptione," if it did exist in the XII Tables as argued above, must have been of the ways in which *manus* was created, and hence at that time *confarreatio* was one of them.[12]

[8] See above all P. Noailles, *Fas et Jus* (Paris, Sirey, 1948), pp. 12f, 31f, who thinks it later than the dedication of the temple to Iuppiter Capitolinus by the Tarquins.

[9] *Ius*, pp. 343ff.

[10] Though as an organic whole it may, he thinks, be later.

[11] It should be observed, moreover, that the mention of payment of price in *mancipatio* is not a demand for payment ("Erfordernis der Preiszahlung") by the transferor, but a statement of payment of the price by the transferee.

[12] Kaser's account does not make it clear when he thinks *con-*

Though some of the details in the sources may represent a later stage of development we can be sure that the accounts do give us an accurate picture of the essentials in our period. Spelt, which was cultivated in Italy long before wheat,[13] was still the basic food[14] and so an eminently suitable symbol to mark the beginning of a life together. The presence of the *pontifex maximus* was also appropriate since the *pontifices* had the duty of ensuring the proper performance of religious rites,[15] and so had general control over *ius sacrum*. At that time, the *pontifex maximus* was not so important as he later became, and he was not the superior of the *rex sacrorum*, the *flamines* and the Vestal virgins. In the official order of precedence of priests—which is an important indication of their earlier ranking—he appears fifth,[16] whereas the *flamen Dialis* is second only to the *rex sacrorum*.[17]

Servius *in Aen.* 4.339 speaks of the use of torches as essential to marriage by *confarreatio*; and in *in Aen.* 4.103, of water and fire perfecting the rite of *conventio in manum*, and of this being proper to *confarreatio*. Nothing in these texts suggests, though, that fire and water were interchanged during the actual ceremony, and other texts indicate that this ritual was performed at the bridegroom's

---

farreatio conferred *manus* on the bridegroom or his father, perhaps even before the xii Tables.

[13] Hence the taboo on the eating of leavened flour by the *flamen Dialis*; Aulus Gellius *NA* 10.15.19: see C. Bailey, *Phases in the Religion of Ancient Rome* (London, Oxford University Press, 1932), p. 28.

[14] Proved by xii Tab. iii.4.

[15] According to Livy (whose authority is more than doubtful) this duty went back to the time of Numa: 1.20.5ff; see Bailey, *Phases*, pp. 162ff.

[16] Festus, *s.v. Ordo sacerdotum*.

[17] The rise in importance of the *pontifex maximus* cannot be precisely dated, but seems to be later in the Republic: see e.g. W. Warde Fowler, *The Religious Experience of the Roman People* (London, Macmillan, 1922), pp. 270ff; K. Latte, *Römische Religionsgeschichte* (Munich, C. K. Beck, 1960), pp. 195ff and the works he cites.

13

threshold. This reception with fire and water at the bride-groom's threshold appears in fact to have been common for all kinds of marriage, including that *sine manu* and seems to have been customary rather than a legal requirement.[18]

Only patricians could be the *flamen Dialis* and *pontifex maximus*[19] and, given their importance and their necessary presence at the ceremony and the reported hostility be-tween plebeians and patricians, we can be reasonably sure that *confarreatio* was restricted to the marriage of pa-tricians.

The *flamen Dialis, flamen Martialis, flamen Quirinalis,* and *rex sacrorum* had to be married by *confarreatio* and to be born of parents who were so married,[20] and in much later times *confarreatio* was chiefly associated with the mar-riage of such persons.[21] But nothing in the texts suggests, and there is no reason to think, that in our period *confar-reatio* was a ceremony restricted to these or other priests.

Coemptio was one particular form of the transaction *per aes et libram* in which the husband fictitiously bought the bride.[22] Though Nonius Marcellus, *s.v. Nubentes,* may give the impression that the woman was thought of, as it were, buying the husband, and though Boethius *II in Top. Cic.* 3.14, Servius *in Verg. Georg.* 1.31, and Isidorus *Etym.* 5.24.26 (who derives directly or indirectly from Servius) talk of mutual purchase by husband and wife, it is certain that *coemptio* was of the wife by the husband. It is, after

---

[18] See also the sources cited by Marquardt for the practice: *Pri-vatleben* 1, p. 56, nn. 2,3.
Likewise customary were the words "Ubi tu Gaius, ego Gaia," which, strangely, Quintilian associates with *confarreatio: Inst.* 1.7.28. Cicero shows they were also used when the marriage was by *coemp-tio: Mur.* 12.27; and Plutarch that they were common and spoken when the bride was led to the bridegroom's home: *Quaest. Rom.* 30.

[19] It was not until the *lex Ogulnia* of 300 B.C. that plebeians could be *pontifices*: Livy 10.6.3ff; 10.9.1ff.

[20] G.1.112.

[21] G.1.112; Tacitus *Ann.* 4.16.

[22] The fundamental texts are G.1.113, 123; Boethius *II in Top. Cic.* 3.14; Servius *in Verg. Georg.* 1.31; Isidorus *Etym.* 5.24.26; Nonius Marcellus, *s.v. Nubentes.*

all, the wife who comes into the *manus* of her husband, and the wife has no power over him. Moreover, the wife in this case has much less independence than in a marriage where there was no *manus*.[23] (Of course, this does not exclude the possibility that as a social—as opposed to a legal—fact there were mutual interrogations especially in later times.) The confusion for these non-legal writers may have arisen over the provision of dowry.

We need not concern ourselves much with the question whether originally *coemptio* was a true sale when a bride-price actually was paid or whether from the beginning it was simply an adaptation of *mancipatio* and never involved a real price.[24] It cannot seriously be doubted that at the time of the xii Tables any purchase was fictitious,[25] and that the wording of the *coemptio* differed from that of *mancipatio*. If bride-purchase, so interesting a topic and so different from the system of dowry prevailing in classical law, had survived into historic times we would, I feel sure, have had some mention of it. Again, if bride-purchase had existed at the time of the xii Tables it is likely that it would have applied also in cases where the *manus* was created by *confarreatio*,[26] and so there, too, we might have expected the point to be mentioned. Further, other variations of *mancipatio*, such as adoption, emancipation of children from *patria potestas*, the *testamentum per aes et libram*, and *fiducia* did not involve a real payment so that we have firm ground for holding that there was no need for a transaction *per aes et libram*—other than the straight *mancipatio*—ever to have, or remain long in, a stage where the payment was real.

[23] See P. Corbett, *Marriage*, p. 80.

[24] But see on this point e.g. R. Köstler, "Raub- und Kaufehe bei den Römern," *ZSS* 65 (1947), 43ff. The name *coemptio* is no indication of original bride-purchase: cf. Köstler, "Raubehe," pp. 56ff.

[25] T. Mayer-Maly leaves the question open: "Studien zur Frühgeschichte der *usucapio* ii," *ZSS* 78 (1961), 221ff, at 260f.

[26] Or that for a single marriage there might be both *confarreatio* and *coemptio*.

Nor need we consider the problem whether, when the bride was *sui iuris*, she was sold by herself or by her *tutor*. In theory this should depend on whether the piece of copper was handed by the bridegroom to her or the *tutor*.[27] In fact there would be no difference legally, and the practical Romans are unlikely to have wasted much thought on the matter.

Any marriage, whether by *coemptio* or another form, would, as later, be accompanied by religious rites. But it should be emphasized that there is no indication that these ever formed part of the *coemptio* itself.

For *usus* the most important text is G.1.111, according to which *manus* was acquired by *usus* if a woman remained married (*nupta*) for a year unless she stayed away from her husband for three nights. The view advanced by J.G.A. Wilms[28] that the nights in question were not any three nights, but the three nights of the Lemuria, 9-10, 11-12, and 13-14 May, when it was believed that the ghosts of ancestors came to homes and had to be warded off by the head of the family, can be confidently rejected. There is nothing in the texts on the Lemuria[29] which indicates or implies in any way that absence on these nights would prevent the acquisition of *manus*. Likewise, nothing in these texts suggests that the Lemuria were significant in any way for the power of a Roman *paterfamilias* over his dependents, for instance, for loss of *patria potestas* if a *filiusfamilias* was absent. The whole ritual is directed toward preventing the ghosts from acquiring any sort of sway over the members of the family, not to giving power over individuals to the

---

[27] See Corbett, *Marriage*, pp. 8off.

[28] *De vrouw sui iuris, Cicero, pro Flacco 34, 84 en de manusvestiging door usus* (Ghent, Mededeelingen van het seminarie voor romeinsch recht aan's Rijks Universiteit te Gent, 1938), pp. 24f; approved as a probability by P. Koschaker, *ZSS* 63 (1943), 447; and by Mayer-Maly, "*Usucapio* II," p. 260. The question is left open by Kaser, *RPR* I, p. 69, n. 9; Watson, *Persons*, p. 20, n. 1. Against the view of Wilms, see R. Yaron, "*De Usurpationibus*," in *Studi Grosso* (Turin, G. Giappichelli, 1968), pp. 553ff, at pp. 554f.

[29] Ovid *Fasti* 5.429ff; Festus, *s.v. Fabam*; Nonius, *s.v. Lemures*.

pater. Moreover, there is no indication and no reason to think that whatever effect the ritual might have had for a dependent in a family was produced only if the dependent was actually present, at the ceremony or in the house. The words of Ovid, in fact, suggest that the head of the household alone arose from his bed and performed the ritual. A text of Aulus Gellius *NA* 3.2.12, shows that for Quintus Mucius Scaevola, in the late second century B.C. absence for any three nights sufficed to break the *usus*, and it is unsatisfactory simply to suggest that this was the result of a change due to juristic interpretation. Gaius 1.111 implies that the *trinoctio abesse* rule was an innovation of the XII Tables, and we can at least accept from what he says that the codification contained an express provision on the subject. But the wording (modernized) of the XII Tables was still very well known in the days of Quintus Mucius—slightly later Cicero mentions that in his childhood the codification was learned by heart at school.[30] In the circumstances arguments for a change in interpretation would have to be produced. A similar argument from Aulus Gellius *NA* 3.2.13 lies against any view that the XII Tables contained no provision on *usurpatio*.

Thus, the wife's absence from the matrimonial home for any three nights would prevent the acquisition of *manus*. The point is of considerable importance, and so is the existence of a specific provision on *usurpatio* in the XII Tables, because the emphasis is then on the avoidance of *manus*, not, as is inherent in Wilms's theory, on the acquisition of *manus*. In other words, there was already in some cases a desire on the part of the woman or her *paterfamilias* to avoid *manus*, and this desire was given legal recognition.

This last conclusion then involves us in a further point, namely, that before the introduction of *usurpatio* the standard marriage was one where the husband had *manus* over the wife. *Usus* was not a device invented to turn a permanent or semi-permanent marriage *sine manu* into a mar-

[30] *Leg.* 2.4.9.

riage *cum manu*, but from the start was intended for marriages which were to be *cum manu*.[31]

The XII Tables' provision also means, of course, that it was possible to have a permanent marital union in which the woman did not ever come under the *manus* of the man. Since positive steps had to be taken to avoid *manus* occurring, and since even as late as the beginning of the second century B.C. marriage with *manus* was probably more common than marriage *sine manu*,[32] we can be confident that at the time of the XII Tables most marital unions involved the woman's being in *manus*.[33] But there is no reason to doubt that such unions where there was no *manus* were nonetheless regarded as true and proper marriages. This is the clear implication of G.1.111[34] and there is no evidence to the contrary.[35]

Where the marriage at the outset was without *manus* no legal formalities or ceremony were required for the creation of the marital bond. There is no direct evidence for this assertion but it can nonetheless be made with some confidence. This was still the position as late as the time of the jurist Cinna in the first century B.C.[36] Only later appears the rule of classical law that there must be *deductio in domum mariti* of the wife, at least when the parties were not present together. Of course, in the fifth century B.C. as later, there would in practice be ceremonies and celebrations at the time of the marriage.

There has been a long controversy as to whether there were two forms of marriage, marriage *cum manu* and marriage *sine manu*—the terms do not appear in the sources—or only one, marriage; whether *conventio in manum* was a

[31] See Kaser, *Ius*, p. 319.

[32] See Watson, *Private Law*, p. 17 and n. 6.

[33] See e.g. Kaser, loc. cit.; R. Yaron, "Minutiae on Roman Divorce," *T.v.R.* 28 (1960), 1ff, at 5.

[34] Even though it can be asserted that words and phrases like *nupta perseverabat* and *maritus* need not be used by Gaius inevitably of valid marriages, the natural understanding is that they are so used unless there are counterindications.

[35] See e.g. Corbett, *Marriage*, pp. 86ff.

[36] D.23.2.6 (Ulpian *35 ad Sab.*); see Watson, *Persons*, pp. 26f.

legal institution independent of marriage; whether *confarreatio* and *coemptio* were marriage ceremonies or only ceremonies creative of *manus*.[37] The discussion seems to me to be fundamentally sterile. Certainly, *manus* might accompany marriage or be created only subsequently (by *usus*); the marriage might end by the death of a *filius* husband and still the wife would remain under the power of his *paterfamilias*. Yet *manus* (in developed law at least)[38] is inextricably linked with marriage: where the parties lacked the capacity for marriage no *manus* would be created, no matter what ceremonies were used. Without marriage there could be no *manus*. Though it be conceded that no form of ceremony was actually needed for a marriage, nevertheless, ancient authors do talk of the ways of creating *manus* as forms of marriage or of ways in which wives were acquired.[39] It must be stressed that socially and historically the important fact is that sometimes a wife came under the power of her husband and sometimes she did not.[40]

Up to this point, for convenience, we have used the word *manus* as a technical term for a husband's power over his wife, just as the word was used later. But now it must be emphasized that many terms were far less precise and technical at the time of the XII Tables than they were in classical law. Thus, though *manus* was almost certainly the term normally used for the authority over a wife, and the content of this authority would be known, yet the word *manus* would once also have been used in other contexts to denote authority, and the extent of this authority would vary according to the institution involved. The exposition of this point will be found in the Excursus to chapter four.

[37] For a bibliography of the controversy see E. Volterra, "*La conventio in manum* e il matrimonio romano," *RISG* 12 (1968), 205ff.

[38] In developed law at least. The qualification is added because of the evidence that in early times *manus* was a wide, non-technical concept, and was used of various kinds of power; see infra, pp. 49ff.

[39] Arnobius *Adv. gent.* 4.20; Boethius *II ad Top. Cic.* 3.14; Servius *in Verg. Georg.* 1.31; *in Aen.* 4.339, 374; Isidorus *Etym.* 5.24.26.

[40] In the later Republic there was a technical term, *materfamilias*, for a wife *in manu*: Cicero *Top.* 3.14.

TWO

Capacity and Requirements for Marriage

With one very significant exception we have no evidence that the XII Tables contained any provisions on capacity and conditions of marriage; on the requirements of age, nationality, personal status; on the prohibited degrees of relationship and on the necessary consents. We can in fact be confident that the XII Tables did not contain any such provisions, and that the essential requirements for marriage were simply assumed. Fortunately we can largely reconstruct these requirements.

The exceptional case, where there was a provision (and for which we have evidence) was contained in one of the two last *tabulae* (Tab. XI.1), those which we are told were added by the decemviri in the subsequent year after they had turned tyrannous,[1] and this abolished the right of intermarriage between patrician and plebeian. The sources[2] present the prohibition of intermarriage as an innovation and this view of the matter is generally accepted today.[3] Indeed, it is only as an innovation that we can explain the presence of the clause in the XII Tables since no other requirement for marriage was set out. Intermarriage was restored by the *lex Canuleia*, a plebiscite of 445 B.C. The whole matter is of

[1] The existence of a second decemvirate is sometimes denied; see e.g. Gjerstad, *Early Rome* 5, p. 98.

[2] Cicero *Rep.* 2.37.63; Livy 4.1.1,2; 4.2.6; 4.4.5-12; 4.5.5; 4.6.2; Dionysius of Halicarnassus 10.6.5.

[3] See above all H. Last, "The Servian Reforms," *JRS* 35 (1945), 30ff, at 31ff; also F. de Visscher, "*Conubium* and *civitas*," *RIDA* 1 (1952), 402ff, at 408ff; Kaser, *RPR* 1, p. 75. But the contrary view has been held, e.g. by Corbett, *Marriage*, p. 50; Gjerstad, *Early Rome* 5, pp. 187f; 6, p. 133. R. M. Ogilvie, *Early Rome* (to appear in 1976, London, Fontana).

the greatest importance; in the relationship of patricians and plebeians, the structure of *gentes*, and the legal force of *plebiscita*. Only the first of these matters will concern us in this chapter, but at the outset we should stress that the prohibition found its way into the xii Tables—and into one of the additional two, at that—because it was an innovation.[4]

Unless we think that the decemviri had wished to insult the plebeians gratuitously we must hold that the prohibition was in response to what was seen as a problem. Intermarriage between a rich and powerful patrician and a poor and weak plebeian must always have been rare, but one situation can be found where intermarriage might have been less uncommon and been seen as a threat. Originally the Romans formed a single political unit[5] but differences in wealth, power, and reputation between families gradually hardened into the distinction between patricians and plebeians before the close of the regal period. One of the striking aspects of this distinction was that only patricians could be senators. Though there were now two rigidly distinct orders in society, the rise and decline of individuals and households would continue and some plebeian families would become rich and important. Tradition, which in this case seems acceptable, relates that plebeians became eligible for membership in the senate early in the Republic.[6]

---

[4] Mommsen declares that we have no control for the division of the xii Tables into ten good and two bad or for the dating of the *lex Canuleia: Staatsrecht* 3, p. 80, n. 1.

[5] The arguments listed by Last, "Reforms," pp. 30f are convincing: (1) that of the seven canonical kings of Rome, all except the eponymous Romulus and the two Etruscan Tarquins bear names which are otherwise only attested as borne by plebeians; (2) that of the seven places united in the Septimontium the only three bearing names which are also personal had names belonging in historical times to plebeian families alone.

[6] Livy 2.1.11; Festus, *s.v. qui patres, qui conscripti*; Plutarch *Publicola* 11.2. Livy makes Menenius Agrippa—famous for the fable in 494 about the belly and the rest of the body—a senator and a plebeian: 2.32.8. It is, however, probably a rationalization for these writers to claim that this occurred in the first year of the Republic. Ogilvie,

Here patricians and plebeians could mingle at the right level and the breakdown of this great class barrier would much increase the chances of intermarriage. Plebeians, having won the legal right of membership in the senate and taken their seats, would actively seek fulfillment of the existing legal right of intermarriage. Some patricians would be won over—perhaps by a large plebeian dowry—hence the feeling among other patricians of a threat.[7]

It is from time to time observed that Cicero *Rep.* 2.37.63 reports the xii Tables' prohibition *conubia . . . ut ne plebei cum patribus essent,* and Livy 4.4.5, *ne conubium patribus cum plebe esset.* It is then argued that, though there is no guidance here as to the exact wording of the provision, the texts are evidence that in the tradition the word *patres* stood for the patricians, and that *patres* was the word used in the law. Conclusions are then sometimes drawn from the observation.[8] But this approach does not seem fruitful: *patres* is frequently used in various contexts by Livy to mean patricians, its appearance here in Livy need tell us nothing about the verbal tradition of the *lex*, and its occurrence also in Cicero may be nothing more than ordinary coincidence.[9] Even if *patres* was the designation used for pa-

---

Commentary, pp. 236f, thinks it was not until the middle of the 5th century that discrimination was practiced on the plebeians as senate members: for F. de Martino, on the other hand, plebeians could not become senators until the city magistracies were opened to them and the first of these was the military tribuneship *consulari potestate*, which is later than the xii Tables: *Storia della costituzione romana* i (Naples, Jovene, 1951), 211ff, 262ff.

[7] Conjecturally but credibly, a proportion of such intermarriages would be into the weaker patrician families which wished to restore their finances or power by dynastic alliances. If this conjecture is right, then *a fortiori* other patricians could see intermarriage as a threat to the order.

[8] Thus, Mommsen claims that *patres* was not used of the purely patrician senate because that term was still used in the xii Tables to designate the patricians in general: *Staatsrecht* 3, pp. 836f. And B. Kübler argues that at that time the patricians were still identified with the senators: *RE* 18, *s.v. Patres, patricii*, 2222ff, at 2224.

[9] Elsewhere in the *Rep.* Cicero also appears to use *patres* to mean patricians: 1.32.48,49.

tricians in the *lex* it is very doubtful if the fact would be of significance. Certainty is not possible but it seems reasonable to assume that in the early Republic the term *patres* was used with two distinct generic meanings: patricians as a body, and senators as a group. Such usage would be entirely natural.[10]

But if the xii Tables contained an express provision on intermarriage between patrician and plebeian there was no clause on the right of intermarriage between Roman and non-Roman. Yet marriages with the *Latini* had long been recognized as valid,[11] and it seems the right of intermarriage was at first and in our period not restricted to members of particular Latin communities.[12] Livy reports that in the year 338 some Latin peoples were deprived *inter alia* of this right.[13] Probably this *conubium* (and *commercium* and *postliminium*) originated at a time when the concept of a state was not well developed.[14] Very short distances lay between one Latin village or town and another and De Visscher has brought out the social importance of the right of intermarriage for the early Latin aristocracy in establishing alliances among themselves.[15]

[10] It corresponds, moreover, to what is found in Livy.

[11] Diodorus Siculus 8.25.4; Strabo 5.3.4 (c. 231); Livy 1.26.2 (all three refer only to Alba); Dionysius of Halicarnassus 6.1.2. The story of the Rape of the Sabine Women, unhistorical though it must be, shows that the later Romans thought their forefathers had few opportunities of finding wives. Plutarch takes it as showing that the Albans refused the Romans the right of intermarriage: *Rom.* 9.2.

[12] See A. N. Sherwin-White, *The Roman Citizenship*, 2nd ed. (Oxford, Clarendon Press, 1973), pp. 30ff, 103ff.

[13] 8.4.10.

[14] See Sherwin-White, *Citizenship*, p. 14; followed by De Visscher, "*Conubium*," p. 406.

[15] "*Conubium*," pp. 412ff. De Visscher thinks that the patricians maintained their rank and supremacy in this way, and did not intermarry with the plebeians of their own town; and he suggests that, seen in this light, the discussions which took place over the legal prohibition of *conubium* between patrician and plebeian assume a wider significance. There is much to be said for this view but it does not satisfactorily explain why the decemviri felt the need to insert the legal prohibition in the xii Tables.

Slaves were always incapable of entering a legally recognized marriage. Whether a free-born citizen could contract marriage with a freed ex-slave cannot be determined; when the picture becomes clear at a much later period there was no legal obstacle to such a marriage though it could be regarded with disfavor.[16]

There were no restrictions (and no need for special formalities) on marriage with a member of another *gens*: otherwise there could scarcely have been a problem about intermarriage between patrician and plebeian, and there could have been no *conubium* with the members of other Latin communities.[17] Indeed, for many marriage inside the *gens* would have been impossible, since by custom there was no marriage up to and including the sixth degree of relationship which would include a lot of people: "P. Celius patricius primus adversus veterem morem intra septimum cognationis gradum duxit uxorem." This part of a fragment from Livy Book 20[18]—which presumably concerns an event after the middle of the third century B.C.—shows that the rules on forbidden relationship were not contained in a statute, especially not the XII Tables, but derived from custom.[19] Interestingly, there is evidence that the Romans counted up to this degree of relationship and no further;[20] hence the custom would seem to be simply that one did not marry a relative.[21]

[16] For the argument see Watson, *Persons*, pp. 32ff.

[17] Against the contrary arguments which have been drawn from Livy 39.9 see now Watson, "*Enuptio gentis*," in *Daube noster* (Edinburgh and London, Scottish Academic Press, 1974), pp. 331ff.

[18] Published by P. Krüger in *Hermes* 4 (1870), 372. The text is probably not as Livy wrote—it may be an epitome—and there must be doubt as to the hero's name since the *gens Caelia* was not patrician.

[19] We cannot be sure that this marriage was declared void. In the 1st century B.C. when we have a clear picture, marriage between first cousins was permitted; Cicero *Clu.* 5.11; Plutarch *Brut.* 13.2; *Antonius* 9.2: and it seems to have been so even earlier; Livy 42.34.3 (refers to 171 B.C.).

[20] See above all D.38.10.10 (Paul *sing. de grad.*).

[21] See Plutarch *Quaest. Rom.* 6; 108. These texts of Plutarch suggest that between Roman women and their male kinsmen there existed

For the age at which a marriage could be celebrated and the relevance (or otherwise) of the actual onset of puberty we have apparently no evidence and the matter is best left undiscussed. Even for the late Republic the position is not entirely clear.[22]

Of much greater social significance is the question of the consents which were necessary for the validity of the marriage. On the bride's side, if she were a *filiafamilias* the consent of her *pater* was an essential requirement and was the sole consent necessary. Her own wishes were legally irrelevant.[23] If the bride were *sui iuris* the position is more complicated, and in the center of any discussion must be Livy's story of the "Maid of Ardea."[24] We shall look at this to see what it reveals, initially treating the tale as if the conditions reported for Ardea were the same as those at Rome. Whether Livy's account for our purposes is plausible for Rome or not will in fact emerge from the next few pages. If the account is historically plausible, it is a reasonable assumption either that the law of Ardea and the law of Rome were the same on this point, or that Livy is transferring Roman conditions to Ardea.[25]

---

a form of what anthropologists call "a joking relationship"; on which see e.g. A. R. Radcliffe-Brown, *Structure and Function in Primitive Society* (London, Cohen & West, 1952), pp. 90ff.

It should be noted, however, that in the account in Dionysius of Halicarnassus 3.13ff (especially at 3.21), the Roman Horatia was a second cousin of the Alban Curiatius to whom she was betrothed.

[22] See Watson, *Persons*, p. 39.

[23] For the foregoing propositions the available evidence actually relates to the late Republic and is set out in Watson, *Persons*, pp. 41ff. But one cannot really doubt that they also applied in the 5th century. If much later in the Republic the consent of a *filia* was not necessary for her marriage, *a fortiori* this would be the case in our period. And there was no family council of such importance that its consent would be appropriate.

[24] Livy 4.9. It is nowhere stated in the story that the girl was fatherless but this is inherent in the situation: see e.g. R. M. Ogilvie, "The Maid of Ardea," *Latomus* 21 (1962), 477ff, at 479f; E. Volterra, "Sul diritto familiare di Ardea nel v secolo a.c.," in *Studi Segni* (Milan, Giuffrè, 1966), pp. 3ff, at p. 10; D. Daube, *Roman Law; Linguistic Social and Philosophical Aspects* (Edinburgh, Edinburgh University Press, 1969), p. 113.

[25] See infra, pp. 175f.

25

In the year 443 B.C. there was at Ardea a plebeian girl who was famous for her beauty. She had two suitors, one a plebeian who was supported by her tutors, the other a noble who was captivated by her beauty alone. The latter was supported by the girl's mother who wanted as grand a match as possible. The tutors, we are told, mindful even here of party matters held out for their man. Since the dispute could not be resolved privately, the matter was taken to law. The magistrates heard both sides and gave the *ius nuptiarum* in accordance with the judgment of the mother. But violence was stronger. The tutors publicly addressed men of their own party in the forum and then, with help, carried off the girl from her mother's house. And so on. Nothing is anywhere said of the girl's wishes.

The explanation of this situation is, I submit, this. At that time, as later, a well-brought up girl took no part in arranging her own marriage. When she had no father and was living with her mother, the mother in practice found a match for her.[26] Of course, the mother had no power over her, but she was in practice responsible for the girl's well-being. The function of the tutors was the preservation of the girl's property, and her physical well-being was not entrusted to them. Their consent was necessary for the creation of any dowry, and for the marriage, at least if that was to be *cum manu* from the beginning.[27] But the reasonable social expectation was that, provided the financial aspects of the marriage were satisfactory, the tutors would accept the mother's choice of a husband. In this case the normal expectation was disappointed because, for political reasons, the tutors would not accept the mother's choice. One can hypothetically reconstruct the arguments on either side. For the mother it would be maintained that she it was who should choose a husband for her daughter, that the sole concern of the tutors should be satisfactory financial arrangements, and that they should not force on the girl a husband whom they

[26] See Watson, *Persons*, pp. 14f, 17f, 46f.
[27] See Watson, *Persons*, pp. 149ff.

preferred for extraneous reasons. The tutors' argument would be that the mother's wishes were legally irrelevant, that their consent was necessary if the marriage was to take place and they could give or withhold their consent as seemed best to them.

Since the mother and the tutors could not resolve their dispute the matter eventually went before the magistrates, probably at the instigation of the mother. The decision in favor of the mother may be presumed to have been to the effect that the tutors could not unreasonably withhold their consent (and that the patrician suitor was satisfactory as a bridegroom).[28]

This explanation, I submit, has the merit of setting the situation in a reasonable social context while at the same time being in conformity with what we otherwise know about early Roman law.[29] Admittedly it cannot strictly be proved that a woman's tutors could withhold their consent only when it was reasonable for them to do so, but the alternative would be intolerable since it would always be in their own financial interest to prevent marriage *cum manu* and the creation of dowry.[30]

It was suggested above that the tutors' consent might not be needed for the girl's marriage where this was not *cum manu* from the beginning. The argument for this proposition (which should not be regarded as certain) is twofold.

[28] The nature of this action is not clear, possibly because of Livy's lack of interest in law. There seem to have been proceedings only in front of the magistrates. It may be felt that the difficulty in explaining the remedy indicates that the law in question must be Ardean, but not much should be made of this, since if the identical problem had arisen at Rome—as it could have—the same difficulty would face us of knowing the right remedy. Equal problems would arise if the validity of a marriage were questioned, or if there was a dispute as to who was *tutor* and so on.

[29] Some similar explanation may very well account for the very puzzling ruling in C.5.4.1 of A.D. 199.

[30] See Watson, "*Enuptio gentis*," especially at p. 337. For the obligation of a tutor to behave reasonably with regard to the dowry in later Republican law see D.32.43 (Celsus *15 dig.*); Watson, *Persons*, pp. 150f.

First, there is no evidence that at any time the consent of tutors was necessary for marriage *sine manu*. Secondly, in Cicero's time when marriage *cum manu* had become very unpopular, the acquisition of *manus* by *usus* was in effect made obsolete by the jurists' deliberate misinterpretation of an irrelevant provision of the xii Tables so that the tutors' consent became essential for *usus*. Hence this consent could not have been needed before.[31]

The story of the Maid of Ardea indicates that the consent of a girl under tutelage to her marriage was not considered very important, but the story cannot be taken as evidence that the consent was not relevant. Probably a marriage could not occur when she objected to it.[32]

On the bridegroom's side, if he were *sui iuris* no other consent would be needed. If he were a *filius familias*, that of his *pater* was essential[33] but we cannot determine whether, as later, the consent of the bridegroom was also necessary. Evidence from Plautus shows that the *pater* then often made the marriage arrangements[34] and we can assume that this was even more the case in our period since the fifth century B.C. was the high-water mark of *patria potestas*.

Finally, on the requirements it should be noted that a widow was forbidden to marry within ten months—the old Roman year—of the death of her husband. If she did remarry the marriage appears to have been valid but a penalty was imposed.[35]

[31] For the argument see Watson, *Persons*, pp. 19ff.

[32] The main argument—other than any *a priori* one—must be that apparently the consent of a tutor was not needed for a marriage initiated otherwise than by *confarreatio* or *coemptio*. Yet some assent to the marriage, with full legal effect, must have been necessary from the girl's side, and this could only have been provided by the girl herself.

[33] As it was later.

[34] For texts and literature see Watson, *Persons*, pp. 17f.

[35] According to Plutarch *Num.* 12.2, the woman had to sacrifice a pregnant cow, but whether this remained in our period cannot be established. In the later Republic there were disabilities in legal proceedings: see Watson, *Private Law*, p. 21, n. 2; Kaser, *RPR* 1, p. 75.

Betrothal, which should have been discussed first, has been left till last. There is no sign of any provisions on it in the XII Tables and, though it certainly existed then,[36] our knowledge is fragmentary at best. At some early time—it is difficult to be more precise, an unprovable hypothesis for the mid-fifth century—a promise was taken from the person by whom the girl would be given in marriage that she would be so given, and an equivalent promise was given by the bridegroom.[37] For these promises the contract of *sponsio* was used, and failure to perform without good reason would give rise to an action on either side, which would be the standard action of the XII Tables for the *sponsio* or *stipulatio*, the *legis actio per iudicis postulationem*.[38] According to Servius, the *iudex* would estimate the *lis* in money.[39] In a passage in which he is clearly discussing an obsolete practice, Varro reports that the promiser promised either money or the girl for marriage.[40] Those modern scholars[41] who feel that in early times an action for an uncertain sum of money could not be brought upon a stipulation see this as the original promise of betrothal which gave rise to a civil law action.[42] No action would lie to compel the marriage, hence, the argument goes, since damages for failure to carry out the marriage would be of an uncertain sum (and so could not be sued for), the sum specified as an alternative in the *sponsio* would be the amount for which an *actio certi ex sponsione* would be brought. This argument fails to convince, really because it cannot be shown that originally the *legis actio per iudicis postulationem* was granted only for *certa pecunia*.[43] If from the start, as later,

36 It will be recalled that according to Livy 1.26.2ff, a sister of the Roman Horatii was betrothed to one of the Curiatii of Alba.

37 Aulus Gellius *NA* 4.4.1ff; see Watson, *Persons*, pp. 11f.

38 G.4.17a.   39 Aulus Gellius *NA* 4.4.2.

40 *Ling.* 6.70.

41 E.g. Kaser, *RPR* 1, p. 76 and n. 33; *T.v.R.* 36 (1968), 430.

42 Earlier, sacred law might have provided a remedy for breach of promise.

43 See e.g. F. de Zulueta, *The Institutes of Gaius* 2 (Oxford, Clarendon Press, 1953), 240.

the *legis actio per iudicis postulationem* could be used in other circumstances as well, then there is no ground for holding that a *sponsio* would be valid and enforceable only when it was for *certa pecunia*. It seems more reasonable to hold that the alternative promise of the money or the girl is a later development, subsequent to the xii Tables, and was due to the growth of a feeling that actions for breach of promise were immoral: on an action on a *sponsio* of the girl alone, minimal damages would be awarded—at some point, indeed, such a promise ceased to be actionable—and a man contemplating marriage would be well advised to insert into the betrothal agreement a clause which would in effect give him a fixed sum as damages in the event of breach of promise.[44]

[44] For the argument see Watson, *Persons*, pp. 12f.

THREE

Marriage, Divorce, and Dowry

The most important effect of a valid marriage was that any children would be in the *potestas* of the husband or of his *paterfamilias*, if he had one, and be members of the father's *gens*. On the husband's status the marriage had no effect and this was also true of the wife's when the marriage was *sine manu*. Then she continued in her father's *potestas* if she was *alieni iuris*; if she was *sui iuris* she retained her *tutor*. If, as was most often the case, the marriage was *cum manu* she became a member of her husband's legal family and was in his *manus* or that of his *pater*, if the husband had one.[1] There is no evidence, for any period, that a husband was under a directly enforceable legal obligation to support his wife, and it can be presumed that none existed in the early Republic.[2]

Ironically, our best guide to other aspects of marriage is the little we know about divorce.[3] It would seem that from regal times a wife could not divorce her husband, but a husband could divorce a wife for a few specific causes; according to Plutarch,[4] for poisoning a child, for substitution of

[1] Particular social effects, or pressures to marry, cannot be specified but see Watson, *Private Law*, p. 22.

[2] It might be argued that in a marriage *cum manu* the answer would depend on the existence of a father's duty to maintain his child. But the idea of a wife *in manu* being *in loco filiae* postdates the disappearance of *manus* as a matter of practical importance.

[3] For the main outline of early divorce I am relying on the arguments in A. Watson, "The Divorce of Carvilius Ruga," *T.v.R.* 33 (1965), 38ff. The relevant texts are: Cicero *Phil.* 2.28.69; Dionysius of Halicarnassus 2.25.1,2,7; Plutarch *Quaest. Rom.* 14; *Rom.* 22.3; *Thes.-Rom.* 35.(6).3,4; *Lyc.-Num.* 25.(3).12,13; Valerius Maximus 2.1.4; Aulus Gellius *NA* 4.3.1; 17.21.44.

[4] *Rom.* 22.3.

keys, or for adultery. If he turned her out for any other reason the husband had to give the wife one half of his property, the other half going to Ceres (or Tellus). This seems to have continued to be the position until the divorce of Spurius Carvilius Ruga around 230 B.C., which figures prominently in the sources as the first Roman divorce. The first Roman divorce it cannot have been in the eyes of modern scholars, but it may well have been the first when the wife was not guilty of one of the statutory offenses and when the husband also was not behaving badly—the wife was sterile and the husband had sworn an oath to the censors that he was marrying for the procreation of children. Before this divorce there were no *actiones rei uxoriae* and no *cautiones* for the return of dowry.[5]

The picture may not be true in every detail, but is, I think, trustworthy in outline and allows us to draw some very general conclusions for the mid-fifth century. First, divorce could not proceed from the side of the wife, but could from that of the husband. Secondly, divorce was permitted only for a few specific and very restricted reasons. Thirdly, the husband had to pay a severe penalty to a wife who was not guilty of one of these offenses and who was cast out. Fourthly, though divorce was legally possible it was in practice very rare.[6]

The evidence is clear for later times that the husband's *paterfamilias* could bring about a divorce even against the wishes of the husband,[7] and it is safe to assume this was also the case in our period.[8] Nothing could better illustrate the fact that marriage was an arrangement between fami-

---

[5] Aulus Gellius *NA* 4.3.1.

[6] Otherwise there could not have been a tradition that a divorce as late as that of Carvilius Ruga was the first one ever; see Marquardt, *Privatleben* 1, pp. 70f. The only reported earlier divorce is that of L. Annius (Valerius Maximus 2.9.2) which should be assigned to 307-306 B.C. (Livy 9.43.25).

[7] See Corbett, *Marriage*, pp. 239ff.

[8] Since *patria potestas* was then at its strongest.

lies, not just between individuals. Whether, as later in the Republic,[9] a *filius* husband could divorce contrary to his father's wishes must be left undecided.[10]

Nothing indicates that the grounds for divorce were altered in any way by the XII Tables, but too much should not be made of Plutarch's list attributed to Romulus. Apart from other considerations, what these grounds for divorce were is obscure. Adultery is clear enough, poisoning of offspring may reasonably be conjectured to mean abortion, but substitution of keys ($\kappa\lambda\epsilon\iota\delta\hat{\omega}\nu$ $\hat{\upsilon}\pi o\beta o\lambda\acute{\eta}$) remains a mystery.[11] Yet we know of one clause of the XII Tables on divorce (Tab. IV.3) and that too concerned keys. Mark Antony apparently got rid of his *mima* mistress and Cicero —to mock him—pretends there was a divorce; "illam suam suas res sibi habere iussit, ex duodecim tabulis clavis ademit, exegit."[12] The "ex duodecim tabulis" must be taken with "clavis ademit" for the balance of the sentence and for the rhetoric of the situation.[13] Thus, it seems the code had a clause about the husband taking keys from a wife on di-

---

[9] See Watson, *Private Law*, p. 23, n. 5.

[10] Likewise it would be rash to enter into a discussion of whether in a marriage *sine manu* the initiative for divorce would come from the wife's side. Probably the matter had never been in issue and was not regulated.

[11] Suggestions range from the wife's acquisition of a fresh set of house keys to facilitate her adultery to her acquisition of keys to the wine cupboard or cellar so that she might secretly drink. Wine-drinking by women was a very serious offense; infra, pp. 34, 36, 38.

[12] *Phil.* 2.28.69.

[13] As indeed it is taken by Latinists and by editors of Livy: see Watson, "Carvilius Ruga," pp. 42f. Jurists, who in general seem unimpressed by the Latinists' expertise, prefer to link "ex duodecim tabulis" with what precedes it: e.g. recently Kaser, *RPR* I, p. 82, n. 6. There is no real evidence that the XII Tables contained a form of words for divorce, but if they did the form was not compulsory: see Watson, "Carvilius Ruga," especially at pp. 42f, 48f; Kaser, *RPR* I, pp. 81f (believes a customary form was mentioned in the Tables, but was not a legal requirement for divorce); see Gjerstad, *Early Rome* 5, p. 312. See also R. Yaron, "Minutiae on Roman Divorce," *T.v.R.* 28 (1960), 1ff.

vorce. Greater precision is not possible since there is no other evidence for the provision, which accordingly cannot long have retained significance.[14] On divorce, some procedure, probably a *remancipatio*, would be needed to remove the wife from *manus*.[15]

But if the husband's right to divorce his wife was restricted to particular circumstances, then so, we would expect, would be his legal right to impose on her severe punishment, especially death. *Manus*, that is, would have a limited content. And this opinion is supported by the sources. Dionysius of Halicarnassus relates that if a wife misbehaved, the injured party, i.e. the husband, was her judge and determined the punishment,[16] but that for other offenses, including adultery and wine-drinking, she was judged by her relatives together with her husband. Romulus, he says, allowed adultery and wine-drinking to be punished by death.[17] Thus, the severest punishment of a wife was then at the discretion of her relatives acting with her husband, and Dionysius' wording suggests that the relatives played the greater rôle.[18] The fact of most interest is that

[14] We cannot presume the provision was used in Cicero's time or even that Cicero knew what it meant. His whole purpose was to mock Antony; the XII Tables are mentioned to achieve a mock solemnity and are quite irrelevant; see Watson, *Law Making*, p. 118.

It is tempting, but has not proved possible, to connect the provisions about keys in Plutarch *Rom.* 22.3 and Cicero *Phil.* 2.28.69, and also perhaps the information about keys in Festus, *s.v. clavim* and Servius *in Aen.* 10.252.

[15] See for a much later period, G.1.137a; D. Liebs, "*Contrarius Actus*," in *Sympotica Wieacker* (Göttingen, Vandenhoek & Ruprecht, 1970), pp. 111ff, at pp. 124f, and the authors he cites. Liebs has also given strong reasons for suspecting that *diffareatio* may be an invention of Augustus: pp. 123f. The sole texts to mention *diffareatio* are Festus, *s.v. diffareatio* and *CIL* 10, 6662; see also Plutarch *Quaest. Rom.* 50. Possibly in the earliest times a marriage by *confarreatio* could not be dissolved by divorce: this may be the way to understand Dionysius of Halicarnassus 2.25.1,2.

[16] 2.25.5.   [17] 2.25.6.

[18] For the historical accuracy of the text see W. Kunkel, "Das Konsilium im Hausgericht," *ZSS* 83 (1966), 219ff, at 233. The word

even when *in manu mariti*[19] a woman was still very much subject to the authority of her family. This long remained the case. When Lucretia, who had been raped by Tarquin, wished to protest her innocence and protect her honor she summoned to her both her father and her husband, each with a friend, told them the sad tale, declared (in Livy's account) that though she absolved herself from the sin she did not release herself from punishment—" 'nec ulla deinde impudica Lucretiae exemplo vivet' "—and killed herself.[20] Livy's account should not be robbed of its legal significance.[21] Lucretia killed herself because death was the appropriate punishment for infidelity. She summoned both her father and her husband—in that order—because they were the persons who above all others were entitled to exact the penalty. Each was to bring a friend, because in a *iudicium domesticum* friends could help with advice.[22] Tar-

---

Dionysius uses, συγγενεῖς, means "relatives" in general but, as necessarily in 4.66f (cf. infra, n. 22), it should be taken here as "blood-relatives," not "relatives by marriage."

[19] It would be unreasonable to think that Dionysius was concerned only with marriage *sine manu*.

[20] Livy 1.58.

[21] J. Heurgon calls attention to the legal terms in 1.58.9: *Tite-Live Ab Urbe Condita liber primus*, 2nd ed. (Paris, Presses universitaires de France, 1970), p. 190.

[22] The account of Dionysius of Halicarnassus, while differing in important details, leads to the same conclusion. The raped Lucretia proceeds to her father's house and asks him to send for as many friends and relatives as possible so that they could hear the events from her: 4.66ff. Only after the suicide was any attempt made to contact the husband.

In Livy's version there is a touch of conscious or unconscious irony which should be mentioned but need not be stressed. In the contest of womanly virtues which preceded the rape and which the decorous Lucretia won, her rivals, the king's daughters-in-law, were discovered passing the time "in convivio luxuque cum aequalibus": 1.57.9. Presumably these ladies—who seem to be Etruscan—were drinking wine (as one can assume *convivium* implies) which, as we know, was conduct meriting death at Rome. Perhaps this aspect, like other legal details, was more prominent in earlier accounts; see infra, pp. 167f. For the *iudicium domesticum* see infra, pp. 42ff.

Marriage, Divorce, Dowry

quin's threat to kill Lucretia and place a slaughtered slave beside her implies, as Diodorus Siculus 10.20.2 expressly noted, that a husband's close relative had the right to kill a wife whom he caught committing adultery.[23] Gellius[24] quotes from a speech of Cato the Censor which shows an important distinction for the end of the third century: if a wife commits adultery she is condemned to death (*condemnatur*); if she is taken in the act the husband may kill her with impunity without a trial (*sine iudicio*). Presumably, therefore, when the wife was not caught in the act an investigation of some kind was required from the husband.[25] Thus, the husband in Cato's time could not just inflict the ultimate penalty on his wife because he felt like it. Cato's speech also shows that wine-drinking by a wife was still thought an offense worthy of punishment though not by death.[26] No distinction is drawn between the powers of a husband who has his wife *in manu* and of one who has not. By Augustus' *lex Iulia de adulteriis coercendis* a husband was forbidden to kill his wife who was caught in adultery but he might slay the *adulter* if the latter were of a particular low status and if he were found in the husband's house.[27] Here, too, no distinction is drawn between a husband with *manus* and one without. A father, however, could kill his married daughter whom he caught committing adultery in his own house or in that of his son-in-law provided he was either her *paterfamilias* or as *paterfamilias* had given her

[23] See D. Daube, *Civil Disobedience in Antiquity* (Edinburgh, Edinburgh University Press, 1972), p. 23.

[24] *NA* 10.23.4,5.

[25] The text is concerned only with the rights of a husband and tells us nothing about a father's right: contra, J.A.C. Thomas who takes the text as showing that a *pater* could not kill his married daughter: "Lex Julia de adulteriis coercendis," in *Études Macqueron* (Aix-en-Provence, Faculté de droit et des sciences économiques d'Aix-en-Provence, 1970), pp. 637ff, at p. 637.

[26] Pace Watson, *Private Law*, p. 23, *multatur* does not mean that the wife was fined.

[27] D.48.5.23(22).4 (Papinian 1 *de adult.*); 48.5.25(24)pr (Macer 1 *publ.*).

36

in manum. His right to kill an *adulter* was also greater than that of the husband.[28] The *lex*[29] shows that the idea persisted—right from the time of the kings—that a woman's adultery was even more of an insult to her blood relatives, especially her father, than to her husband.[30]

When in 154 B.C. two noble ladies, Publicia and Licinia were supposed to have poisoned their husbands, *consulares*, they were put to death by their relatives, apparently, according to Livy, by their blood relatives, *cognati*.[31] Yet in view of the date and the rank of the offenders and their husbands, it would be surprising if the wives had not been *in manu* though they may well have become *sui iuris* as a result of their husband's death. In 186 B.C. the women participants in the Bacchanalian rites were handed over to their families for execution. Livy has: "mulieres damnatas cognatis, aut in quorum manu essent, tradebant, ut ipsi in privato animadvertant in eas."[32] So this time, women *in manu* were to be put to death by their husband or his *paterfamilias* if he had one. The situation, of course, does not concern the *iudicium domesticum* or the *vitae necisque potestas*; as Yaron puts it, "There is in this case no exercise of a power, but rather the carrying out of a duty by persons

[28] D.48.5.21(20) (Papinian *1 de adult.*); 48.5.23(22); 48.5.24(23) (Ulpian *1 de adult.*).

[29] The law may properly be seen as restricting the right to kill; for relevant literature see Thomas, "Lex Julia." Thomas's own position is rather surprising; he considers the father's "right is not really based on *potestas* as such but is a special power created by the *lex.*" Moreover, "There was, in short, to be no really effective *ius occidendi* —hence the complete reversal of the old position, transferring to the father the privilege of the republican husband" (p. 640). Most recently A. M. Rabello considers the *ius occidendi* of the *lex Iulia* has some connection with *patria potestas*: "Il *ius occidendi iure patris* della *lex Iulia de adulteriis coercendis* e la *vitae necisque potestas* del paterfamilias," in *Atti del Seminario romanistico internazionale* (*Perugia-Spoleto-Todi; 11-14 ottobre 1971*) (Perugia, Libreria editrice universitaria, 1972), pp. 228ff, especially at p. 241.

[30] But see Valerius Maximus 6.3.10.

[31] *Per.* 48. Valerius Maximus is less specific and just mentions *propinqui*, relatives: 6.3.8.

[32] 39.18.6; Valerius Maximus 6.3.7, speaks only of *cognati*.

who have no discretion in the matter."[33] Although the case is therefore not on a level with the other situations looked at, it is useful in reminding us of the strong authority of a husband (or his *pater*) over a wife *in manu*.

The pattern which emerges enables us to draw conclusions for the period which concerns us. A husband had no free right of killing his wife even when he had justification, and a wife *in manu* remained very much under the jurisdiction of her blood-relatives. An investigation involving her family and her husband was expected before she could be put to death for adultery, though probably a husband who caught her in the act was entitled to slay her on the spot. Wine-drinking by a wife was regarded as a very serious matrimonial offense, though perhaps no longer meriting death.[34]

Dowry was a recognized social institution.[35] Yet there was no mention of it whatever in the xii Tables,[36] and we

[33] "*Vitae necisque potestas*," *T.v.R.* 30 (1962), 243ff, at 244.

[34] No theory yet satisfactorily explains why wine-drinking was treated so harshly. The idea that wine was considered to have contraceptive or abortifacient qualities (see M. Durry, "Les femmes et le vin," *Revue des Études latines* 33 [1955], 108ff) is supported only by rather late evidence; and both Dionysius of Halicarnassus 2.25.6 and Plutarch *Quaest. Rom.* 6 show their bewilderment at the rule.

[35] Textual evidence for dowry in the time of the kings is in Dionysius of Halicarnassus 2.10.2. The rule that clients were to assist in providing a dowry for the marriage of patrons' daughters fits so thoroughly into the pattern of law described for the time (and is so similar to the English feudal law of "aids") that its general accuracy must be accepted; for the argument, see Watson "*Leges Regiae*," pp. 100ff. But even *a priori* considerations lead to the conclusion that dowry existed in 5th century Rome: see Corbett, *Marriage*, pp. 147ff.

[36] The main arguments are: (1) there is no evidence for any dowry provision in the xii Tables; (2) the only known action for recovery of dowry—and which relates to the law of dowry—is the *actio rei uxoriae* which is explicitly stated to be much later; (3) Quintus Mucius in his *Ius civile* (and Gaius in his *Institutes*) does not deal with dowry—see Watson, *Law Making*, pp. 153f—and the xii Tables and developments up to the later 3rd century were decisive for the general contents of Mucius' *Ius civile*. The law of dowry was so important by Mucius' time that if there had existed any mention of it

know that *cautiones rei uxoriae* and *actiones rei uxoriae* only came into existence very much later.[37] We are entitled to conclude that there were no specific legal rules on dowry. Things given to the husband as dowry simply became part of his general assets[38] and were in no way distinguishable from his other property. If the marriage ended because of the wife's death the husband simply retained what had been given as dowry and no one else had any claim to it;[39] if the husband died first, all his estate (including dowry) fell to be divided in the ordinary way. If the husband divorced his wife for a matrimonial fault, neither she nor anyone else could demand the return of any part of the dowry; if the husband otherwise put away his wife he had to pay a severe penalty to her, irrespective of whether or not he had received a dowry.

---

in the XII Tables this would have been used as a peg for a full discussion (as *mancipatio* was for *emptio venditio, ercto non cito* for *societas*).

[37] Aulus Gellius *NA* 4.3.1,2.

[38] As at all periods in Roman history.

[39] That is, *inter alia*, that at that time there was no distinction between *dos profecticia* and *dos adventicia*. The action available to the wife's ancestor on the wife's death for return of *dos* which he had given was the *actio rei uxoriae*; hence, until the introduction of an action with that scope, *dos profecticia* could not be recovered.

FOUR

Parent and Child

A child born in a valid marriage was under the legal control, *in potestate*, of his father or of his father's *paterfamilias*,[1] but a child born outside wedlock was in the *potestas* of neither his natural father nor of his mother's *pater*. The presumption of a husband's being the father of any child born to a married woman was such that an infant born within ten months of a husband's death was regarded as his under an actual provision (IV.4) of the Tables.[2]

This *potestas* was not subject to any limitation by age but continued so long as both parties remained alive. On the death of a *paterfamilias* his male and female descendants who did not have an intermediate living direct male ancestor became *sui iuris*; and the males were now in their turn *patresfamiliarum*, a status which did not depend in any way on having children.

Potestas might also be created by adoption, of which in the later Republic there were two types, *adrogatio* and *adoptio*. Of these, the latter (which was used for the adoption of males *alieni iuris*) did not exist as early as our period,[3] the former probably did[4] though no strict proof is possible.

---

[1] For any period for which we have evidence, birth within marriage is the decisive fact for *potestas*, not any act of acceptance by the husband; for literature on this disputed point see Watson, *Private Law*, p. 30, n.1.

[2] Aulus Gellius *NA* 3.16.12; D.38.16.3.9,11 (Ulpian *14 ad Sab.*).

[3] It arose like *emancipatio* from a deliberate misinterpretation of the XII Tables' clause "si pater filium ter venum duit": G.1.134; Aulus Gellius *NA* 5.19.3; see e.g. D. Daube, "Texts and Interpretation in Roman and Jewish Law," *Jewish Journal of Sociology* 3 (1961), 3ff, at 5ff (on *emancipatio*); Kaser, *RPR* 1, p. 67.

[4] As is generally assumed: see e.g. Kaser, *RPR* 1, pp. 66f.

Adrogatio as it appears very distinctly in the first century B.C. was the adoption of a male *sui iuris*. Therefore it involved the extinction of a Roman family and was permitted only if otherwise the family of the adopter would die out. It was very formal and in two stages. First, the *pontifices* inquired into the adoption's advisability, and, if they approved, the matter then went before the *comitia calata* which was summoned by the *pontifex maximus*. The person to be adopted and the adopter were asked in turn if they agreed to the adoption and then a *rogatio* was put to the people asking if they wished and ordered the adoption.[5] Hence this was a legislative act. Only males could be adrogated both because males alone could appear in the *comitia* and also because the purpose of *adrogatio* was the continuance of a family which otherwise would be extinguished.

Conjecture alone can supply further details of early *adrogatio*.[6] But one conjecture seems both plausible and important, namely, that *adrogatio* could then be used for the adoption of males who were already *in potestate*.[7] Adoption of a male *alieni iuris* would seem more acceptable both socially and sacrally than adoption of a male *sui iuris*—no family and no religious cult were being wiped out—and it is not easy to think adoption of the former was impossible when that of the latter was permitted.[8] Yet no machinery for adoption other than *adrogatio* seems to have existed.

[5] For the forms of words as they are known for later times see infra, p. 47.

[6] One might reasonably think that only a male above puberty could be adrogated (if he were *sui iuris*) and also that a formal renunciation of his previous family religious obligations, a *detestatio sacrorum*, was needed; see Kaser, *RPR* 1, p. 66, and for a later period, Watson, *Private Law*, pp. 31f. Possibly D.50.16.238.1 (Gaius *6 ad xii tab.*) refers to this: " 'Detestatum' est testatione denuntiatum."

[7] For those who have previously thought this possible see the references given by M. Kaser, "Zur altrömischen Hausgewalt," *ZSS* 67 (1950), 474ff, at 484, n. 39.

[8] But Kaser thinks there was a principle that *patria potestas* could not be dissolved: "Hausgewalt," p. 484.

The later introduction of the simpler *adoptio* for the adoption of *alieni iuris* would have been just as desirable as it otherwise was, since the full formalities and panoply of religion for *adrogatio* were not there so important. Indeed, it becomes easier to see why the deliberate misinterpretation of the XII Tables on which *adoptio* was based was considered permissible if the intention was no more than to make adoption of *alieni iuris* less formal, rather than to permit adoption of such persons for the first time. But the full proceedings of *adrogatio* would remain desirable where the adoptee was *sui iuris*.[9]

Patria potestas or simply *potestas* was not then a technical term to designate the power of the father,[10] and the *rogatio*[11] for *adrogatio* has "utique ei vitae necisque in eum potestas siet, uti patri endo filio est." Thus, this *vitae necisque potestas* is treated as the kernel of paternal power, and it seems to have been expressly conferred by the XII Tables.[12] But it could not be exercised arbitrarily[13] and there is strong textual evidence that the XII Tables contained a clause that a *paterfamilias* could put a son to death only *ex iusta causa*.[14] It is against a background such as this that we should see the existence even at an earlier date of

[9] Contra, P. Koschaker, ZSS 63 (1943), 449, n. 6.

[10] For the argument see infra, pp. 47f.

[11] Perhaps the exact wording is later but this does not affect the argument: see infra, pp. 47f.

[12] Coll. 4.8 (Papinian *sing. de adult.*).

[13] See on *a priori* grounds R. Yaron, "*Vitae necisque potestas*," T.v.R. 30 (1962), 243ff, at 248f. The original meaning and scope of *vitae necisque potestas*—Yaron's main concern—is not relevant here.

[14] Gai Inst. fr. Augustod. 85; 86: The text is not complete but this point at least seems secure: for the full argument see W. Kunkel, "Das Konsilium im Hausgericht," ZSS 83 (1966), 219ff, at 242ff; also Kaser, RPR 1, p. 61. A. Guarino thinks it most improbable that the XII Tables would restrict the *vitae necisque potestas* in this way and regards the text as too mutilated for such conclusions to be drawn from it: Labeo 13 (1967), 124.

the family council or domestic tribunal. The power to punish severely, to put to death, a member of a family belonged to the *pater* but he had to act with good reason, which would mean in the normal case that the son or other person had to have committed a crime.[15] To establish the facts and also protect himself from any charge of having acted arbitrarily[16] the *pater* would summon members of the family or friends to sit in judgment with him and would accept their opinion. But this family council developed as a social fact; it had no legal standing and the *pater* was under no legal obligation to summon it.

The family council appears prominently in the lay sources and it would be wrong to deny its existence or its importance.[17] Yet its extra-legal position is shown by a number of facts. Above all, the sources for all periods concur in giving the *vitae necisque potestas* to the *pater* as an individual and not to the family,[18] but the decision in a family council was by a majority vote.[19] The language of the texts

[15] See Kunkel, "Konsilium," p. 243. But see Dionysius of Halicarnassus 2.26.4,5,6, who obviously thinks a father in early times had an unfettered right to kill his son. Interestingly, Dionysius draws his boundaries too wide and includes cases where the father was exercising his powers as a military commander: see Yaron, "*Potestas*," p. 243. Dionysius seems to be romanticizing the *vitae necisque potestas*, contrasting the Romans favorably with the Greeks: "Mild punishments are not sufficient to restrain the folly of youth and its stubborn ways": 2.26.3.

[16] Q. Fabius Maximus was *damnatus* around 105 to 103 B.C. because he behaved improperly as a *pater* in having his son killed: Orosius 5.16. On the text see Kunkel, "Konsilium," p. 241 and the authors he cites, n. 44.

[17] See now above all G. Wesener, *RE, supp.* 9, 373ff; Kunkel, "Konsilium." The latter thinks the family council had to be summoned when a *filiusfamilias* was thought to have committed an offense worthy of death, except when he was caught in the act.

[18] E.g. Dionysius of Halicarnassus 2.26.4 (for time of Romulus); *Gai Inst. fr. Augustod.* 86 (for the XII Tables); Cicero *Dom.* 29.77 and Aulus Gellius *NA* 5.19.9 (both for the forms used in *adrogatio*). See also Livy 1.26.9.

[19] See the arguments drawn by Kunkel, "Konsilium," pp. 220ff, from Seneca *Clem.* 1.15.2ff.

is incomprehensible if in fact the power resided in the council. Again, friends who were not members of the family might be asked to sit on a council.[20] If the family council had legal standing this is hard to explain. Thirdly, none of the legal sources, such as Gaius' *Institutes* and the *Digest*, mention the family council.[21]

In one case and one case only did the family council have legal recognition and that was where a woman who was no longer in the *potestas* of her *pater* was thought to have misbehaved. Romulus himself is said to have decreed that for adultery and wine-drinking a woman could be judged and put to death by her relatives acting with her husband.[22] Very reasonably the right of inflicting the supreme penalty was not simply entrusted to the husband even when the wife was in his *manus*. For later times, moreover, there is evidence that the family had the right to punish and put to death a woman who was *sui iuris*,[23] and this is unlikely to have been an innovation posterior to the fifth century.

The *paterfamilias* also had the right to inflict lesser punishments on his dependents, above all to sell them into foreign slavery,[24] and he could almost certainly deliver at least

---

[20] See Seneca *Clem.* 1.15.2ff where the *pater* summoned his friend Augustus to sit on the council; Valerius Maximus 2.9.2 (relates to 307-306 B.C.), where the censors removed L. Annius from the Senate because he divorced his wife "nullo amicorum [in] consilio adhibito." The latter episode is no evidence of a legal duty to summon a family council.

[21] Though Kunkel, "Konsilium," pp. 248f, would reconstruct D.48.8.2 (Ulpian *1 de adult.*) so that it does; contra, Guarino, loc. cit.

[22] For this see supra, pp. 34f.

[23] Valerius Maximus 6.3.8 and Livy *Per.* 48 (both texts refer to the same instances around 154 B.C. Possibly, despite their husbands' deaths, the ladies in question remained *in manu* [of their fathers-in-law]): Tacitus *Ann.* 13.32 (refers to A.D. 58); Suetonius *Tib.* 35; see Kunkel, "Konsilium," pp. 237f. For the 2nd century B.C. there is evidence that women convicted after a public trial might, for decency's sake, be handed over to their relatives for execution: Livy 39.18.6, and Valerius Maximus 6.3.7 (both refer to 186 B.C.).

[24] Cicero *De Or.* 1.40.181,182; *Caecin.* 34.98.

sons into noxal surrender for any delict they had committed.[25] The power of the *pater* to control the marriage of his family has already been seen.[26]

Any child whom he did not wish to bring up the *pater* could expose, and restrictions on the right of exposure which apparently existed earlier appear to have disappeared.[27] The XII Tables expressly ordered (Tab. IV.1) that a child born deformed should be quickly killed.[28]

A strange provision of the code which is more appropriately discussed elsewhere should be mentioned here, namely, that if a pater sold a son three times the son was to be free from the pater.[29]

Much less dramatic, yet of far greater social significance, was the fact that only persons *sui iuris*—women as well as *patresfamiliarum*—could own property. Likewise, only persons *sui iuris* had the right to bring a private law action,[30] and they alone could be sued.[31] In practice, however, it did happen that the *pater* allowed at least male descendents to have control of a fund of property which they could deal with as if it were their own.[32] But there was no legal content to the *peculium*, as it is called.

A male who became *flamen Dialis* or a female who became a Vestal virgin ceased to be in *patria potestas*.[33]

[25] Noxal surrender is best discussed in the chapter on slavery since the known XII Tables' clause speaks only of slaves: infra, pp. 85f.

[26] Supra, pp. 25, 28.

[27] Dionysius of Halicarnassus 2.15.2; see Watson, "*Leges Regiae*," p. 102.

[28] Cicero *Leg.* 3.8.19.

[29] G.4.79; see infra, pp. 118f.

[30] Even much later when a *filius* entered a contract the right of action accrued to the *paterfamilias*: D.44.1.14 (Alfenus Varus *2 dig.*); see Watson, *Persons*, pp. 99f.

[31] See Kaser, *ZPR*, p. 46.

[32] There is no direct evidence for this statement but we know that a *peculium* might be granted to slaves—*Epit.Ulp.* 24; see infra, pp. 93f —hence *a fortiori*, we can assume, to sons.

[33] G.1.130; Aulus Gellius *NA* 1.12.9. The XII Tables actually contained a provision that a Vestal virgin was free from *tutela*; see infra, p. 76. If the Romans had by the 5th century established a colony

Parent and Child

The early Republic can properly be regarded as the high-water mark of *patria potestas*. Restrictions recorded for the regal period[34] are no longer to be traced at the time of the xii Tables. Gradually, though mainly well after the years which concern us, limitations on paternal power creep in.[35]

---

in Latium—the only possibility might be at Ostia at the salt workings —then the colonists might also have been freed from *patria potestas*: see G.1.131.

[34] For these and the general reliability of the tradition see Watson, *"Leges Regiae,"* especially at pp. 102f.

[35] The question whether a Roman's power over his wife (*in manu*) and children was the same as that over his slaves and other property is briefly discussed, infra, p. 133.

Potestas and *Manus*

In chapter One we were primarily concerned with how a wife entered the *manus* of her husband, in chapter Four with the power of a father over his children. In this excursus we will consider more closely the meaning of the words *manus* and *potestas* in a legal context. The usages of the word *potestas* emerge more clearly from the legal sources, so we shall look at that term first.

In classical law *potestas* is used technically or semi-technically above all of *patria potestas*, of the head of a family's power over his children (of whatever age) and remoter descendents. When a son was adopted by *adrogatio* a *rogatio* was put to the people: "Velitis, iubeatis, uti L. Valerius L. Titio tam iure legeque filius siet, quam si ex eo patre matreque familias eius natus esset, utique ei vitae necisque in eum potestas siet, uti patri endo filio est. Haec ita, uti dixi, ita vos, Quirites rogo." And at an earlier stage of the proceedings the person to be adopted was asked, "Auctorne es, uti in te P. Fonteius vitae necisque potestatem habeat ut in filio?" These formulations are very old, even if they do not reach back to the XII Tables. From them we can deduce first that the power of a father over his descendents was very great—*vitae necisque potestas*—and was well known and established, and secondly that nonetheless there was no technical concept of *patria potestas*, and certainly no technical usage of that phrase. If there had been such a technical usage, it would have appeared in the *rogatio* instead of "vitae necisque potestas uti patri endo filio est," and in the question to the adoptee instead of "vitae necisque potestas ut in filio."[1] Of course, should these formulations be later than the xII Tables, then *a fortiori* there cannot then have been a technical use of *potestas* in respect of a father's power over his descendents.

The xII Tables contained a clause (v.7a), "Si furiosus escit, adgnatum gentiliumque in eo pecuniaque eius potestas esto."[2] Thus, relatives were to have *potestas* over a lunatic and over his property. Now this *potestas* is not more closely defined, though its limits would have been known. However complete it may have been, the *potestas* over the lunatic is unlikely to have had the same content as the *potestas* over descendents. Presumably, at least, the *adgnati* and *gentiles*, were not the owners of the lunatic's property.[3] And again, *potestas* over the lunatic is likely to have meant something different from the *potestas* over his property.

After Gaius declares[4] that, of persons *alieni iuris*, some are *in potestate*, others are *in manu*, and yet others *in mancipio*, he considers first those *in potestate* and starts with slaves. Slaves, he says, are "in potestate" of their owners who have over them "vitae necisque potestas."[5] He shows that this power is limited, and then tells us that the slave is in the *potestas* of him who has the slave *in bonis*, not of him who is the bare owner *ex iure Quiritium*.[6] The only other instance of being *in potestate* which he mentions is that of descendents. The idea of the slave's being *in potestate* is likely to go back, I suggest, some considerable time before

---

[1] It might be felt that a mention of *vitae necisque potestas* was appropriate because of the awesomeness of that power, and one would not want to deny force to that assertion. But, as we have seen, the father's power to put to death was very severely restricted; and the power would be less noticeable (and important) than the incapacity of a *filius* to have property of his own. At the least, if *patria potestas* had been a technical legal concept we would expect to find the term expressed in the *rogatio* and the question to the adoptee even if, because of its awesomeness, *vitae necisque potestas* was also specifically mentioned.

[2] See infra, pp. 76f.

[3] Though Cicero claims the xII Tables forbade a lunatic to be owner of his own property: *Tusc.* 3.5.11.

[4] G.1.49.   [5] G.1.52.   [6] G.1.54.

potestas came to be thought of so predominantly in terms of the power over descendents; and hence to be much older than Gaius' *Institutes*, even if not so old as the xii Tables. The view that the person with *potestas* is he who has the slave *in bonis* and not the bare Quiritary ownership probably developed later than the xii Tables. However this may be, we seem to have another type of case where *potestas* was used—even long after the xii Tables—to signify the existing power-relationship. A much more doubtful case, which should not be insisted on here, is whether a *tutor* had *potestas* over his pupil.[7]

Thus, legal sources indicate that in the earlier Republic, *potestas* was used at least of a father's power over his children, of a master's power over his slaves, and of relatives' power over a lunatic and over his property. It should not be argued from this that *potestas* was a unitary conception,[8] that, for instance, the *adgnati* had a *vitae necisque potestas* over the lunatic, that his property was theirs, and so on. Rather, we should admit that *potestas* was not at all a technical term—most clearly revealed by the *rogatio* in *adrogatio*—that it simply signified "power" or "control," and that the legal extent of that power would be defined by the circumstances.

In the legal sources, *manus* is used before Justinian[9]

[7] As is maintained by the dominant opinion: contra, Watson, *Persons*, pp. 106ff; see infra, p. 73.

[8] Though from the ancient wide usage of *potestas*, *manus*, and *mancipium* it is generally held that ancient Roman law had only one unitary private "power of ownership" over everything subject to the *paterfamilias*, over free members of his family, slaves, animals, and inanimate property: see e.g. Kaser, *Eigentum*, pp. 1ff; Diósdi, *Ownership*, p. 50.

[9] Long before Justinian, of course, marriage *cum manu* had disappeared. In legal writings of his time *manus* appears to be used in the context of release from paternal power almost as a synonym for *patria potestas*; C.7.40.1.2 (A.D. 530); 8.48.6 (A.D. 531); J.1.12.6 (does not derive from any classical model; see Ferrini, *Opere* 2 [Milan, U. Hoepli, 1929], 342); Theophilus *Paraph.* 1.12.6; *Nov.* 81.1pr (539). This usage cannot be regarded as a survival, but is innovatory and is the result of the disappearance of *manus* in marriage.

only in respect of a wife with one solitary exception.[10] The single exception is in D.1.1.4 (Ulpian *1 inst.*) where Ulpian, explaining the derivation of the word *manumissio*, says that a slave "manui et potestati suppositus est." In the circumstances not too much should be made of the text.[11] Perhaps it is important, too, that in the context of a wife the word *manus* is never used in the nominative, but always in a phrase such as "in manu" or "in manum convenire."[12] But a few very important legal words—*mancipium, mancipatio, emancipatio, manumissio*,[13] all compounded with *manus*—reveal that once *manus* was used much more widely to signify power over things,[14] descendents, and slaves, though the restriction in legal usage seems to have occurred earlier than was the case with *potestas*.

The significance of the usage in the literary sources is difficult to judge. When Livy, whose legal knowledge is notoriously imprecise, uses *in manu* of women—always of women—who are in the charge of a father or *tutor*,[15] we

[10] Even Gaius when discussing entry into *manus*, G.1.108ff, does not say that *coemptio fiduciae causa* puts the woman *in manu*: G.1.114-115b.

[11] U. Coli holds the text interpolated in part; "*Regnum*," *SDHI* 17 (1951), 1ff, at 128f.

[12] More likely, though, the fact has no legal significance. One would expect that *in manu* and *convenire in manum* would be much more common than *manus* by itself just as in legal contexts *in potestate* is much more common than *potestas*. Indeed, only when the control over a wife was actually being described could one reasonably hope to find *manus* by itself, and the absence of legal sources drastically cuts down the likelihood of this occurrence. Actually, the very existence of *in manu* and *in manum convenire* presupposes a form of control called *manus*. And what about "alienos manu emittitis" in Plautus *Curc.* 497? For opinions held see Diósdi, *Ownership*, p. 54, n. 36 and the authors he cites.

[13] See Voigt, *XII Tafeln*, 2 (Leipzig, A. G. Liebeskind, 1883), pp. 83ff.

[14] The conclusion holds good even if we think that the word *mancipatio* derives from "a taking by the hand" and that originally "hand" was understood mainly in its primary sense. Very quickly the idea of power would come to predominate, especially since the actual taking by the hand is not the most prominent element in the ceremony.

[15] 3.45.2; 34.2.11; 39.18.6. The last text may refer exclusively to wives *in manu*.

should perhaps see here his lack of legal knowledge rather than a genuine survival of an earlier usage.[16] But Plautus had a keen interest in law[17] and when he says "alienos manu emittitis"[18] of the transfer of slaves, and "illi suam rem esse aequomst in manu"[19] of the control of one's property (especially a female slave) it is tempting to see everyday language which would not sound odd to the jurists.[20]

[16] And the same may be true of some other authors who were writing after *manus* became obsolete (except for religious purposes): Seneca the Elder *Con. Ex.* 3.3 (of a son *in potestate*); Pliny the Younger *Ep.* 8.18.4; Lactantius *Div. Inst.* 4.29 (of a son *in potestate*).

[17] See e.g. Watson, *Private Law*, p. 3 and n. 2.

[18] *Curc.* 497.　　　　　　　[19] *Merc.* 454.

[20] No conclusions need be drawn from the verse of Caecilius Statius which is quoted by Cicero *Tusc.* 4.32.68. Poetic license can explain the idea of a person being *in manu* of Love, but it is possible that similar conclusions should be drawn as for Plautus.

FIVE

Succession

The picture of the family unit which we have been looking at in early Roman society is dominated entirely by the *paterfamilias*. When we turn to consider wider groupings of relatives and quasi-relatives, or persons *sui iuris* but of less than full capacity we find, significantly, that the simplest approach is via succession, testate and intestate, to the *paterfamilias*. Only persons *sui iuris* could own property, hence only they could leave any behind. Only a *paterfamilias* above the age of puberty would have any right to make a will. Unsystematic though it may seem, succession will therefore be discussed before we look at the remaining topics in the law of persons.

By the time of the XII Tables, succession could be by will or on intestacy, and the code contained express provisions on both. The former we will treat first as did the XII Tables themselves,[1] and we must at the outset reconstruct as far as possible the original wording of the provision on testate succession, which is given in the editions as Tab. v.3.

This clause appears in the sources in three different versions.

Cicero has: "Paterfamilias uti super familia pecuniaque sua legassit, ita ius esto."

Gaius: "Uti legassit suae rei, ita ius esto."

---

[1] The arguments for this proposition are: (1) Ulpian in D.38.6.1.1 expressly states that intestate succession was dealt with after testate in the XII Tables; (2) Quintus Mucius Scaevola's *Ius civile* also treats testate before intestate succession, and the influence of the code on that work was enormous; (3) Cicero *Inv. Rhet.* 2.50.148 and *Rhet. Her.* 1.13.23 quote the provisions of the XII Tables in the order testate, intestate.

And Ulpian: "Uti legassit super pecunia tutelave suae rei, ita ius esto."

Thus, in one the object of the *legare* is *familia pecuniaque*, in another *sua res*, and in the third *pecunia tutelave suae rei*. The differences here, of course, go far beyond mere matters of wording, and it becomes essential to decide which version is closest to the original. All three have had their supporters.[2] For the text of Cicero is urged his less remoteness in time from the XII Tables and the fact that he had to learn the XII Tables by heart at school; for that of Gaius, his acknowledged study of the XII Tables, and a fragment of Pomponius (D.50.16.120), which gives the same reading; for that of Ulpian, a text of Paul (D. 50.16.53pr), and that testamentary tutelage can be traced to the XII Tables. Recently Diósdi has claimed that it seems impossible to decide which version is most accurate or to ascertain the original wording.[3] If this verdict is correct then any attempt to reconstruct the law on any point as it appeared in the XII Tables is bound to fail. If we cannot determine the original wording when we have three versions, then *a fortiori*, we cannot judge the accuracy of the tradition when we have only one.

I submit that it is possible to decide which version is closest to the original wording of the XII Tables. In the first place, the reading of Cicero, which appears both in *Inv. Rhet.* 2.50.148 and in the celebrated work by an unknown author, the *Rhet. Her.* 1.13.23, can be excluded.

It is well known that either Cicero's *Inv. Rhet.* derives from the *Rhet. Her.*—an outdated opinion!—or else *Rhet. Her.* derives from *Inv. Rhet.* or that both used a common source.[4] The connection between the two works is clear

[2] See the authors cited by Diósdi, *Ownership*, p. 24, n. 34.

[3] *Ownership*, p. 24.

[4] See e.g. H. M. Hubbell, *Cicero de inventione, de optimo genere oratorum, topica* (Loeb Classical Library, London, Cambridge, Mass., 1949), pp. viiif; H. Caplan, *Rhetorica ad Herennium* (Loeb Classical Library, London, Cambridge, Mass., 1968), pp. xxviff; G. Kennedy, *The Art of Rhetoric in the Roman World* (Princeton, Princeton University Press, 1972), pp. 103ff.

even from the very passages in question and one text must not be regarded as corroborating the accuracy of the other. Both texts purport to quote more than one provision of the XII Tables, but there are two extreme oddities in the supposed quotations. First, it was not necessary to specify that the testator is a *paterfamilias*—since only a *pater* could have property—and normally the XII Tables omit unnecessary words. It cannot be argued that this well-known characteristic of omission is due to later tampering with the other texts since later legal style was itself fuller and also the texts with omitted subjects and objects—see especially Tab. 1—are less easy to understand. Deliberate alterations would have the aim of making the Tables more comprehensible. Secondly, another apparent provision, "Si paterfamilias intestato moritur, familia pecuniaque eius agnatum gentiliumque esto," is a conflation of two separate clauses of the XII Tables which we shall consider shortly: v.4, "Si intestato moritur, cui suus heres nec escit, adgnatus proximus familiam habeto." v.5, "Si adgnatus nec escit, gentiles familiam [habento]."[5] The Ciceronian version with these peculiarities does not reappear in later sources. It seems, therefore, to have been a version in rhetorical use which did not survive. Obviously, despite its flaws which make it unreliable, it has some connection with the original.

Thus, we are now left with the versions of Gaius and Ulpian.

Gaius' reading, "Uti legassit suae rei, ita ius esto" in G.2.224, receives support from Pomponius who gives the same reading in D.50.16.120 (*5 ad Quintum Mucium*) and who uses the wording to illustrate the wide scope of early testaments. Further support is to be found in Justinian's *Nov.* 22.2pr which has "Uti legassit quisque de sua re, ita ius esto." The other version, that of Ulpian in the *Epit.Ulp.* 11.14, "Uti legassit super pecunia tutelave suae rei, ita ius esto," has some backing from Paul who in D.50.16.53pr

---

[5] For this see infra, pp. 66ff.

(*59 ad ed.*) cites as a quotation the words "super pecuniae tutelaeve suae" to prove that disjunctives may be used as conjunctives.

There is nothing in the forms which would allow us to choose between the version of Gaius and the version of Ulpian. Likewise, both versions are well established in juristic tradition; so well established, indeed, that deductions are made from the wording. Nonetheless, the version closest to the original must be that of Ulpian. Firstly, *legare suae rei* could make sense in classical Latin if *suae rei* were treated as a partitive genitive or as a dative of respect. But no such explanation can be found for *legare super* + ablative. Secondly, *tutela* after *legare* makes no sense in classical law or in the law of the later Republic whereas *res* after *legare* does. Hence on both these counts a principle akin to that of *difficilior lectio potior* very much favors Ulpian. One can see why someone who was puzzled by the provision would excise "super pecunia tutelave" if that phrase had been in the clause in front of him, but not why someone would insert the phrase if it were not there. Thirdly, the strange *legare super* appears in both Ulpian and Cicero. It has already been argued that Cicero's account was from an inaccurate rhetorical version—with, of course, some connection with the original—which did not survive in use. If this is correct then Cicero's *legare super* provides us with independent evidence of the accuracy of Ulpian's version.

Moreover, if "Uti legassit super pecunia tutelave suae rei" were the original, both of the variations can be simply explained. "Super familia pecuniaque" would represent a deliberate change made in an attempt to recover the original reading because *tutela* was thought to make no sense. Similarly, dissatisfaction with *tutela* could lead to "super pecunia tutelave" being purposely excised as an unwarranted and undesirable gloss which had crept into the text. But it is not easy to account for both variations if either "Uti legassit suae rei" or "Uti super familia pecuniaque sua legassit" were the original. If the former, we have to suppose that of the two variations one derived (directly or indirectly) from the original, the other from the variation, and we have to account for the alteration to the absurd "tutela." Above all, we could not claim that the variations were due to dissatisfaction with the original. If the latter, we have to imagine that in one variation the satisfactory "familia" became changed to the absurd (for Ulpian) "tutela," and that "suae rei" was inserted; that the other variation derived from this one and not from the original—hence the "suae rei"—but that dissatisfaction with *tutela* caused the excision of "super pecunia tutelave." Finally (if the choice lay between the versions of Cicero and of Ulpian) the word *familia* is the unquestioned word used to signify the heritable estate in the provisions of the XII Tables which appear in the editions as v.4 and v.5. Any Roman from the late Republic onward might be forgiven for expecting to find the word "familia" also in v.3; and hence for substituting it for the strange "tutela." Significantly perhaps, v.4 (or a version of it) is quoted both in Cicero *Inv. Rhet.* 2.50.148 and *Rhet. Her.* 1.13.23, beside their version of v.3.

Thus, by the XII Tables there could be a *legare* in respect of *pecunia* and *tutela suae rei*. These terms all require elucidation though consideration of the meaning of *tutela suae rei* which appears to refer to guardianship may be postponed to a later chapter.[6]

Pecunia seems to occur in the XII Tables not only in v.3, but also in v.7a;[7] "Si furiosus escit, adgnatum gentiliumque in eo pecuniaque eius potestas esto." Strikingly, in the two provisions on succession without a will, v.4 and v.5, which have been quoted above, the term indicating the deceased's property is *familia*. It is very likely that the code dealt with intestate succession immediately after the clause on testate succession,[8] hence on general linguistic grounds we must assume that the use of *pecunia* in v.3 and of *familia* in v.4

[6] See infra, pp. 72f.   [7] And further in Tab. x.7.
[8] See supra, p. 52, n. 1.

and v.5 indicates that these words did not have the same meaning at the time of the XII Tables. A wanton proliferation of terms with the same significance is not to be expected.

But it has been amply shown that, whatever the earlier and subsequent history of *pecunia* and *familia*, both words at the time of the XII Tables referred to property of all kinds which a man could own, and neither was restricted to certain kinds of things.[9] A solution which seems to fit the sources is that *pecunia* means "property," and *familia* means "a man's property considered as a unit." Thus, both could designate owned things of all kinds, and could refer to everything which a person owned. But when the code was concerned with succession on intestacy to everything a man had the appropriate term was *familia*, just as later *hereditas* was a convenient word to designate a dead man's property conceived of as a unit. The term *paterfamilias* expresses the same idea, the head of the unit.[10] Indeed, one can plausibly reconstruct this stage in the history of the word *familia*. Perhaps the word originally connoted the slave members of a household, and eventually widened to include the free members, especially the dependent members. At this point a term such as *paterfamilias* might be introduced. The transition then to the meaning for *familia* of all the combined

[9] Many attempts have, of course, been made to show that *pecunia* referred to one sort of thing, *familia* to another, but for the failure of these views see e.g. Kaser, *RPR* 1, pp. 97f, and above all Diósdi, *Ownership*, pp. 23ff. The main arguments against such views are (1) that only certain kinds of thing, the *familia*, would be open to intestate succession; (2) that only certain other kinds of thing, the *pecunia*, would come under the control of a lunatic's relatives; and (3) that *pecunia* in Tab. x.7 is used to include both slaves and horses—Pliny *HN* 21.3.7—hence (a) *familia* as opposed to *pecunia* cannot mean "slaves" and (b) *familia* cannot mean the *res mancipi*, and *pecunia* the *res nec mancipi*. One should also add that all later Roman writers take both *pecunia* and *familia* to cover individually all the things which a man owned.

[10] And when there were no *sui heredes*, the *familia* for the *paterfamilias* would have exactly the same content as the *familia* for the *agnati* and *gentiles*.

assets and rights of a *pater* presents no difficulties. An important, perhaps even the main, use of *familia* with this sense would be to denote the assets which a *pater* had at the time of his death; but this rôle of *familia* was in time taken over by the word *hereditas*.[11]

Pecunia, "property," has no such connotation, hence is the right word to designate the object of individual bequests,[12] and the belongings of a lunatic which require looking after. The danger in the latter case is not so much that the lunatic may dispose of all he owns as a unit, but that he may lose his property by various unwise transactions.

If these are the meanings properly to be attributed to *familia* and *pecunia* for the XII Tables then *pecunia* in Tab. v.3 does greatly assist in the elucidation of the scope of testamentary succession at that time. But it should first be stressed that there is no implication in the use of the word either that all property of the testator must fall under the *legare* or that the testator could not so dispose of everything he owned. All that emerges is that the testator could make testamentary arrangements by *legare* for all kinds of owned property.

The significant point, I should like to suggest, is the omission from Tab. v.3 of any mention of *familia*. This contrasts not only with Tab. v.4 and v.5, but more strikingly with the wording—as it has come down to us—of the *mancipatio* in the *testamentum per aes et libram*: "Familiam pecuniamque tuam endo mandatela tua custodelaque mea esse aio, eaque quo tu iure testamentum facere possis secundum legem publicam, hoc aere aeneaque libra esto mihi empta."[13]

---

[11] The meaning of *familia* is not clear in Cato *de agr.* 138: "Mulis, equis, asinis feriae nullae, nisi si in familia sunt." The most likely explanation seems to be that of Diósdi who takes *feriae* as the subject of the final clause: *Ownership*, pp. 27f. In any event in the case of a word like *familia* which underwent several shifts of meaning, Cato's usage is not necessarily illuminating for the sense of the word in the mid-5th century.

[12] Even if these might exhaust all the inheritance of the testator.

[13] G.2.104. None of the problems on the wording of the *mancipatio* affects the point which here concerns us.

The dating of this precise form of wording cannot be established[14] but it was in use at a time when the *testamentum per aes et libram* was used to institute an heir and it provided in addition a means of awarding legacies. The presence in the developed *testamentum per aes et libram* of both the words *familia* and *pecunia* and the known function (at least by the later Republic) of that *testamentum*, plus the meaning to be attributed to *familia* in Tab. v.4 and v.5 leads to the conclusion that the absence of *familia* from "Uti legassit super pecunia tutelave suae rei" indicates that that clause was not envisaging the appointment of an heir. The testamentary provisions involved relate only to the making of individual bequests and the appointment of tutors.

The etymology and early history of the verb *legare*[15]— both obscure—do not seem to help to explain the scope of Tab. v.3. But in classical Latin, the verb *legare* has *inter alia* the technical legal meaning, "to leave a legacy" and the noun *legatum* means "legacy." The verb is not used to denote the institution of an heir, and the noun is not used to designate the deceased's property in general or the part of it which goes to the heir. The meaning of *legare* and *legatum* at the time their meaning is readily apparent to us is easier to explain if *legare* at no time was used of the institution of an heir. This argument seems to support the conclusion reached on other grounds that "Uti legassit super pecunia tutelave suae rei" in the XII Tables did not relate to the appointment of an heir. Probably one can go further. It does seem that an early meaning of *legare* is "to give instructions"; hence the very common sense of "to send as an ambassador, etc." and indeed the derivative *legatus*, "ambassador." Our clause, then, could well be translated: "As he gave instructions with regard to his *pecunia* and the guardianship of his property." This approach would likewise lead to the conclusion that at this time the *testamen-*

---

[14] On the argument advanced here, this wording must be post-decemviral.

[15] From *lex* (itself of very doubtful etymology)? Or from *legere*?

tum per aes et libram was not concerned with the appointment of an heir. Very much in favor of this interpretation
of *legare* is that it makes possible an easy understanding
(for that period) of *legare super tutela suae rei*.

The clause, it should be noted, does not speak of the making of a *testamentum*, and it may be an anachronism to
think of the provision as concerning a "last will and testament." However that may be and whatever Tab. v.3 may
have concerned, the xii Tables had otherwise no provision
on testate succession. This emerges from the total lack of
evidence of any further provision, the treatment in the later
sources of Tab. v.3 alone as the early statutory basis for
testate succession, and the very prominence of Tab. v.3 in
these later sources. But one cannot conclude that in the
mid-fifth century b.c. there was no testate succession apart
from what was contained in that clause. The xii Tables did
not aim at a complete statement of the law.

Further progress on testate succession can be made from
an examination of Tab. v.4: "Si intestato moritur, cui suus
heres nec escit, adgnatus proximus familiam habeto." According to this, apparently, the nearest agnate is to take the
familia when there is no *suus heres* if the deceased died
intestato.[16] Hence it would seem that if the testator had
died *testatus*, the *agnatus proximus* would not take the
familia and so—if the arguments given above on the meaning of *familia* were justified—a *paterfamilias* could appoint
an heir by will. Accordingly, if the arguments on Tab. v.3
are also correct, there must have been two ways (at least)
at the time of the xii Tables by which a *paterfamilias* could
make arrangements for property distribution after his
death; one, the subject of Tab. v.3, which did not permit the
appointment of an heir; the other, evidenced indirectly in

---

[16] A further translation of Tab. v.4 is possible which, however, does
not affect the present issue; cf. infra, pp. 65f. H. Lévy-Bruhl has a very
different—and, to me, impossible—interpretation of this clause: *Nouvelles Études sur le très ancien Droit romain* (Paris, Sirey, 1947), pp.
40f; *"Intestatus"* in *Studi Albertario* i (Milan, Giuffrè, 1953), 545ff.
But see Kaser, *RPR* i, p. 102, n. 7 and the work he cites.

Tab. v.4, which did. It therefore seems that at this time the *testamentum comitiis calatis* existed in some form and permitted the institution of an heir; and that the *testamentum per aes et libram* also existed in some form but no heir could be appointed under it. This conclusion is, of course, not new,[17] but the way in which it has been reached may put it on a firmer basis. Above all, it seems there are positive arguments against propositions such as that the *testamentum per aes et libram* did not exist even as a "Legatentestament" at the time of the xii Tables,[18] or that it already existed as a full testament with the institution of an heir, or that the *testamentum calatis comitiis* did not allow the institution of an heir.[19]

The *testamentum per aes et libram* and the *testamentum comitiis calatis* should be considered separately and in greater detail. The former arose in practice as an adaptation of *mancipatio* without "official" authority. This is why it is the subject of a specific provision, Tab. v.3: the decemviri are expressly ratifying existing but doubtful legal practice. The latter, on the other hand, was well established and did not need to be reinforced by a clause of the code.

For the *testamentum per aes et libram* were required the usual elements for a valid *mancipatio*.[20] The transferee, who is known in later times as the *familiae emptor*, uttered the appropriate words and went through the appropriate motions. The wording cannot be precisely reconstructed but it will have had similarities with that known for later times (which has been quoted above)[21] though, of course, the

---

[17] See e.g. Kaser, *RPR* 1, pp. 101f, 105ff.

[18] This opinion is held by P. Voci, *Diritto ereditario romano* 1, 2nd ed. (Milan, Giuffrè, 1967), 14ff; and Watson, *Succession*, p. 11.

[19] The opinion of O. Lenel, "Zur Geschichte der *heredis institutio*," in *Essays in Legal History*, ed. P. Vinogradoff (London, Oxford University Press, 1913), pp. 125ff (reprinted in *Labeo* 12 [1966], 355ff): but now generally rejected; see Kaser, *RPR* 1, p. 106, n. 13. It is, of course, from time to time suggested that if no heir could be appointed by will, then "intestato" in Tab. v.4 must be a later insertion: cf. Wieacker, "xii Tafeln," p. 317.

[20] See infra, pp. 134ff.   [21] Supra, p. 58.

form will not have used the word *familia*. The testator himself will have indicated both his intention to create legacies and the content of them[22] by an oral declaration (known as the *nuncupatio*) in a form concluding in words such as "ita do, ita lego, ita testor, itaque vos Quirites testimonium mihi perhibitote."[23] This wording clearly dates back to a time when an heir was not appointed by this will. The *testamentum* presents some problems of a theoretical character. First, why could tutors be appointed under it? Presumably this practice also troubled the Romans until it was given statutory authority by Tab. v.3. Secondly, where was the ownership of the property legated between the time the *testamentum* was made and the death of the testator? The *familiae emptor* apparently does not claim to be owner in the form of words for the *mancipatio* which is known to us, though Gaius states that in early times the *familiae emptor* "heredis locum optinebat."[24] There is no sign that any action ever existed against a *familiae emptor* who refused to hand over the property entrusted to him, which may suggest that at no time was he treated in any real sense as an owner. (Likewise, there is no evidence that there was ever a sacral sanction.) What the *familiae emptor* does claim is that the property is in the *mandatela* of the testator and in his own *custodela*. The problem is perhaps best considered in two stages. First, in the period before the xii Tables when the *testamentum* still had no official support, the *mancipatio* may have given the *familiae emptor* a title, but no right. Practical problems may well have been rare since it is reasonable to suppose that such a will would be made only when the testator was on his deathbed. After the xii Tables, when the *testamentum* had official backing, it may easily

---

[22] Though the latter may have been in writing.

[23] G.2.104.

[24] G.2.103. This suggests the *familiae emptor* did become owner at some point though perhaps only at the testator's death. No argument here can be drawn from the preceding "id est qui a testatore familiam accipiebat mancipio" since the sole point of that clause is to explain the term *familiae emptor*.

have been the case that the *familiae emptor* was not even regarded in any sense as having title. Otherwise there would have to be some way of transferring his title to the legatees, and for this there is no evidence.[25] It would seem that we can regard Tab. v.3 as going beyond the form of the *mancipatio* and establishing the bequests as legacies. But this problem alerts us to a real question, the nature of the *legata*, and we see that they are the direct forerunners of the classical *legata per vindicationem*.[26] We can now understand two peculiarities of the *legata per vindicationem*: why the testator had to be owner *ex iure Quiritium* of the thing legated at the time the will was made,[27] and why the formulation "do lego" appeared to Gaius as the prime way of creating a *legatum per vindicationem*.[28] Since in the *legatum per vindicationem* (as opposed to the *legatum per damnationem*) the legatee automatically became owner of the thing legated when the *hereditas* was accepted, it seems reasonable to think that the legatee in the *testamentum per aes et libram* at the time of the XII Tables became owner without ado on the testator's death.[29]

Though the contrary has been asserted,[30] it seems unlikely that a forerunner of the classical *legatum per damnationem* also existed at the time of the XII Tables within the ambit of the *testamentum per aes et libram*. The *legatum per damnationem* did not give automatic ownership of the object legated to the legatee but gave the legatee a right of action against the heir, and the testator did not need to be

[25] There seems no need to think in terms of divided ownership between the testator and the *familiae emptor*, and between the *familiae emptor* and the legatees; but see Kaser, *RPR* 1, p. 108 and the references he gives.

[26] See e.g. Kaser, *RPR* 1, p. 110.   [27] G.2.196.

[28] G.2.193: see Watson, *Succession*, pp. 122f.

[29] Thus, the *familiae emptor* was little more than a figurehead at this time.

[30] E.g. by Kaser, *RPR* 1, p. 111. The argument is that the executive force of the wording of the legacy, "damnas esto," would be based on Tab. vi.1; "Cum nexum faciet, mancipiumque. . . ." The argument may justify the recognition of *legatum per damnationem* in later times.

owner of the object legated at the time the testament was made. Both these facts tell against a *legatum* with these characteristics existing as early as the XII Tables for the *testamentum per aes et libram*. To begin with, there was no heir for the legatee to sue, and if one were to argue that for this purpose the *familiae emptor* is to be regarded as heir, one has also to claim that property to satisfy the legacies ended up in the hands of the *familiae emptor* on the testator's death, and for this there is not the slightest evidence. Again, the requirement that the object left by *legatum per vindicationem* be owned at the time the will was made is closely tied to the form of the will as a *mancipatio*. Within the framework of the mancipatory will a legacy of property which need not have been owned when the will was made must be a subseqent development. But we have seen that the mancipatory will was in its juridical infancy in the mid-fifth century, that it was a practice which was ratified by the XII Tables, hence a forerunner of the *legatum per damnationem* will be later.

Before we leave the *testamentum per aes et libram* it is well to call attention to what it has revealed about *mancipatio*. We have seen that a *mancipatio* could be used for purposes—e.g. the appointment of a *tutor*—other than the transfer of *res mancipi*. Indeed, the possibility of appointing a *tutor* by *mancipatio* reveals the extent to which social reality and social needs had resulted in modifications of its function. Again it has become apparent that the wording of a *mancipatio* was not invariable or rigidly fixed, but was chosen to fit the circumstances. Further, since the *familiae emptor* would not make a real payment to the testator in return for the *mancipatio*, we can see that the ceremony with copper and scales need not involve a real weighing out.[31]

---

[31] There is evidence (see infra, p. 94) that in early Latin *emptor* meant a "recipient" or "taker" of any kind and was not restricted in use to a "purchaser," and likewise that *emere* meant simply "to take." Hence it is possible that the idea of a sale is totally absent from the *testamentum per aes et libram* despite the use of the words "empta esto" in the *mancipatio* and despite the term *familiae emptor*.

Finally, it would seem that a *mancipatio* need not entail an immediate transfer of ownership.[32]

The *testamentum calatis comitiis* was a true will and permitted the institution of an heir. It died out at an early date and so the surviving information is very sparse.[33] Gaius tells us that this and the *testamentum in procinctu* were the two original forms and that the *testamentum per aes et libram* was a later addition.[34] This seems very plausible. The will was made in front of the *comitia calata* which met twice a year for the purpose of making wills,[35] on 24 March and 24 May. This will was, therefore, very public whether one thinks of the assembled *populus* simply as witnessing or, as in the case of *adrogatio*, approving the will by a legislative act. In the latter eventuality especially, it may have been the case that the will could be made only in limited circumstances, originally indeed only if the testator had no *suus heres*. But it should be stressed that there is no evidence[36] unless an interpretation of Tab. v.4, different from that already proposed,[37] be adopted. "Si intestato moritur cui suus heres nec escit . . ." might be translated as "If a man who

___

[32] One matter of considerable importance for the *testamentum per aes et libram* has not been discussed, namely, could there then be a legacy of a *res nec mancipi*? The problem is that (apart from succession) *mancipatio* would not transfer ownership of *res nec mancipi* when there was no delivery, so how could rights to *res nec mancipi* be acquired either by the *familiae emptor* or the legatee without physical delivery? My *a priori* answer—justified by evidence for later times but not for the 5th century—is that the theoretical difficulty would be ignored, as it was in the creation of *tutela*, and legacies of *res nec mancipi* would be valid.

[33] G.2.101-103; *Epit.Ulp.* 20.2; Aulus Gellius *NA* 15.27.3; J.2.10.1; Theophilus *Paraph.* 2.10.1.

[34] G.2.101, 102.   [35] G.2.101.

[36] Nor for the rather attractive view that this *testamentum* was originally an *adrogatio* whose effects were postponed until the death of the *adrogans*. Pace Kaser, *RPR* 1, p. 106, n. 6 and the authors he cites, there is nothing in Aulus Gellius *NA* 15.27.3 to suggest that a *detestatio sacrorum* was linked with the *testamentum calatis comitiis*. For views which are held see Kaser, *RPR* 1, pp. 105f, and the authors he cites.

[37] Supra, p. 60.

has no *suus heres* dies intestate . . ." and the implication would be that if he *had* a *suus heres* no question of testating would arise.

The *testamentum in procinctu* should probably be regarded as a military form of the *testamentum calatis comitiis*. It was made when the army was drawn up in battle array after the general had taken the auspices. Probably in its early days as later in the Republic no formalities were required.[38]

The order of intestate succession was the subject of two clauses of the XII Tables, Tab. v.4 and v.5,[39] and is straightforward; first a *suus heres*, then the nearest agnate, then the *gentiles*.

A *suus heres*[40] was a free person in the *potestas* or *manus* of the deceased and who became *sui iuris* on his death. No priority for succession was given to the firstborn or eldest, and women inherited equally with men. For this purpose, a wife *in manu* ranked equally with a son or daughter. *Impuberes* were also fully heirs.[41] Grandchildren whose father had predeceased their grandfather would take the share which would have come to their father had he survived. On the death of the *pater* the *sui heredes* became the heirs automatically without any activity on their part.[42]

Agnates were persons with an unbroken line of descent through males from a common ancestor (though the line could be created artificially as by *adrogatio*). Thus, apart

[38] For the *testamentum in procinctu*, see Cicero *Nat. D.* 2.3.9; *De Or.* 1.53.228; G.2.101; Aulus Gellius *NA* 15.27.3; see Kaser, *RPR* 1, pp. 106f; Watson, *Succession*, pp. 8ff and the authors they cite. Plutarch *Coriolanus* 9.2,3 reports that the *testamentum in procinctu* was used by Roman soldiers in the Republic even before the XII Tables. Professor Wieacker has kindly suggested to me the conjecture that the *testamentum in procinctu* was restricted to what the soldier had with him, such as weapons, horse, booty.

[39] Quoted supra, p. 54.

[40] See e.g. Kaser, *RPR* 1, pp. 95ff.

[41] This point is disputed but is best considered in connection with *tutela*; infra, p. 72.

[42] On *consortium* and division of an inheritance see infra, pp. 69f.

from *sui heredes*, a person's nearest agnates would be his brothers and sisters, failing these his father's brothers and sisters, and his own brother's children. The nearest agnate became heir only if he showed his willingness to accept the inheritance.[43]

The *gentiles inter se* are, according to Cicero, those who have the same name, who are born of freeborn parents, none of whose ancestors was ever a slave, and who have not undergone *capitis deminutio*.[44] The private law rights of the *gentiles* were restricted to intestate succession, and the guardianship which is connected with this.[45] In addition the *gentiles* had in common *sacra* and burial rights.[46] It may well be that[47] at an earlier stage the *gens* was a political unit, but if so its importance was gone before the XII Tables. There is no evidence that in historical times a *gens* had any formal organization or a leader. The question therefore arises how the *gentiles* would take an inheritance or exercise the right of guardianship. It is clear that the *gentiles* profited individually from the *hereditas*[48] and that the property was not used just for the upkeep of the *sacra* or of the burial place. The sources provide no material for an answer to the question but it may be reasonably conjectured that the *hereditas* (and guardianship) went to those persons who claimed as *gentiles* and were able to prove their claim. When Rome was small and few slaves had been manumitted the difficulties inherent in this would be slight.

[43] Infra, p. 69.

[44] *Top.* 6.29. The definition may be due to Quintus Mucius Scaevola, the *Pontifex*.

[45] See infra, p. 71. For the strange right of *enuptio gentis* granted to Hispala Faecenia in 186 B.C. see now Watson, "*Enuptio gentis*," in *Daube noster* ed. A. Watson (Edinburgh and London, Scottish Academic Press, 1974), pp. 331ff.

[46] See e.g. Kübler, *RE* 7, *s.v. gens*, 1176ff, at 1184ff.

[47] We need not be more precise, but it seems very likely that the *gens* was once a political unit.

[48] Emerges clearly from Catullus 68.119ff and *Laudatio Turiae* 1.13-26; perhaps also from Cicero *Flac.* 34.84 if Valerius Flaccus did take the *hereditas* of Valeria as a *gentilis*; see Watson *Succession*, p. 181; all the evidence is for a much later period.

At a later stage the onus (presumably) would be very much on the individual claimants to show that they were *gentiles* and in practice this would greatly favor the upper classes, particularly the patricians, who kept such proud records of their ancestry.[49] Because the *gentiles* were the ultimate heirs, there would be no rival claim from a person outside the *gens*.[50] Since in early law a *hereditas* could be usucapted in one year,[51] a successful claimant need not fear for long that he would unexpectedly have to share the inheritance with others.

Interestingly, the xii Tables' provisions on intestate succession do not set out the rule that the *sui heredes* are to take the inheritance. That is simply assumed, and Tab. v.4 enacts that where there is no *suus heres*, the nearest agnate is to have the *familia*. Tab. v.5 then proceeds to state that if there is no agnate, the *gentiles* take the *familia*. This rather surprising formulation of the order of succession should be seen in conjunction with the interpretation of "agnatus proximus" which was still current in the late Republic, namely that the succession opened only to the nearest agnate; if he refused the inheritance or if he died before he accepted it, no other agnate was called but the inheritance went to the *gentiles*. This excessively narrow interpretation which was certainly not necessary in the later Republic is best explained on the hypothesis that at one time succession went first to the *sui heredes*, whom failing, then to the *gentiles*. Tab. v.4 then represents an innovation allowing succession by an agnate, but since it could also be viewed as reducing existing rights (of the *gentiles*) it was interpreted

---

[49] But it is not suggested that only patricians had *gentes*.

[50] The practical consequence of this is that while a claim of a would-be inheritor to be a *gentilis* would be investigated, the status of the deceased might not be. Where what was claimed was *tutela*, especially over a woman, the tutee might argue that the family was not in a *gens*; *Laudatio Turiae* 1.13-26.

[51] G.2.54. The evidence does not allow us to state definitely that this was the position as early as the xii Tables.

restrictively.[52] It emerges, therefore, that as with Tab. v.3, so with Tab. v.4 and v.5, there was a particular reason for the existence of the clauses in the XII Tables. None of these three clauses had as its main purpose the setting out of established and accepted rules of law.[53]

Sui heredes would become the heirs automatically on the death of the *paterfamilias*, but others only when they actually signified their acceptance of the *hereditas*.[54] The heirs, as well as taking the assets, were also liable for the deceased's debts, and there seems to have been a provision of the XII Tables establishing that heirs were liable for debts in the same proportion that they took the assets.[55] The code also provided that debts outstanding to the deceased were to go to the heirs in the ratio of their entitlement to the *hereditas*.[56] The heirs were also bound to perform the deceased's *sacra familiaria*.[57]

The action available to heirs to claim the inheritance was a *legis actio sacramento in rem*[58] probably with a variant formulation.[59] A further action, the *actio familiae erciscun-*

---

[52] See the references given by Kaser, *RPR* 1, p. 102, n. 2; Watson, *Succession*, pp. 176ff; Kaser, "Die Beziehung von *Lex* und *Ius* und die XII Tafeln," in *Studi in Memoria di G. Donatuti* 2 (Milan, La Goliardica, 1973), 523ff, at 529f.

[53] For intestate succession to a freedman see infra, p. 109.

[54] See e.g. Kaser, *RPR* 1, p. 103. From the wording of Tab. v.4 and v.5 Gjerstad deduces that the *agnatus proximus* and the *gentiles* could take the estate but were not heirs: *Early Rome*, 5, p. 314.

[55] C.2.3.26 (Diocletian, A.D. 294); 4.16.7 (idem); D.10.2.25.13 (Ulpian *19 ad ed.*); see Kaser, *RPR* 1, p. 151 and the authors cited, n. 12.

[56] C.3.36.6 (Gordian); 8.35(36).1 (Caracalla, A.D. 212); D.10.2.25.9.

[57] Doubt has been expressed as to whether this was originally the case for *extranei heredes*: see e.g. F. Wieacker, "Hausgenossenschaft und Erbeinsetzung," in *Festschrift Siber* (Leipzig, Leipziger rechtswissenschaftliche Studien, 124, 1940), p. 8; Kaser, *Ius*, p. 339; *RPR* 1, p. 151. The oldest set of rules known to us for the obligation to perform the deceased's *sacra* is in Cicero *Leg.* 2.20.49, and it must be older than the middle of the 3rd century B.C., see Watson, *Succession*, p. 4; Kaser, *RPR* 1, p. 151.

[58] See infra, pp. 125ff.

[59] See Watson, *Succession*, pp. 195ff; Kaser, *RPR* 1, pp. 104f. That

dae, deserves especial mention in this place. The XII Tables established that the procedure for it was the *legis actio per iudicis postulationem*.[60] The function of the action was the division of the estate between *coheredes*, and the name of the action is of great importance in view of the earlier discussion of the meaning of the word *familia*.[61] Here, too, it signifies a person's property considered as a unit and is virtually a synonym of "hereditas." One could not imagine a remedy with this scope being called "actio pecuniae erciscundae."

When *sui* were *coheredes* a *consortium* called *ercto non cito* automatically came into existence on the death of the *pater*. *Ercto non cito*, which existed until the inheritance was divided, if it ever was, was a complete common ownership.[62]

---

in this period a *hereditas* might be usucapted is very probable but not certain: for modern literature see Kaser, *RPR* 1, pp. 103ff and nn. 21, 22.

[60] G.4.17a; D.10.2.1pr (Gaius 7 *ad ed. prov.*).

[61] Supra, pp. 57ff.

[62] G.3.154a; see the authorities cited in Kaser, *RPR* 1, p. 99, nn. 30, 31.

SIX

Incapacity and Guardianship

Particular classes of persons *sui iuris*—those under puberty, women, lunatics, and prodigals—were regarded as not (or not fully) capable of managing their own affairs, and guardians of one kind or another were appointed. Each class should be considered separately, though the cases have in common the protection of the inherent proprietary rights (on the death of the person protected) of the persons appointed guardians as well as of the property of the wards.

Impuberes

A *tutor* might be appointed to an *impubes sui iuris* either by operation of law or by express direction of the *paterfamilias*. In the former case agnates would first be called, apparently by an express provision of the XII Tables (Tab. v.6),[1] all those above puberty in the same degree of relationship being called equally. When there were no agnates *gentiles* could claim the *tutela*.[2] *Tutores* in this category came to be known as *tutores legitimi*.[3] Since, if the child died these *tutores* would be his heirs, they had a particular interest in looking after the property as carefully as possible.

Authority for the appointment of a *tutor* by the *pater* is

[1] G.1.155.

[2] There is no evidence for *gentiles* exercising *tutela impuberum* but their right to do so can be presumed from its existence for *tutela mulierum; Laudatio Turiae* 1.13-26.

[3] There is evidence for later law that a *tutor legitimus* could not refuse to be *tutor* but he was under no duty to act. There is no indication that he could transfer the *tutela* by *in iure cessio*: see Watson, *Persons*, p. 122; Kaser, *RPR* I, p. 88, n. 28.

in Tab. v.3: "Uti legassit super pecunia tutelave suae rei, ita ius esto."⁴ Since this clause refers to the *testamentum per aes et libram* which could not be used at this period for the appointment of an heir, the necessary implication is that the *impubes* became heir in some other way, presumably on intestacy, and that the appointment of a *tutor* was independent of the institution of the heir. The fact is important since it establishes that at this time in this context the appointment of a tutor had nothing to do with pupillary substitution.⁵ Though there is no evidence it might well be that a *tutor* could also be appointed for an *impubes* heir in the proper will before the *comitia calata*.⁶

The XII Tables' clause indicates something more. The *legare* is "super tutela suae rei," "in respect of the protection of his property." If this is an accurate translation of the Latin for that time,⁷ the implication is that the *tutela* was

⁴ For the accuracy of the wording of this version of Tab. v.3 see supra, pp. 52ff. The best meaning of *legare* in this context is probably "to give instructions": see supra, pp. 59f.

⁵ Contra, e.g. Kaser, *RPR* 1, p. 89. I wish to add nothing to my arguments in *Succession*, pp. 59ff against the common view (based largely on the existence of pupillary succession) that in early times an *impubes* was not really heir until he reached puberty: see now for that view Kaser, *RPR* 1, p. 96. Nor do I intend to discuss the theory that ownership was functionally divided between pupil and *tutor*: for this see now Kaser, *RPR* 1, p. 87. The arguments specifically from *tutela* for that theory—see e.g. Kaser, *ZSS* 59 (1939), 40—do not appear weighty (since there is little point in *tutela* unless the *tutor* is granted powers of administration), and the main support is the general theory of relative and divided ownership so stoutly maintained especially by Kaser; for a summary see e.g. his "The Concept of Roman Ownership," in *Tydscrif vir Hedendaagse Romeins-Hollandse Reg* 27 (1964), 5: and contra, Watson, *Property*, pp. 91ff.

⁶ Livy 1.34.12 and 1.40.2 reports, accurately or not, the appointment of a testamentary tutor, Lucius Tarquinius Priscus, to the children of King Ancus, during the regal period.

Though there is no evidence for this time, the *tutor testamentarius* in later law could refuse the *tutela* or resign it, but he could not transfer it to another; see Watson, *Persons*, p. 117.

⁷ Theories on the scope and meaning of Tab. v.3 occasionally lead individual scholars to the view that *tutela* here cannot refer to guardianship in the normal juridical sense. Thus Albanese takes *tutela* here as having the general sense of "custodia"; "La successione ereditaria

of the testator's property, not of the person of the *impubes*.[8] The *tutor*, indeed, had no control or authority over the person of the pupil.[9] Any doubts on this point should be removed when the wording of Tab. v.3 is compared with that of Tab. v.7a which gives *potestas* to the guardian of a lunatic "in eo pecuniaque eius." The difference should not be thought to be merely accidental; control over the person of a lunatic was necessary, though not over an *impubes*.

Once an *impubes* was capable of speech he could enter into legal transactions—though he could not marry or make

---

in diritto romano antico," *Annali Palermo* 20 (1949), 127ff, at 435; and Wieacker thinks *tutela suae rei* means "property"; most recently, "XII Tafeln," p. 301. But the explanation I have given of the meaning of *pecunia* and *familia* and the general scope of Tab. v.3 (supra, pp. 57f) permits me to take *tutela* in that clause as meaning what it did in periods for which there is more evidence; and this is, happily, the simplest approach. Moreover, later Romans themselves considered that the XII Tables permitted the appointment of a testamentary tutor, and they must be thinking of this clause: D.26.2.1pr (Gaius *12 ad ed. prov.*); 26.2.20.1 (Paul *38 ad ed.*); 50.16.120 (Pomponius *5 ad Quintum Mucium*).

[8] The famous idea that tutors are appointed "personae, non rei vel causae" does not intend to suggest that tutors have control over the persons of their pupils. As the context shows, the idea is that tutors cannot be appointed for a particular property, etc.: D.26.2.14 (Marcian *2 inst.*); J.1.14.4.

[9] The contrary dominant opinion is primarily based on Servius' definition of *tutela* in D.26.1.1pr (Paul *38 ad ed.*); cf. J.1.13.1: see now Kaser, *RPR* 1, pp. 86f and the authorities he cites. I wish to add nothing to my opposing arguments on D.26.1.1pr in *Persons*, pp. 102ff, especially at pp. 106ff; and *Private Law*, p. 36, n. 7. Rightly, the dominant opinion lays little stress on Aulus Gellius *NA* 5.19.10 (though see Kaser, *ZSS* 59 [1939], 38). Gellius reports for his own day that a *pupillus* could not be adrogated, "tutoribus in pupillos tantam esse auctoritatem potestatem fas non est ut caput liberum fidei suae commissum alienae dicioni subiciant." The thought that the non-jurist Gellius is trying to express is probably that there could in his day be no *adrogatio* of a *pupillus*, and that if there had been this would have given too much power to the *tutor*. The *tutor's* consent to the *adrogatio* would have been necessary for the same reason—protection of property rights—that his consent was needed to a woman's marriage *cum manu*, and this right of consent together with his general authority with regard to the *pupillus* could lead to abuse.

a will—and the function of the *tutor* was to interpose his authority when the transaction might cause financial loss to the property of the *impubes*.[10] This authority was needed for the transaction to be effective against the pupil.

Two remedies specifically for *tutela* were expressly given by the xii Tables (Tab. viii.20) against fraudulent *tutores*,[11] but neither can be considered wholly satisfactory. Against a *tutor legitimus*[12] lay an action—which was eventually called the *actio rationibus distrahendis*[13]—for double the value of property which the *tutor* embezzled. The action could apparently be brought only when the *tutela* came to an end,[14] and to judge from later evidence (as is here reasonable) did not lie against the heir of the *tutor*.[15] There could be proceedings against the *tutor testamentarius* during the continuance of the *tutela* on suspicion of fraud for what is called *crimen suspecti tutoris*.[16] Whether this involved criminal proceedings or a civil action is not clear; the sole outcome, to our knowledge, was the removal of the *tutor*.

Tutela impuberum would be ended by the pupil's attaining puberty, by his death or that of the *tutor*, by the *capitis*

---

[10] It is not intended to go further into this matter since we have no real evidence for the period. Arguments for the propositions set out above are: (1) the law so set out is evidenced for later in the Republic and it is difficult to believe that the rights of an *impubes* to enter into a legal transaction had increased; (2) interposition of authority of the *tutor* is evidenced for the xii Tables in *tutela mulierum*; see infra, pp. 75f.

[11] D.26.7.55.1 (Tryphoninus *14 disp.*); 26.10.1.2 (Ulpian *35 ad ed.*). It is not clear to which of these two remedies Cicero *Off.* 3.15.61 refers.

[12] D.26.7.55.1.

[13] The name suggests the purpose of the action was to compel the *tutor* to separate his accounts from those of the pupil; see e.g. O. Karlowa, *Römische Rechtsgeschichte* 2 (Leipzig, Veit, 1901), 280. Kaser prefers to take the name as meaning "for the examination of the accounts in detail"; *RPR* 1, p. 89, n. 40.

[14] D.27.3.1.24 (Ulpian *36 ad ed.*); but substantive interpolations have been suspected; see *Index Itp.*

[15] D.27.3.1.23.   [16] D.26.10.1.2.

deminutio of either,[17] or as a result of an *accusatio suspecti tutoris*.

Though there is no direct evidence, it is reasonable to hold that in the case of boys the physical attainment of puberty was needed before the *tutela* was terminated;[18] perhaps, indeed, the *tutela* continued until the religious festival of the Liberalia on 17 March when the symbols of boyhood were set aside, and those of manhood accepted.[19] Probably 12 was the age at which a girl notionally reached puberty[20] but this has little importance in this connection since the woman would continue to have the same *tutor*.

Mulieres

The legal capacity of adult women *sui iuris* did not differ greatly from that of *impuberes*. They were under permanent tutelage,[21] and their *tutores* were appointed in the same way as *tutores impuberum*. Even when a woman married she retained her *tutor* unless and until she entered the *manus* of her husband.

In this case, too, the function of the *tutor* was to interpose his authority, when the transaction could worsen her financial position. His authority or consent was thus needed for her marriage *cum manu* by *confarreatio* or *coemptio*, the creation of dowry,[22] and transfer of *res mancipi*.[23] A woman was incapable of making a will; she did not have the right to appear before the *comitia calata* and it would appear that even after the introduction of the *testamentum per aes*

---

[17] If, as seems likely, a *pupillus* could not be adrogated, then there could be no *capitis deminutio minima* of him.

[18] The argument is that in the early Empire when the Proculians held that *tutela* ended when a boy became 14, the Sabinians required actual physical capacity—see G.1.196—and the latter is presumably the older view.

[19] For this see Marquardt, *Privatleben* 1, pp. 123ff.

[20] As in later law.   [21] G.1.144.   [22] Cf. supra, pp. 25ff.

[23] Cicero *Flac.* 34.84; *Att.* 1.5.6; *Vat.Fr.* 1: see Watson, *Persons*, p. 152.

et libram time elapsed before any sort of testamentary capacity was permitted her. Even much later in the Republic a woman who was *sui iuris* could make a *testamentum per aes et libram* only if she had undergone *capitis deminutio*, and she required the consent of her *tutor* to the will.[24]

An honorific exception was made for the Vestal virgins. On a girl's being taken for that priesthood, escorted to the House of Vesta and delivered to the pontiffs, she was automatically freed from *patria potestas*[25] and did not become subject to *tutela*. Gaius says that this freedom from *tutela* was expressly provided for in the XII Tables (Tab. v.1),[26] and Plutarch even ascribes the rule to King Numa.[27] The Vestal was also given the right to make a will[28]—according to Plutarch this was likewise the work of King Numa[29]— though we have no information on the procedure followed. The Vestal was not heir to any intestate person, nor was anyone heir to her if she died intestate,[30] presumably because her agnatic ties were broken when she became a priestess.[31]

Furiosi

The care of the lunatic and his property was the subject of an express provision of the XII Tables (Tab. v.7a) of which we have the wording: "Si furiosus escit, adgnatum gentiliumque in eo pecuniaque eius potestas esto."[32] This care

[24] For the development see Watson, *Persons*, pp. 152ff; contra, Kaser, *RPR* 1, p. 324.

[25] Aulus Gellius *NA* 1.12.9. [26] G.1.145.

[27] *Num.* 10.3. [28] Aulus Gellius *NA* 1.12.9.

[29] *Num.* 10.3. [30] Aulus Gellius *NA* 1.12.18.

[31] Though Labeo thought the legal principle involved was an unsettled question: Aulus Gellius *NA* 1.12.18. For all matters affecting the legal position of Vestals see now F. Guizzi, *Aspetti giuridici del sacerdozio romano, il sacerdozio di Vesta* (Naples, Jovene, 1968).

[32] Cicero *Inv. Rhet.* 2.50.148; *Tusc.* 3.5.11; *Rhet. Her.* 1.13.23; cf. G.2.64; D.27.10.13 (Gaius *3 ad ed. prov.*); 26.1.3pr (Ulpian *27 ad Sab.*); *Epit.Ulp.* 12.2.

was not regarded as a form of *tutela* but was known as *curatio*.[33] It extended over both the person[34] and the property[35] of the lunatic, and the same word, *potestas*, was used for both aspects.[36] The xii Tables are not more specific about the nature and extent of the *potestas* involved in either case, which is significant for the drafting of the code. Nor can we determine the extent of control which was then deemed appropriate. Likewise significant for drafting is the wording "adgnatum gentiliumque." The order of precedence for being appointed to the *potestas* must have been agnates first (in order of closeness of the relationship), and failing any *agnatus*, then the *gentiles*, but this does not appear from the Latin, whether -*que* is taken conjunctively or even disjunctively, or from the fact that in the phrase the *agnati* come before *gentiles*.[37] Yet it would be difficult to hold that the original wording was more precise.[38] Presumably the decemviri, insofar as they considered the matter at all, thought the meaning obvious, and this might indicate that the editors are justified in placing this clause close to but after Tab. v.4 and 5.

A further interesting difference from *tutela* should be stressed; it does not appear that a *paterfamilias* by will could nominate someone to look after the lunatic and his property.[39] It is, however, possible that there was a further

[33] The term may not be as old as the xii Tables though *Epit.Ulp.* 12.2 says: "Lex duodecim tabularum furiosum, itemque prodigum, cui bonis interdictum est, in curatione iubet esse agnatorum"; see D. 27.10.13 (Gaius *3 ad ed. prov.*).

[34] For the Empire see D.27.10.7pr (Julian *21 dig.*).

[35] For the meaning of *pecunia* see supra, pp. 56ff.

[36] See supra, p. 48.

[37] See also M. Kaser, "Die Beziehung von *Lex* und *Ius* und die XII Tafeln," in *Studi in Memoria di G. Donatuti* 2 (Milan, La Goliardica, 1973), 523ff, at 530.

[38] Varro *Rust.* 1.2.8, offers confirmation of the reading: ". . . mente est captus adque adgnatos et gentiles est deducendus."

[39] Much later Tryphoninus declares that if a *pater* nominates a *curator* by will to his lunatic son who was grown up, the praetor should appoint the *curator* in accordance with the father's wishes: D.27.10.16pr (*13 disp.*).

clause in the XII Tables on the appointment of a protector when none emerged from Tab. v.7a: an unattached fragment begins "ast ei custos nec escit,"[40] and it is usually assigned to this context. Certainty is by no means possible,[41] but the conjecture is plausible. When no *agnatus* or *gentiles* claimed *potestas*, a guard of some kind might be considered desirable, and not just for the protection of the lunatic's property.

Prodigi

A prodigal who had inherited on intestacy[42] and who was wasting his substance was interdicted from dealing with his property by a clause of the XII Tables.[43] The *interdictio* was presumably pronounced by a magistrate,[44] and, in later times for which evidence is available, it ran: "Quando tibi bona paterna avitaque nequitia tua disperdis liberosque tuos ad egestatem perducis, ob eam rem tibi aere[45] commercioque interdico."[46] The wording would suggest that only a person who inherited as a *suus heres* might be interdicted but possibly the wording was not invariable. The XII Tables also expressly provided (Tab. v.7) that the property of the prodigal—though not his person—should be in *cura*, and the *curatio* went to the agnates.[47]

---

[40] Festus, *s.v. nec.*

[41] See Kaser, *RPR* I, p. 90 and the authors he cites. U. von Lübtow thinks the provision allowed the appointment of a *custos* to an absent *agnatus proximus* so that *usucapio pro herede* might be avoided: "Die Entwicklungsgeschichtlichen Grundlagen des römischen Erbrechts," in *Studi de Francisci* I (Milan, Giuffrè, 1956), 407ff, at 463f.

[42] Appears from *Epit.Ulp.* 12.3.

[43] Tab. v.7c in the editions: D.27.10.1pr (Ulpian *I ad Sab.*); *Epit.Ulp.* 12.2.

[44] Later by the praetor: *Epit.Ulp.* 12.3; D.27.10.1pr; 27.10.10 (Ulpian *16 ad ed.*); *P.S.* 3.4a.7.

[45] The text has *ea re* but for the emendation see Kaser, "Vom Begriff des *commercium*," in *Studi Arangio-Ruiz* 2 (Naples, Jovene, n.d.), 131ff, at 152ff.

[46] *P.S.* 3.4a.7.

[47] *Epit.Ulp.* 12.2. Whether *sui heredes* were called first is doubtful.

Roman legal tradition claims that the *interdictio* of prodigals existed even before the XII Tables and was introduced by custom.[48] Since the jurists, at all periods, attribute very few rules to custom they must in this instance, as in others,[49] have had a reason. At any event, the interdiction of prodigals from dealing with their property at the time of the XII Tables is probably the strongest indication there is both for the strength of feeling that the latent property interests of members of a family deserved protection, and that the protection of such interests was a large part of the functions of *tutores* and *curatores*. Why the *interdictio* was available—at this time—only when the prodigal had inherited *ab intestato* is not clear. (It seems to have been already possible for a testator—at least if he had no *suus heres*—to appoint an outsider as heir by the *testamentum comitiis calatis*, and this heir might later become prodigal.[50] The simplest solution is perhaps that a family was thought to have a special interest in property which had descended from a *paterfamilias*: a man should pass that on to his relatives whatever he did with any other acquisitions.

One must also wonder whether the existence of an *interdictio* and *curatio* here is evidence that the decemviri might make provision for relatively unusual situations or whether at that time prodigals were frequent. There are indications that Rome was suffering an economic crisis around the middle of the fifth century B.C.,[51] and it may be conjectured that

---

Certainly in the Empire sons were not appointed *curatores* (though there was a relaxation when the son of a *furiosus* was regarded as worthy): D.27.10.1.1.

For the foregoing paragraph see e.g. S. Solazzi, "Interdizione e cura del prodigo nella legge delle XII Tavole," now in *Scritti di diritto romano* 3 (Naples, Jovene, 1960), 245ff; Kaser, *RPR* 1, pp. 85, 91.

[48] D.27.10.1pr; *P.S.* 3.4a.7.

[49] For the attribution of a few rules of later Republican law to custom see Watson, *Law Making*, pp. 168ff.

[50] See supra, p. 65.

[51] Commerce with Athens was reduced to a minimum around 450 B.C.; see Gjerstad, *Early Rome* 4, pp. 517f. And there had been a general slowing down of cultural and economic life from c. 470.

relatively slight extravagance was enough to bring a man into disfavor.[52] But the possibility cannot be excluded that *interdictio* arose following a *cause célèbre* not very long before the XII Tables, and that the code was following the custom.

Finally, the unique nature of the *interdictio* should be noted, and we must ask why this procedure came into being. Once it was determined that a man was a prodigal, why was he not just deemed incapable—as was a lunatic—with the *curator* looking after his affairs? The *interdictio*, of course, does not declare that the *prodigal* is not competent to transact, but forbids him to act. It must be that his capacity is regarded as continuing, though inhibited by the *interdictio*.[53] The conclusion is important—and not just in this context—since it shows that as early as the XII Tables intention, *voluntas*, was occupying a central rôle in matters such as contract and testation. A male *sui iuris* above puberty who could form an intention could make a contract or a will; one who could not form the intention—namely a lunatic—could not. A person who could form the intention, but often formed an undesirable intention, retained his capacity, though he might be officially forbidden to transact and though his acts might have no force.

[52] Cf. the restrictions on luxurious mourning contained in Tab. x.
[53] This conclusion holds even if any contract entered into after the *interdictio* is void.

SEVEN

Slaves

A child born to a slave mother was automatically a slave and the status of the presumed father was irrelevant. Capture in war was another cause of slavery and even Latins with whom the Romans were fighting could be enslaved.[1] Moreover, any person belonging to a people which did not have *hospitium*[2] or a treaty of friendship with the Romans could be seized at any time as a slave.[3] Finally, a person might be purchased as a slave from a non-Roman and it seems that in this way even Latins whose people did have a treaty with the Romans might become Roman slaves.[4] A Roman could not become a slave at Rome.[5]

But this bare recital of the legal causes of slavery simply raises questions of the origins and functions of slaves in early Republican Rome. Were there many or relatively few slaves? Were many of them born to slave mothers? What were the main racial or tribal origins of the others? How were the slaves distributed among the free population? What work did they do—were they farm workers or do-

---

[1] See Livy 2.22; refers to 495 B.C.

[2] For this see R. Leonhard, s.v. *Hospitium*, RE 8, 2493ff.

[3] No textual evidence seems to exist for this period, but such was the legal position later in the Republic—D.49.15.5.2 (Pomponius 37 *ad Quintum Mucium*); for the argument see Watson, *Persons*, pp. 162ff—and it is inconceivable that this right of seizure was an innovation subsequent to the XII Tables. For a different opinion see Kaser, *RPR* 1, p. 35.

[4] Again the evidence is for later in the Republic—Livy 41.8.10; 41.9.11; see Watson, *Persons*, p. 165; *Private Law*, p. 43 and n.4—but is conclusive for our period.

[5] See, e.g. H. Lévy-Bruhl, "Théorie de l'esclavage," in *Quelques problèmes du très ancien droit romain* (Paris, Domat-Montchrestien, 1934), pp. 15ff, at pp. 16ff.

mestic servants or were they used in incipient industry? On these questions only the xii Tables can give help. Analogies drawn from other places and other times are valueless since we do not know enough about the early Roman society and economy even to know where to look for a possible analogy.

The slave presence at Rome was considerable. This emerges not so much from the provisions in the code about slaves as from that on testamentary manumission conditional upon payment by the slave to the heir, and by the rules on succession to freedmen. Only when slaves were reasonably common (and not too expensive) would they be freed in sufficient numbers to explain the interest of the decemviri in freedmen. Again, birth to a slave mother was a common cause of slavery. This is likewise shown by the provision on manumission and freedmen.[6] Slaves born in the house are more likely to be close to their master (and hence to be manumitted) than those acquired at a later stage of their lives. But more significantly, the rules on succession to freedmen indicate that they—at least those whom the provisions concern—would remain in Rome. Yet persons whose enslavement was the result of capture might be expected to want to return to their place of origin.[7] Those born slaves would have no other homeland. The racial origin of those born slaves is of secondary importance but most would descend from neighboring tribal stock, including Latins.[8] It is a reasonable conjecture that many would

[6] No argument can be drawn from the term *verna* for a slave born in the household. Festus' explanation, *s.vv. Vernae*, that they have that name because spring is the most natural time for birth may be illuminating for later ideas. But the derivation from *ver* is unconvincing. Both the time of introduction of the word in Latin and its etymology are uncertain even if we accept E. Benveniste's view that it is of Etruscan derivation: *Revue des Etudes Latines* 10 (1932), 437f.

[7] Unless their economic standing would have been better at Rome.

[8] That there had been many Latins taken prisoner and made slaves during the regal period is suggested by the fact that the day of the foundation of the temple of Diana on the Aventine by Servius Tullius was the slaves' feast day, and Diana was originally a Latin goddess: see Wissowa, *Religion*, p. 250.

be half-Roman—the father being the slave mother's *dominus* or the son of the *dominus*. It is very doubtful whether the Romans of the time had the economic resources to buy slaves from outsiders, so purchase from foreigners would not be a frequent source of enslavement at Rome.[9] This argument also favors the idea that many slaves were born slaves, since of slaves by capture only those whose homeland was at a considerable distance were likely to remain at Rome. Likewise, piracy cannot have had a marked effect on slave numbers since the Romans then were not a seafaring people. As for the slaves who were taken as the spoils of war, they would be from neighboring peoples: Etruscans, Sabines, Volsci, and Aequi. There may have been Latins, too, taken captive before the *foedus Cassianum* reputedly of 493,[10] but like 6,000[11] of those captured after the Roman victory over the Latins at Lake Regillus in 496, some may have been released and returned. Since for the half century following the expulsion of the kings, Rome was not generally in a dominant military position,[12] we should beware of exaggerating the number of captive slaves. How frequently in practice outsiders might simply be seized as slaves in time of peace cannot be determined. It certainly

[9] There seems to have been a general slowing down of cultural life which becomes marked from around 470 with the cessation of building of new temples after the dedication of that to Dius Fidius in 466. Imported Greek pottery becomes rather scarcer after 500, still more so after about 480, and is virtually nonexistent between 450 and 400: see the list of finds in Gjerstad, *Early Rome* 4, p. 515. (These figures seem at variance with Gjerstad's own claim, p. 599, that "there is no evidence that the import of Greek goods decreased considerably in the later part of the first half of the 5th century B.C.)

[10] Dionysius of Halicarnassus 6.95.2. Despite frequent expressions of doubt this date seems now generally accepted: see H. Last in *CAH* 7 (Cambridge, Cambridge University Press, 1928), 491; T. Frank, *An Economic Survey of Ancient Rome* 1 (reprinted Paterson, N.J., Pageant Books, 1959), 8f; H. H. Scullard, *A History of the Roman World, 753-146 B.C.*, 3rd ed. (London, Methuen, 1961), p. 65 and n. 2. Gjerstad accepts the mid-490s as the date; *Early Rome* 6, p. 185.

[11] Livy 2.22.5.

[12] See e.g. Last in *CAH* 7, pp. 485ff; Scullard, *Roman World*, pp. 64ff.

was not the automatic fate of foreigners who came to Rome,[13] or even what little trade there was would have been impossible. Notably among those who could *not* be seized as slaves were the Carthaginians after the treaty of friendship of 509[14] and the Latins after the *foedus Cassianum.*

All in all, we can conclude that at this time a large proportion of the slave population was born in slavery, and that many of the slaves would be half or even three-quarters Roman in blood. As we shall see, this makes it easier to understand some of the legal rules and their working.

On the distribution of slaves among the free population and on the work done by slaves little can be said with confidence. That very considerable inequalities of wealth already existed among the free citizens is incontestable,[15] and it seems reasonable to assume that rich families might have several slaves whereas poor families would have none. Again probably, some slaves would be primarily domestic servants (especially in the wealthier households), others would be agricultural workers. That in early times slaves were much used for field work[16] is seen in that the festival of the Compitalia was for the slaves above all, and that the

---

[13] Thus around 505 Attius Clausus, afterwards known as Appius Claudius, who was a Sabine championing peace fled to Rome with many *clientes.* They were given citizenship and land, and Appius was himself enrolled in the senate: Livy 2.16. Again (during the regal period), when as a result of conquest a neighboring town was incorporated into Roman territory its citizens were normally given Roman citizenship; see Gjerstad, *Early Rome* 6, pp. 153f, 181.

[14] Polybius *Hist.* 3.22.1-13. For the historical accuracy or otherwise of this treaty see e.g. Frank, *Economic Survey* 1, pp. 6ff; N. Lewis & M. Reinhold, *Roman Civilization* 1 (New York, Harper Torchbooks, 1966), 70; and the authors cited by Scullard, *Roman World*, pp. 434ff.

[15] It is enough to refer to the Servian constitution.

[16] The point has to be made since the extensive use of slaves for agricultural purposes in 4th century Attica has been doubted by e.g. A.H.M. Jones, "Slavery in the Ancient World," *Economic History Review* 9 (1956), 185ff, at 187; contra, e.g. M. I. Finley, "Was Greek Civilization Based on Slave Labour?" *Historia* 8 (1959), 145ff, at

Lares worshiped at the Compitum were the protectors of the fields within sight (though also of the house).[17]

In law, slaves were fully owned by their master and were *res mancipi*.[18] The master could inflict any punishment including death, and there were no legal limits to his power over his slaves. When a slave committed a civil wrong he could not himself be sued—since only persons *sui iuris* could be parties to a *legis actio*[19]—but an action lay against the master who had the choice of either paying the appropriate amount of damages to the injured party or transferring the wrongdoing slave to him. A clause of the XII Tables (Tab. XII.2a) permitting noxal surrender, as it is called, began: "Si servus furtum faxit noxiamve no[x]it."[20] "Noxiamve no[x]it" would cover any kind of damage whether to property or to a person's body.[21] The slave could own nothing, but in practice the master might allow him to control a fund, the *peculium*, as if it were his, and with it

---

148f. Archaeology has shown that the size of some households in 5th century Rome would make domestic servants very desirable; see Gjerstad, *Early Rome* 4, pp. 401ff.

[17] See Wissowa, *Religion*, pp. 166ff.

[18] See infra, p. 136.

[19] Cf. e.g. Kaser, *ZPR*, p. 46.

[20] D.9.4.2.1 (Ulpian *18 ad ed.*); cf. D.47.6.5 (Marcellus *18 dig.*); 50.16.238.3 (Gaius *6 ad leg. xii tab.*); Festus, *s.v. Noxia*. It seems almost certain that, as later, a *paterfamilias* could also hand over a *filius* in noxal surrender, and it is sometimes suggested that this clause of the XII Tables also expressly referred to the *filius*; most recently, Kaser, *RPR* 1, p. 163, n. 5. But there is no evidence that any statute including the XII Tables or edict *expressly* allowed the noxal surrender of a *filius*: see Watson, *Obligations*, pp. 277f. (The suggestion made in *Obligations*, p. 278, n. 1 as showing the sort of thing which might possibly explain how the word "servus" came to be used to designate all persons liable to noxal surrender should be ignored. It does not fit since there is no evidence that in the earliest days a *filius* could be sued by *legis actio*). The legal basis for noxal surrender of a *filius* is a mystery. Perhaps "servus" in this clause of the code was understood more broadly just as in *Vat. Fr.* 307 the word "servus" was used to signify "freedman": infra, p. 109 and n. 42.

[21] See above all D. Daube "*Nocere* and *noxa*," *Cambridge Law Journal* 7 (1939-41), 23ff.

the slave might eventually be allowed to purchase his freedom. If a slave made a contract, any rights or property acquired under it were acquired for his master, but no obligation was incurred by the master and the slave himself could not be sued. Satisfactory as this might seem for the owner at first sight, the consequence would be that a slave could not be used for commercial transactions. Since slaves, in law, were not persons they could not enter a marriage recognized in law, nor was their killing—even by an outsider—murder.[22]

But an injury to a slave gave the master a right of action; and the penalty for the *os fractum* of a slave was half that for a freeman.[23] It is in the highest degree significant for social attitudes that in the XII Tables serious injuries to slaves were assimilated with those to free citizens whereas centuries later, under Chapter 3 of the *lex Aquilia* the same injuries to slaves were equated with those to animals.[24]

Later in the Republic there were three ways in which a slave could be manumitted by his master, by will, *censu*, and *vindicta*, all of which gave the ex-slave Roman citizenship as well as freedom. The XII Tables contained no specific provisions on manumission[25] but manumission by will is incidentally evidenced by a clause (Tab. VII.12) concerning the *statuliber*.[26] There is no conclusive evidence for the existence of the other two—which alone could be operated to give a slave freedom during his master's lifetime—but the balance of probability is that they were already available.

Manumissio vindicta was an application of the *vindicatio*

---

[22] The evidence for most of the statements in this paragraph relates to later periods (see e.g. Watson, *Private Law*, pp. 45f), but we can be sure of the state of the law for our time.

[23] Apparently *talio* was appropriate for *membrum ruptum*, whether of a slave or freeman.

[24] The assimilation of slaves to animals in the *lex Aquilia* may also rightly be regarded as an indication of greater legal sophistication.

[25] Thus, manumission is not dealt with in Quintus Mucius' *Ius civile*; see Watson, *Law Making*, p. 153.

[26] See infra, pp. 91ff.

in libertatem,[27] the claim that a free man was wrongly held as a slave. For this manumission a master who wished to free his slave arranged that a friend should claim before a magistrate that the slave was free, the master would put up no defense, and the magistrate would then declare the slave free. The process is obviously a juristic invention and dodge,[28] but it requires the cooperation of the magistrate. Moreover, since the ex-slave also becomes a citizen the approval—at least the tacit approval—of the state is a prerequisite for the full efficacy of the procedure, and it may be that at an early stage of development a slave so freed did not become a citizen.[29]

A first argument that is at times adduced for the early existence of *manumissio vindicta* seems to me, it must be admitted, of no weight. The argument appears to be that we are informed that *cessio in iure* was in existence by the time of the XII Tables[30] and that *manumissio vindicta* must be about the oldest form of *cessio in iure*.[31] The support adduced for the second part of the argument is very flimsy and is drawn from the name "manumissio vindicta." If *in iure cessio* were well developed earlier then, it is suggested,[32] the name of this form of manumission would have been linguistically dependent on the term "in iure cessio." But first, in the nature of things, there seems no reason for this linguistic dependence ever to have occurred. Secondly, it by no means follows that the standard name of an insti-

[27] See infra, pp. 95ff.

[28] See now e.g. D. Daube, "Two Early Patterns of Manumission," *JRS* 36 (1946), 57ff, at 63.

[29] See e.g. Mommsen, *Staatsrecht* 3, p. 59; M. Kaser, "Die Anfänge der *manumissio* und das fiduziarisch gebundene Eigentum," *ZSS* 61 (1941), 152ff, at 154.

[30] *Vat. Fr.* 50; see Kaser, *RPR* 1, p. 116, n. 8.

[31] So M. Wlassak, "Der Gerichtsmagistrat im gesetzlichen Spruchverfahren," *ZSS* 28 (1907), 1ff and 39 (cited approvingly by Kaser, loc. cit.); following *inter alios* A. Bechmann, *Der Kauf nach gemeinem Recht* 1 (Erlangen, Deichert, 1876), 555, who is rather more positive. But from Bechmann's n. 3 one must doubt whether he thought *manumissio vindicta* existed as early as the XII Tables.

[32] By Wlassak, loc. cit.

tution is as old as the institution itself. Either "cessio in iure" or "manumissio vindicta," or indeed both, might be very much later than the practice of *cessio in iure* or *manumissio vindicta*. Thirdly, *manumissio vindicta* was a very special case of *cessio in iure*, both because it was not modeled on the *vindicatio* but on the *vindicatio in libertatem* and because it was concerned with the giving of freedom and citizenship to a slave, not with the transfer of rights or property. Hence it is natural that the name "manumissio vindicta" should emphasize this.[33]

A different, and perhaps rather more successful, argument might be drawn from Livy 2.5. In the first year of the Republic, the story goes,[34] some young aristocrats sought to restore the monarchy, but a slave learned of the conspiracy and informed the consuls. The conspirators were executed, and the informer was rewarded; money was granted from the treasury, freedom and citizenship were given him. Livy then relates that this slave is said to have been the first freed *vindicta*, and that some people hold that the term "vindicta" comes from him since his name was Vindicius: "After him the rule was maintained that those who were freed in this manner were regarded as having been admitted to the rights of citizenship." It has long been recognized, of course, that one cannot take this story as straight history.[35] Above all, the derivation of *vindicta* from Vindicius is impossible and betrays the attempt to improve on fact. But we should notice one fundamental point which is common both to this account and the looser version in Plutarch *Publicola* 7.5, namely, that the manumission was *vindicta*.[36] This means that the slave was freed by his master,[37]

---

[33] This point is made also against the argument of Bechmann, loc. cit. (accepted by Wlassak, "Gerichtsmagistrat," p. 39, n. 1), that the name is taken from only one outstanding part of the institution and that this points to its great age.

[34] Livy 2.3ff.

[35] See now for all, Ogilvie, *Commentary*, pp. 241ff.

[36] To be exact, Plutarch talks of a decree being passed which made Vindicius the first freedman to be a citizen of Rome, and then he

not, as we might have expected and as happened later in such circumstances in the Republic, directly by the state.[38] The story seems to have the characteristics of an aetiological legend.[39] The question to be answered is: Why does a private act, *manumissio vindicta*, by an owner have public consequences, namely, citizenship, for the slave? Answer: Because the first *manumissio vindicta* was at the wish of the state which desired citizenship to be acquired by the manumitted slave.[40] As an aetiological myth, of course, "the date and circumstances are apocryphal, belonging to the fantasy world of legal precedents."[41] Yes, but the story is certainly not Livy's invention and more than one scholar has observed that at the end of the text the language is properly legal.[42] And at the same time the myth indicates the belief that *manumissio vindicta* was in existence with full effect for more than fifty years before the xii Tables. There is some support for this in that the xii Tables made no mention of *manumissio vindicta* yet we could have expected this dodge to be ratified—as was the *testamentum per aes et libram*[43]—if it were of recent origin.

A further argument has greater weight. *Manumissio vin-*

---

relates that "from this Vindicius, as they say, a perfect manumission is to this day called *vindicta*."

[37] Livy's *praemium indici pecunia ex aerario* may be an abridgment of an earlier version in which the money, or part of it, was paid to the master for the manumission.

[38] E.g. Cicero *Balb.* 9.24; see Kaser, "Anfänge," p. 167. Kaser, indeed, p. 168, suggests that the manumission of Vindicius (if he were a historical personage) would have been by an act of the state.

[39] See Ogilvie, *Commentary*, p. 241.

[40] Ogilvie, loc. cit., is right that the story is told to illustrate *manumissio vindicta*, and not as Daube thinks ("Patterns," p. 74) that the detailed mode of manumission is added because of Vindicius' name. The argument also holds against M. Lemosse, "L'Affranchissement par le cens," *RHD* 27 (1949), 161ff, at 191.

[41] Ogilvie, loc. cit.

[42] Daube, "Patterns," p. 75; Ogilvie, *Commentary*, p. 247. Daube, indeed, observes that Livy's "post illum observatum ut qui ita liberati essent in civitatem accepti viderentur" is reminiscent of "qui ita manumissus erit . . . liber esto" in the *lex Salpensana*, lines 25f.

[43] See supra, p. 61.

dicta involves a juristic dodge, *manumissio testamento* does not. There seems no theoretical reason why the purpose and intention of one should be concealed whereas the purpose and intention of the other could be left apparent. Both clearly have their origin in practice. Presumably one arose when manumission (giving citizenship) was not legally recognized, hence a dodge was needed; the other, after manumission was an accepted fact, hence no dodge was required.[44] Thus *manumissio vindicta* is older than *manumissio testamento*. If this argument is accepted it is further confirmation that *manumissio vindicta* is considerably older than the xii Tables, since in that code the validity of *manumissio testamento* is simply assumed *en passant*, and hence was already well established.

Manumissio censu was the enrollment of a slave, with the consent of his master, on the *census* list of Roman citizens. It must surely have had the effect of making the slave a citizen from its origin or at least before *manumissio vindicta*.[45] It is so formal and could be used only when the *census* was taken, about once in four or five years, that it is unlikely to have ever come into existence if the simple *manumissio vindicta* was available with full effect.[46] This view has the support of Roman tradition. Dionysius of Halicarnassus, 4.22.4, relates that King Servius Tullius permitted slaves who had been manumitted and who did not choose to return to their own countries to be enrolled in his *census* and to acquire citizenship. Indeed, in this account the whole purpose of the ex-slaves' being enrolled in the *census* was to make them citizens. These slaves, therefore, must have been manumitted in some other way and must not have acquired citizenship. Much of the account is presumably legendary, but as Daube insists there must be some truth in it: "The notion

[44] See W. W. Buckland, *The Roman Law of Slavery* (Cambridge, Cambridge University Press, 1908), p. 443. The opposite conclusion has also been inferred from the same evidence.

[45] See e.g. Daube, "Patterns," p. 73.

[46] Professor Wieacker kindly tells me that, in his opinion, this argument is not convincing.

that manumission *censu* was the first mode of manumission to confer not only liberty but also citizenship is rather too specific, too technical, too alien from the interests of an inventor of pleasant tales or sensational reports, to be thrown on the dust-heap of fiction."[47]

Of the existence of *manumissio testamento* at the time of the XII Tables there can be no doubt. There is no express provision on it, but the clause (Tab. VII.12) on the *statuliber*, which we shall look at shortly, indicates that *manumissio testamento* was well known and accepted. But the question does arise whether the manumission could be by *testamentum per aes et libram*, by *testamentum calatis comitiis*, or by both.

The first opinion seems to be widely held[48] but it (and therefore also the third) can, I suggest, be excluded. The argument in favor of that opinion is that manumission, it is said, is within the scope of the verb *legare* in the XII Tables' clause which accepts the validity of the *testamentum per aes et libram*, and that Roman jurists of the classical period consider "Uti legassit super pecunia tutelave suae rei, ita ius esto" to be the clause which permitted manumission by will.[49] But it is not the (obscure) scope of *legare* which should be decisive here, but the absence of any mention of manumission in the list "super pecunia tutelave suae rei."[50]

[47] "Patterns," p. 74. Lemosse thinks that before 443 B.C., the date of creation of the censorship, *manumissio censu* operated only spasmodically: "L'Affranchissement," p. 190, but C. Cosentini thinks it operated properly before the XII Tables: review of Lemosse, *IURA* 1 (1950), 535. Kaser thinks *manumissio censu* rather later than the XII Tables: now *RPR* 1, p. 117. Jolowicz-Nicholas, *Introduction*, p. 136, declares we do not know whether *manumissio censu* and *manumissio vindicta* existed as early as the XII Tables.

The weight of Appius Claudius' reforms in 312 B.C. was on suffrage for freedmen: Plutarch *Publicola*, 7.5; cf. Livy 9.46.10f.

[48] E.g. by Kaser, "Anfänge," pp. 154ff; *RPR* 1, p. 116.

[49] G.2.224; D.50.16.120 (Pomponius 5 *ad Quintum Mucium*); *Epit. Ulp.* 1.9.

[50] But if the version of the clause with *familia* which is found in Cicero is the original—contra, see pp. 52ff—and *familia* meant, as later, "the slaves," then it might be arguable that *legare super familia* included manumission.

The clause expressly allows the giving of legacies and the appointment of a tutor, but says nothing about manumission.[51] However, the conclusive argument is another. The purpose of the "Uti legassit" clause was to ratify and validate a practice which had no previous authority, the making of a will *per aes et libram*.[52] The clause on the *statuliber* shows that the validity of a *manumissio testamento* was clearly established and needed no ratification. It is obviously impossible that the accepted validity of manumission by will should depend on the doubtful validity of a form of will making. Moreover, the theoretical argument[53] favors the *testamentum calatis comitiis*. Not only was that the only full and proper will of the period, but—unlike the *testamentum per aes et libram*—it was an act which involved the people, assembled in the *comitia calata*. Since manumission had public consequences—citizenship—one would expect in early times that it could not be effected simply at the whim of the owner without some outside form of control. This, of course, is observably the case for both *manumissio vindicta* and *manumissio censu*.

It has already been several times stated in this chapter that, though slaves are mentioned in more than one provision of the xii Tables, there was not even one clause which dealt specifically with the law of slavery: not with the causes of enslavement, the institution of slavery, or with manumission. The argument for this proposition is first that we just do not have any evidence of any such clause; secondly, and more significantly, Quintus Mucius Scaevola's *Ius civile* which was so heavily dependent on the xii Tables also did not deal expressly with slavery.[54] The fact is of considerable importance for our understanding of the xii Ta-

---

[51] The authority of the classical jurists is weakened on this matter since Pomponius considers that this clause also permitted the institution of an heir, which cannot be correct: supra, pp. 58f.

[52] See supra, p. 61.

[53] See e.g. Daube, "Patterns," p. 59.

[54] See Watson, *Law Making*, p. 153.

bles: the code was not comprehensive and was scarcely meant to be.[55] The reason for the omission cannot be that there was no law on slavery, or that slavery was so accepted as not to be noticed. Slavery might be so accepted that its existence was not questioned but that would be no reason for not treating the law of slavery. Rather, it would seem that on the matters discussed in this chapter there were no innovations and the law was settled. And slaves were no "pressure group." The need to set it out was not felt.

Finally, it ought to be mentioned that what was said earlier in this chapter about the racial origins of slaves is very consistent with the law of this early period. Most slaves, however freed, would be likely to be descendants of the owner,[56] hence it was reasonable for all three methods of manumission to give citizenship.[57] Likewise, it is not surprising that in private law the position of a *filiusfamilias* is not greatly different from that of a slave, and that both sons and slaves might have a *peculium*. Again there is no sign of any fear that slaves might flee and there was no repressive legislation: hard to understand if slaves had been taken from neighboring people, but not if they had no other homeland. For what it is worth, Plutarch claims that in the early Republic the Romans treated their slaves with great kindness because they worked and ate with them.[58] The converse is that the masters were not afraid of an attack from their slaves.

More than once in this chapter mention has been made of the XII Tables' clause (Tab. VII.12) on the *statuliber*. The *statuliber* was a slave who was ordered in his master's will

[55] See infra, p. 185.

[56] Cf. the word *liberi*, "descendants."

[57] The social situation would be different at the time when Servius Tullius, it is said, introduced enrollment on the *census* so that slaves freed by another method could attain citizenship. The motive expressly attributed to Tullius was the increase of the number of citizens: Dionysius of Halicarnassus 4.22.2ff.

[58] *Coriolanus* 24.4.

to be free on the fulfillment of a condition. The clause in question was to the effect that if a slave were ordered to be free if he made a certain payment to the heir, and the heir transferred him to another, then the slave obtained his freedom on paying that amount to the purchaser.[59] The clause shows both that the *statuliber* remained very much a slave until the condition was fulfilled (and that he could be sold) and that his prospective right to freedom could not be taken from him at the whim of his owner. We also see that such a thing as a condition could be validly imposed.[60]

The texts[61] show that in the tradition of the clause either the word *emptor* described the recipient from the heir or *emptio* was used of his taking; or perhaps both *emptor* and *emptio* appeared in the provision. No fanciful theory—whether on the original scope of the provision or on its subsequent interpretation, or on later modifications of the provision, or even its complete invention by later generations—should be constructed on this fact. Quite simply, the original meaning of *emere* was "to take,"[62] and this sense of the word was still in use at the time of the XII Tables. In a way, the very appearance of *emptio* or *emptor* with such a meaning in the texts is the strongest evidence that the tradition of the provision's wording is accurate.[63]

[59] *Epit.Ulp.* 2.4; D.40.1.25 (Modestinus *9 diff.*); h.t. 29.1 (Pomponius *18 ad Quintum Mucium*).

[60] Interestingly, it is primarily his unwillingness—based on *a priori* grounds—to accept that there could be a conditional transaction as early as the XII Tables which leads P. Voci to doubt that the status of the *statuliber* then existed; *Diritto ereditario romano* 1, 2nd ed. (Milan, Giuffrè, 1965), 75. And G. Impallomeni's similar doubts stem also from his *a priori* view that it is difficult to believe that *mancipatio familiae*, a complex institution, was in use in the mid-5th century; *Le manomissioni mortis causa* (Padua, CEDAM, 1963), pp. 16f. Against both see Kaser, *RPR* 1, p. 114 and n. 15.

[61] *Epit.Ulp.* 2.4; D.40.1.29.1.

[62] See e.g. Ernout & Meillet, *Dictionnaire*, p. 195; E. Benveniste, *Le Vocabulaire des institutions indo-européennes*, 1 (Paris, Éditions de Minuit, 1969), 137. This was also the opinion of Festus, *s.v. Emere*.

[63] On the topic see now A. Watson, "Emptio, 'taking,'" to appear in *Glotta* 54 (1975).

A claim might be made that a person treated as a slave was really a free man or that a person acting as a free man was someone's slave. Both procedures are forms of the *legis actio sacramento in rem*[64] but with their own peculiarities.

A person held as a slave could not himself start or act in the proceedings, but any citizen could behave as *adsertor in libertatem*,[65] summon the apparent master before the magistrate, and make the claim that the supposed slave was free. This was one of the very few exceptional cases where the *legis actio* procedure could be used by one person on behalf of another.[66] Moreover, again to protect liberty, the *vindicatio in libertatem*, if it once failed, could be brought time and time again.[67] In the normal case the master would counter the plea of the *adsertor*, claiming that the man belonged to him. The challenge would then be made and the oath taken as to whether the plaintff had claimed justly.[68] The xii Tables provided (Tab. ii.1) that the oath in the *legis actio sacramento* should be for 500 *asses* if the suit concerned a matter worth 1,000 *asses* or more, for 50 if the matter was worth less.[69] But the code also expressly declared that where the matter at issue was a man's freedom the *sacramentum* would always be for 50, whatever the man's value.[70] A further provision of the xii Tables (Tab. vi.6) created another exceptional rule, namely, that between the procedure *in iure* and that *apud iudicem, vindiciae* would always be given *secundum libertatem*, that is, that the person who was the object of the proceedings would remain in *de facto* freedom. According to Roman

[64] See infra, pp. 125ff.

[65] See E. Ferenczy, "L'*adsertor libertatis* nell'età della repubblica romana arcaica," in *Studi in memoria di G. Donatuti* i (Milan, La Goliardica, 1973), 387ff.

[66] J.4.10pr; cf. G.4.82. See G. Franciosi, *Il processo di libertà in diritto romano* (Naples, Jovene, 1961), pp. 150ff.

[67] Cicero *Dom.* 29.78. The rule in all other cases was that an action could not be brought twice on the same matter.

[68] See infra, pp. 126ff on the *legis actio sacramento in rem*.

[69] G.4.14. Of course, coined money was not then in existence.

[70] G.4.14.

tradition this provision in the code was due to Appius Claudius,[71] and Pomponius states that it repeated existing law.[72]

Procedure in the *vindicatio in servitutem* was basically similar. The person who maintained that another was his slave would seize him by the procedure known as *manus iniectio* and lead him before the magistrate.[73] Since the person seized might indeed be a slave he could not act on his own behalf in the proceedings, and had to rely on some citizen's maintaining his defense. The course of events was then as in the *vindicatio in libertatem* except that the supposed master was plaintiff instead of defendant, and the citizen maintaining the man's freedom was cast in the rôle of defendant.

Prominent in the tales of early Rome is the story of freeborn Verginia who was claimed as a slave to satisfy the lust of Appius Claudius the decemvir.[74] We need lay little stress on the story here since we do not require it to reconstruct the working of the early *vindicatio in servitutem*. If the story has no basis in reality[75] we are (for present purposes)

[71] D.1.2.2.24 (Pomponius *sing. enchirid.*); Livy 3.44.12-45.1.

[72] In the late Republic, at any rate, the action was heard before the *decemviri stlitibus iudicandis*: Cicero *Dom.* 29.78; *Caecin.* 33.97. But they do not seem to have existed in our period, and any connection with the early plebeian (*iudices*) *decemviri* is very doubtful: see e.g. Franciosi, *Processo*, pp. 10ff; Kaser, *ZPR*, p. 40; most recently, E. Ferenczy, "Vom Ursprung der *decemviri stlitibus iudicandis*," *ZSS* 89 (1972), 338ff.

Franciosi, *Processo*, pp. 1ff thinks the *vindicatio in libertatem* is later than the xii Tables and would come into existence only when slavery was practiced on a vast scale, that is, not before the second half of the 4th century. But on this view we should be forced to deny the Roman tradition not only on the *vindicatio in libertatem* but also at least on manumission and on freedmen. Also against Franciosi, see Kaser, *RPR* 1, p. 114, n. 18.

[73] Cf. Livy 3.44.6ff.

[74] The main sources are Livy 3.44ff; Dionysius of Halicarnassus 11.28ff; Diodorus Siculus 12.24; Cicero *Rep.* 2.37.63; *Fin.* 2.20.66; 5.22.64; D.1.2.2.24.

[75] As modern historians believe; see e.g. H. Gundel, *RE* 8A, 1530ff; J. Bayet, *Tite-Live, histoire romaine* 3 (Paris, Belles Lettres, 1954), 133ff; Ogilvie, *Commentary*, pp. 476ff.

no worse off; if it is historically true or accurate in its portrayal of legal conditions, it mainly confirms what we otherwise know or can assume.[76]

[76] Some elements in the story can at once be discarded as later inventions: the girl's name is too good to be true, and her plebeian status (in most sources) is the result of subsequent struggles between the orders. Yet I cannot accept the widely held view that Livy's sources presented the tale as a paradigm of the *causa liberalis* as defined by the XII Tables: see e.g. E. Täubler, *Untersuchungen zur Geschichte des Dezemvirats und der Zwölftafeln* (Berlin, Historische Studien 148, 1921), p. 32; Bayet, *Tite-Live* 3, p. 145; Ogilvie, *Commentary*, p. 478. One would not choose as a paradigm a story where the wrong decision was given on the legal issues (apart altogether from the accuracy of the facts), and where Appius Claudius' legal argument for his absurd decision to give *vindiciae secundum servitutem* at the first hearing could be thought plausible. (That its plausibility can still mislead is shown by its acceptance in Ogilvie, *Commentary*, p. 483.)

EIGHT

Patronus and *Cliens*: *Patronus* and *Libertus*

In the clear light of the late Republic four different relationships can be seen comprehended within the idea of *patrocinium*: that with a Roman of lower social standing; that between a former master and his freedman; that between a pleader in court and the party he appears for; and that between an important Roman on the one hand, and provinces, colonies, *municipia*, and individual members of these on the other.[1] Of these four, the last—I should like to suggest—is outside the scope of this work and need not be discussed. The third is a natural development from the first and second and as a distinct relationship with its own characteristics is in all probability later than our period. The second may be regarded as a special instance of the first relationship, though it is also much more.

The first-mentioned relationship therefore ought to be discussed first. It was, it can be said, fundamental to Roman society from the earliest times, and remained important in some form for more than a thousand years. Dionysius of Halicarnassus[2] relates that Romulus entrusted the plebeians to the care of the patricians and that each plebeian was allowed to choose himself a patron. We are, of course, in the present context not concerned with the origins of the relationship, but the reports of its nature in the regal period are of great importance because they appear to be reliable in the general picture which they present,[3] and they are a

---

[1] See M. Gelzer, *The Roman Nobility* (Oxford, Blackwell, 1969), pp. 62f. A. von Premerstein does not keep these relationships sufficiently apart and the result is very confusing: *RE* 4, 23ff, *s.v. Clientes.*
[2] 2.9.1.
[3] For the argument see Watson, "Leges Regiae," pp. 100ff. Some

guide to conditions in the early Republic. The patricians' duties were to interpret the law for their clients, bring actions for them if they suffered injury, and to help them when they sued.[4] The clients were to assist their patrons in marrying off daughters if the parents lacked funds, ransom the patrons or patrons' children from the enemy if they were captured, and pay the damages awarded against their patrons in private actions and the fines imposed in public actions. Also, we are told, the *clientes* were to share the costs incurred by their patrons in magistracies and positions of honor. It was contrary to *ius fasque* for either patron or client to accuse the other, or give evidence against him, or cast a vote against him. If anyone was convicted of such an evil deed he was liable under the law of treason established by Romulus and any person could kill him as someone *sacer* to Dis. This account by Dionysius[5] may give an overly legal tone to the relationship but its essential character is plain. The *clientes* are to be the general supporters of the patron, communally maintain him in his political ambitions and social position, and cushion him economically when he has serious problems. The patrons' duties are of a nobler sort, the protection of a weaker man.

Yet the *cliens* emerges as an independent legal personal-

---

scholars think that in the archaic period plebeians were citizens, but *clientes* were not: e.g. Gjerstad, *Early Rome* 5, pp. 188ff. But for the mid-5th century Gjerstad admits that the *clientes* were plebeians and citizens: pp. 310f.

[4] Dionysius also says that patrons had to take the same care of *clientes* when they were absent as when they were present; and, with regard to money and to contracts concerning money, to do for them everything fathers do for their sons. The first aspect stresses that the relationship is based on *fides*. The second must not be taken as giving the wording of the rule or as implying a relationship akin to *patria potestas*, otherwise there would be an intolerable conflict with Dionysius' account of the duties of the *clientes*. Dionysius is writing to explain Rome to a Greek audience (cf. 1.4.2). Not surprisingly, collections of the *leges regiae* do not quote this part of Dionysius 2.10.1; see Bruns, p. 4; P. F. Girard, *Textes de droit romain*, 6th ed. by F. Senn (Paris, A. Rousseau, 1937), p. 5; *FIRA* 1, p. 4.

[5] 2.10.1ff.

ity. His very duties show that he can own property of his own, and he is clearly capable of bringing a legal action[6] (though the patron may be expected to assist). No legal rights over the person of the *cliens* are given to the patron who—qua patron[7]—has no right, so far as we are made aware, to punish an erring *cliens*. All this must be made explicit for our understanding both of the *patronus* and *cliens* relationship at the time of the XII Tables and for the relationship between patron and freedman. The evidence, as we shall see, is that the patron's legal rights and duties in respect of his *clientes* diminished with time, and were much reduced even by the mid-fifth century. If the term *potestas* were to occur in this context it ought not simply to be construed as involving a legal power like *patria potestas*, nor should the fact that the word *patronus* is derived from *pater* suggest a similar conclusion.[8] Likewise, if it should be thought—as it is by some scholars—that the *patronus* has *potestas* over his *libertus*, this should be considered as a special feature of that relationship, and not as a general mark of the patron/client situation. Moreover, since *clientes* existed and were important earlier than *liberti*, no arguments for the *patronus*/*libertus* relationship should be drawn from the etymology of *patronus*.[9]

[6] Though for our purposes there is no need to insist upon it, the story of Verginia in Livy 3.44ff depends upon a *cliens* being competent to start legal proceedings.

[7] Of course, for a breach of *patrocinium*, anyone could kill the *cliens*, and one might think that the patron could feel he had greater cause and justification than others. Likewise, since a *cliens* could not accuse his patron, the *patronus* might be tempted to abuse his position. Yet whatever might be the case in practice, the legal theory was that the *patronus* might also be killed for a breach of *patrocinium*, and he, too, could not accuse a *cliens*.

[8] Thus, not much can be made of Festus, *s.v. Patronus*, even if the usual reconstruction of this extremely corrupt text is accurate: "Patr[*onus a patre cur ab antiquis dictus*] sit, manifestum: quia [*ut liberi, sic enim clientes*] numerari inter do[*mesticos quodammodo possunt*]."

[9] There is nothing which suggests the word *patronus* came into being to describe the former master of a freedman.

But in fact the term *potestas* does not seem to be used in this context. Von Premerstein writes, "Ebenso wie das durch die Dedition entstandene Verhältnis als *dicio* und *potestas* des römischen Volkes, charakterisiert ist, erscheint auch die Clientel einzelner als ein Herrenrecht (*potestas*)."[10] Yet the sole textual authority for this influential statement[11] appears to be Cicero *Font.* 18.40: "frugi igitur hominem, iudices, . . . videtis positum in vestra fide et potestate atque ita ut commissus sit fidei, permissus sit potestati." But even if we accept the idea that the jury is to regard Fonteius as if he were a client entrusted and also subject to them, the image conveyed is much more that of public than of private law, that of a client state or inhabitant of such. In the public sphere, moreover, we do find *potestas* used as one term among several to designate the authority over dependent peoples.[12]

To come at last to the law at the time of the XII Tables. We know of one provision (Tab. VIII.21) which that code contained, "Patronus si clienti fraudem fecerit, sacer esto."[13] This clause, of course, does not specify the rights and duties of patron and client. Since for the Republic (and later) there is no evidence for precise *legal* rights and duties between patron and client it is plausible to claim that the XII Tables contained no other clause on the subject.

Two things immediately strike one about the provision. First, it is essentially negative. Positive activity is not commanded: the patron is merely ordered to abstain from *fraus*

---

[10] *RE* 4, 24.

[11] The idea (and use of the term) of *potestas* is taken over, for instance, by M. Kaser (particularly in the context of freedmen): "Die Geschichte der Patronatsgewalt über Freigelassene," *ZSS* 58 (1938), 88ff, at e.g. 96; *RPR* 1, p. 118, "Wie alle privatrechtlichen Gewalten ist der *patronatus* zunächst eine Vollgewalt"; and now in "Die Beziehung von *Lex* und *Ius* und die XII Tafeln," in *Studi in Memoria di G. Donatuti* 2 (Milan, La Goliardica, 1973), 523ff, at 535.

[12] See the references given by Mommsen, *Staatsrecht* 3, p. 723, n.1. For usages involving *fides* see the sources in von Premerstein, *RE* 4, 23f, and add Dionysius of Halicarnassus 2.9.1.

[13] Servius in *V. Aen.* 6.609.

on his *cliens*. Secondly, the order is directed unilaterally: the patron, not the client, is to abstain from *fraus*.

The patron's legal obligations reported for the regal period no longer exist as such. Yet they remained important, morally and socially. The giving of legal advice continued throughout the Republic to be a mark of the superior Roman even though, with time, it ceased to be tightly tied to the relationship of *patronus* and *cliens*.[14] The same applies with equal force to appearing for another in court.[15] How strong this obligation was felt to be in later times—and *a fortiori* how strong it was in the mid-fifth century—is best seen in a passage from Plautus:

> How we are bound to this stupid and exceedingly troublesome custom! The better men are, the more they are tied to it. Everyone wants a large number of *clientes*. Whether they are good or bad, they don't ask. They consider more the wealth of *clientes* than their reputation for *fides*. If he is poor and not a bad chap, he is regarded as worthless. But if he is rich and wicked he is held to be a splendid *cliens*. But those who have no concern for law or for what's fair keep their patrons anxious. They deny that what was given was given, are full of lawsuits, they are rapacious and fraudulent fellows who have made their money by usury or perjury. Their mind is always on their lawsuit. The day fixed for the hearing is likewise fixed for their *patroni*. The case comes up before the people, or *in iure* or in front of the aedile. In that way, today a certain *cliens* kept me extremely worried. Nor could I do what I wanted or be with whom I wanted, so much he delayed me, so much he kept me. I pled the case before the aediles for his very numerous evil deeds, I put forward terms both twisted and difficult. I had put the case more or less as was needed for the *sponsio* to be made. What did he do? He gave a surety.[16]

[14] For the later Republic see Watson, *Law Making*, pp. 194ff.
[15] See Watson, *Law Making*, pp. 106ff.
[16] *Men*, 571ff:
Vt hoc utimur maxume more moro,
molesto atque multo atque uti quique sunt op-
tumi maxume morem habent hunc!
clientes sibi omnes volunt esse multos:

It appears that *patroni* felt strongly that they were under an obligation to conduct a case for a *cliens* who had a lawsuit, whether they thought the *cliens* was honorable and had a reasonable case or not, and whether or not they had other things to do. From another source we learn that Sabinus in the third book of his *Ius civile* stated that for the old Romans the obligation to a *cliens* ranked after that to one's *pupillus* and to one's *hospes*, but before that to a *cognatus* and to an *adfinis*.[17] Thus, it was very important. Again, we are told that one might give evidence for a *cliens* against *cognati*, but no one gave evidence against a *cliens*.[18] Conceivably there was a legal obligation not to testify against a *cliens*, but it is not easy to see law in this ranking of duties.[19]

Little need be said here specifically on the provision of

---

bonine an mali sint, id hau quaeritant; res
magis quaeritur quam clientum fides
   quoius modi clueat.
si est pauper atque hau malus nequam habetur,
sin diues malust, is cliens frugi habetur.
qui nec leges neque aequom bonum usquam colunt,
   sollicitos patronos habent.
datum denegant quod datum est, litium pleni, rapaces
   uiri, fraudulenti,
qui aut faenore aut peiiuriis habent rem paratam,
   mens est in quo
eius ubi dicitur dies, simul patronis dicitur,
   quippe qui pro illis loquimur quae male fecerunt:
   aut ad populum aut in iure aut ad iudicem rest.
sicut me hodie nimi' sollicitum cliens quidam habuit neque quod
   volui
agere aut quicum licitumst, ita med attinit, ita detinit.
apud aedilis pro eius factis plurumisque pessumisque
deixei caussam, condiciones tetuli tortas, confragosas:
aut plus aut minu' quam opus erat dicto dixeram controuorsiam,
   ut sponsio fieret. quid ill' qui praedem dedit?
nec magis manufestum ego hominem umquam ullum teneri uidi:
omnibus male factis testes tres aderant acerrumi.

The situation involved is so Roman that we can be sure the passage is Plautine and not taken over from a Greek model.

[17] Aulus Gellius *NA* 5.13.5.   [18] Aulus Gellius *NA* 5.13.4.
[19] See Watson, *Persons*, pp. 104f, especially p. 105 n. 1.

the XII Tables. Exactly what punishment was meant for the offending patron by "sacer esto" need not be discussed here.[20] *Fraus* in early Latin, and for a long time in legal Latin, had a wider meaning than the English "fraud."[21] Here the best translation is probably "wrong": "If a patron does wrong to a *cliens*." I should like to link this clause—conjecturally since there is no firm textual evidence—with the disappearance of legal obligations on the *clientes* to pay money in certain circumstances to their patrons. There is, it should be stressed, no evidence that any such duties existed for *clientes* after the regal period. Indeed, Plutarch, after relating the duties imposed by Romulus, goes on, "But in later times, when all other rights and privileges remained in force, the taking of money by those of high degree from the more lowly was held to be disgraceful and ungenerous."[22] This, I suggest, had come to be the position before the XII Tables, and one purpose of the clause in question was to stop patrons putting unwarranted pressure on *clientes* to make payments to them.[23]

There is no indication that any original restriction that only patricians could be *patroni* survived into the Republic.

That a freedman was a *cliens* of his manumitter and former master—who is also termed his *patronus*—is beyond doubt. But this patron/freedman relationship had its own characteristics to such an extent from at least as early as the XII Tables that it is best to treat it on its own.

The nature of this relationship between *patronus* and *libertus* has been, I suggest, obscured by the conception which some scholars have of *potestas*. Thus, for instance,

[20] According to Dionysius 2.10.3, both a patron and a client who were guilty of a specified act of treachery against the other would be consecrated to Dis. The provision is quite different from that of the XII Tables.

[21] See Ernout & Meillet, *Dictionnaire*, p. 252; TLL 6, 1267.

[22] *Rom.* 13.6.

[23] It is convenient to leave D.47.2.90(89) (Paul *sing. de poen. pag.*) until the discussion of *patronus* and *libertus*; infra, p. 108.

Kaser writes,[24] "Like every *potestas*, that over freedmen also at first included the right of life and death." But to argue from the term or concept *potestas* to the content of the relationship between patron and freedman is, in my view, unacceptable. Before in this book I have maintained that in early times *potestas* was not a technical term but merely meant "power" or "control" and that its extent would be defined by the legal context. Of even greater importance here is the fact that the term *potestas* just does not seem to be used of this relationship between *patronus* and *libertus*. If the patron did have the right to kill his freedman this must be shown by other particular evidence.[25] We should notice before going further that the xii Tables' provision[26] on succession to freedmen makes it abundantly plain that, unlike slaves and sons *in potestate*, freedmen could own property.

To establish the extent and nature of the legal relationship we should look for an answer to specific questions. Did a patron have the right to kill or to re-enslave a freedman? Could he send him into *relegatio*[27] or subject him to lesser punishment? What restrictions existed on actions between patron and client? Was the freedman under any legal obligation to perform services for his patron or to show him any outward marks of respect? Did the patron have any rights to property belonging to the freedman during the latter's lifetime or when he died?

There is no evidence, or at any rate no unambiguous evidence, that the patron had a right to kill a freedman. For the contrary view three much later texts are adduced.[28] Valerius Maximus 6.1.4 records that P. Maenius, probably

[24] "Geschichte der Patronatsgewalt," p. 96; see also the quotation from his *RPR* i, supra, p. 101, n. 11.

[25] As, of course, those who believe in the patron's right to kill attempt to do.

[26] Tab. v.8.

[27] *Relegatio* is not a real possibility for our period, but was a standard punishment later.

[28] Above all by Kaser: most recently *RPR* i, pp. 118, 298.

in the late Republic, killed a freedman for kissing his daughter. But Valerius Maximus is not interested in the legal aspects of the story, and nothing indicates that Maenius had a legal right to act as he did, or indeed that his behavior did not lead to criminal proceedings against him. From Suetonius *Iul.* 48 we learn that Caesar inflicted capital punishment on a favorite freedman for adultery with the wife of an *eques*. But this behavior of Julius Caesar, perhaps even as *praefectus morum* or *dictator*, cannot be taken as real evidence that any patron had the legal right to put a freedman to death. The third text, Suetonius *Aug.* 67, which concerns a compelled suicide, is plainly irrelevant.[29] In the absence of evidence that a patron was legally entitled to execute a freedman at any period, and in the sure knowledge that in the time of Nero no such right existed,[30] it is preferable to hold that in our period, too, the patron had no *vitae necisque potestas*. It is evident, moreover, that until the early Empire a patron could not have his freedman re-enslaved, even for ingratitude.[31] *Relegatio* seems to have been introduced as a penalty for ungrateful freedmen by the *lex Aelia Sentia* of A.D. 4.[32]

The evidence—both in respect of *relegatio* and re-enslavement—suggests that in the early Empire there was a sharp increase in the legal powers of punishment avail-

[29] The arguments are set out in full in Watson, *Persons*, pp. 227f: S. Treggiari, *Roman Freedmen during the Late Republic* (Oxford, Clarendon Press, 1969), pp. 72f.

[30] Tacitus *Ann.* 13.26.

[31] See e.g. Kaser, *RPR* 1, pp. 292ff; Watson, *Persons*, p. 229. The main sources are D.37.14.5pr. (Marcian *13 inst.*); Suetonius *Claud.* 25.2; Tacitus *Ann.* 13.26f; D.25.3.6.1 (Modestinus *sing. de manum.*).

[32] The evidence is not unambiguous: D. 50.16.70pr (Paul *73 ad ed.*) shows that the *lex Aelia Sentia* introduced an *accusatio liberti ingrati*; Tacitus *Ann.* 13.26 that the sole punishment available to *patroni* in the time of Nero was *relegatio*. See above all Treggiari, *Freedmen*, p. 74, against the view that Augustus was reviving an obsolete right. Quintilian *Inst.* 7.7.9 does not show that patrons had the right of *manus iniectio* over freedmen; the legal rule, like that for instance, in 7.7.10, is imaginary: contra, Kaser, *RPR* 1, p. 298.

able to *patroni*. Perhaps changing social conditions or social awareness was responsible for the trend.[33]

As for any legal right of the patron at the time of the XII Tables to inflict minor punishment on a freedman, the answer *from the sources* must be *non liquet*. For a much later period, certainly the *actio iniuriarum* was not granted against a patron except for *atrox iniuria*, and Ulpian declares that slight punishment was granted to a patron against a *libertus*.[34] But Ulpian's comment might be a rationalization. Reasons of public policy might decree that the *actio iniuriarum* for ordinary *iniuria* should not be allowed against the *patronus*; and this refusal need not imply that the patron had a right to inflict minor punishment on the *libertus*, just as the fact that a *tutor* was liable only for fraud does not imply that he had a right to be negligent. It may be observed that an emancipated son had similar restrictions placed on his bringing the *actio iniuriarum* against his father.[35] Again, the refusal of the *actio iniuriarum* might be but one instance of the edictal rule that a freedman could not summon his patron, etc., *in ius* without the permission of the praetor:[36] the law had stabilized to the extent that the praetor would automatically refuse the action for ordinary *iniuria* but grant it for *atrox iniuria*. The edict might even have been refusing a remedy where one had existed before. Again, I suggest that very little can be deduced from the fact that at least in the Empire the *patronus* had no *actio furti* against the *libertus* in respect of *furta domestica*.[37]

[33] In general, criminal law penalties became harsher in the Empire than they had been in the Republic; see P. Garnsey, "Why Penal Laws become Harsher: the Roman Case," *Natural Law Forum* 13 (1968) 141ff.

[34] D.47.10.7.2 (Ulpian 57 *ad ed.*); h.t. 11.7 (idem); 2.4.10.12.

[35] D.47.10.7.3.

[36] For the edict see Lenel, *EP*, pp. 68ff; cf. pp. 106ff.

[37] D.47.2.90 (Paul *sing. de poen. pag.*); 48.19.11.1 (Marcian 2 *pub. iud.*). (The latter text concerns the criminal law action, not the delictal *actio furti*.) For the contrary opinion see e.g. Kaser, *RPR* 1, p. 298.

Certainly the very existence of this rule implies that the patron could punish the freedman himself, but the basis of the rule is not that the thief is a freedman; the rule equally applied where the thief was a *mercennarius*, a free man who had hired out his services to the injured party, and where he was a *cliens*.[38] The rule would seem to have operated only when the thief resided in the home of his victim.[39]

There is no evidence that specific duties of *obsequium* and *operae* existed for the freedman by operation of law. When a patron wished to be in a position to enforce any such right he would probably have to create the obligation by contract with the freedman at the time of manumission.[40]

In the last few paragraphs we have rightly been concerned only with the theoretical legal position. In practice, the relationship between patron and freedman could look very different. It is unlikely, given that slaves would not be anything like so numerous as they were later, that manumission was awarded on a grand scale, but would be the reward to a select few for excellent and trustworthy service. The freedman would continue to reside with his former master and serve him as before. Indeed, prominent Romans might place more trust in the loyalty of freedmen than of anyone else.[41] Socially the freedmen would be very dependent upon his patron. Indicative of this is the fact that in early times the word *servus* could include the sense of

---

[38] D.47.2.90; 48.19.11.1. Consistently, Kaser claims that the householder had very great powers of punishment which he exercised over *mercennarii* as he did over his own slaves, but Kaser does recognize that *mercennarii* were independent in their personal rights: *RPR* 1, p. 301.

[39] See e.g. Kaser, "Geschichte der Patronatsgewalt," pp. 101ff.

[40] The argument for this derives from the information on the edict of Rutilius (and of subsequent praetors) on *obsequium* and *operae*: D.38.2.1 (Ulpian *42 ad ed.*).

[41] This is the real significance of Cicero *QFr.* 1.1.13. The reference to freedmen must be understood in its context: see Treggiari, *Freedmen*, pp. 68f.

"freedman" within its meaning.[42] The respect due from a freedman to his patron would be understood by everyone.

The XII Tables (v.8) did, however, contain one provision on patron and freedman, and it regulated intestate succession to the latter: if a freedman died and had no *suus heres*, the inheritance went to the *patronus*.[43] In the context of this provision (or one closely connected with it) occurred the words *ex ea familia . . . in eam familiam*,[44] but any reconstruction is hazardous and cannot increase our knowledge.[45] There was no obstacle to a freedman making a will, and he could completely pass over his patron.[46] Finally, it seems extremely unlikely that there existed any *legal* obligation on a patron to give material support (*alimenta*) to a needy freedman,[47] or vice versa.

Before we leave the subject of patron and freedman it

[42] It is difficult to assess the significance of this, but one need not derive far-reaching conclusions about private law. After all, freedmen and slaves—despite the usages of the word *servus*—were very different in status: to say no more, the former were citizens and the latter not. (And the word *servus* was not used of the slave only with reference to his relationship with his owner.) Little weight need be attached to the few inscriptions (collected in Mommsen, *Staatsrecht* 3, p. 428, n. 1) where *servus* or *ancilla* is used of a freed person; these might be nothing more than a token of the respect which was felt to be due to the patron. In the context, especially of the freedman's name, no confusion of status is possible. The real evidence that the word *servus* might objectively be used to signify freedman is *Vat.Fr.* 307 (plus 308 and 309) which concerns the *lex Cincia* and it may be that the relevant provision of the *lex* is not yet fully understood; see G. G. Archi, *La donazione* (Milan, Giuffrè, 1960), pp. 17ff. On the usage see e.g. Mommsen, *Staatsrecht* 3, pp. 427ff; Treggiari, *Freedmen*, pp. 265f.

[43] *Epit.Ulp.* 29.1. Later at least, it was apparent that any *suus heres*, including an adopted child or a wife *in manu*, would exclude the *patronus*: G.3.140. Likewise it was established—probably by interpretation after our period—that if a patron were dead his rights of succession would pass to certain descendants; G.3.45f.

[44] D.50.16.195.1 (Ulpian *46 ad ed.*).

[45] The meaning ascribed, supra, pp. 57f to *familia*, "a man's property considered as a unit" seems also to make sense here.

[46] G.3.40f. Restrictions were introduced much later by a praetorian edict.

[47] Contra, apparently, Kaser, *RPR* 1, p. 119.

should be stressed that there is something unreal in considering this relationship primarily in terms of law. Little law was actually involved. The freedman was bound to his patron by gratitude, by (generally) continuing to live in the patron's house as a subordinate member, and by what was expected in that society from a freedman.[48]

[48] Freedmen and the children of freedmen suffered from disabilities vis-à-vis *ingenui* in public law, but we need not consider these here.

NINE

Nexum

The problem of debt and debtors looms large in the stories of social discontent in early Rome. The worst *abuses* were those perpetrated on debtors bound by *nexum*.[1] The details of *nexum* are confused in our sources, really for two reasons. First, because the institution was obsolete long before the texts were written; it disappeared as a result of the *lex Poetilia* probably of 313 B.C.[2] Secondly, because in early times law was less formal and rigid than later, and our viewpoint is from classical times. Terminology at the time of the XII Tables was not so technical, legal logic not so rigid. In addition the texts are not numerous enough to give a clear picture of the details.

The XII Tables contained a clause on *nexum* (Tab. VI.1) which we shall come across again: "Cum nexum faciet mancipiumque, uti lingua nuncupassit, ita ius esto."[3] *Nexum* was an act *per aes et libram* by which a free man was bound to a creditor and was subject to his control until an amount of bronze which had been weighed out was repaid. Such an account of the transaction, which conceals many problems, would be generally acceptable. Of the few texts which use the word *nexum* in any legal way, that of Varro *Ling.* 7.105 merits discussion first and it should be quoted in the standard edition of G. Goetz and F. Schoell.[4]

---

[1] The literature on *nexum* is immense. See in addition to the works cited in this chapter those listed in Kaser, *RPR* 1, p. 166, n. 2; and G. MacCormack, "The *lex Poetilia*," *Labeo* 19 (1973), 306ff. It is not proposed to discuss the numerous theories which exist.

[2] See Watson, *Law Making*, pp. 6ff.

[3] See infra, pp. 144f.

[4] M. *Terenti Varronis de lingua latina quae supersunt* (reprinted, Amsterdam, Hakkert, 1964), pp. 121f.

"Nexum" Manilius scribit, omne quod per aes et libram geritur, in quo sint mancipia. Mucius, quae per aes et libram fiant ut oblige[n]tur, praeter quom mancipio dentur. Hoc verius esse ipsum verbum ostendit, de quo qu⟨a⟩erit: nam id ⟨a⟩es[t] quod obligatur per libram neque suum fit, inde nexum dictum. liber qui suas operas in servitutem pro pecunia quam debebat, dum solveret, nexus vocatur, ut ab aere obaeratus. hoc C. Poetilio Libone Visolo dictatore sublatum ne fieret, et omnes qui bonam copiam iurarunt, ne essent nexi dissoluti.

Thus, there was a difference of opinion between Manilius and Mucius. For the former, *nexum* meant all acts *per aes et libram* including *mancipatio*, but the latter excluded *mancipatio* from the meaning of *nexum*. More important for us at the moment is Varro's resolution of this conflict by the use of etymology. Varro sides with Mucius that *nexum* does not include *mancipatio*, and he argues that the word itself shows this: "nexum" derives from "neque suum." Ownership, that is to say, is not transferred in a *nexum*; hence the term *nexum* does not cover *mancipatio*. Whatever it is which is not being transferred is the main subject matter of the transaction, not the bronze. Hence the emendation to be found in Goetz and Schoell of "nam id est quod obligatur" to "nam id aes quod obligatur" is to be excluded.[5] If it be wondered why Varro chooses this formulation in the neuter, "nam id est quod obligatur," when the subject matter will always be a human being, the answer is that he needs the neuter "neque suum" for his demonstration of the derivation of the word *nexum*.[6] The text shows that in Varro's opinion the person bound by *nexum* did not become the property, the slave, of the creditor, and there is no evidence elsewhere for the existence of a contrary opinion.

[5] It goes back to Mommsen and is widely accepted: see e.g. F. de Zulueta, "The Recent Controversy about *nexum*," LQR 94 (1913), 137ff, at 139, n. 4; C. St. Tomulescu, "*Nexum* bei Cicero," Iura 17 (1966), 39ff, at 49, n. 16.

[6] In a similar way is to be explained Varro's unexpected use of *suus*: "neque suum" was what was needed for his etymology, not "neque eius."

Varro, indeed, after explaining the etymology of *nexum*,
"neque suum," declares that the free man who is bound *in
servitutem* for the money is called "nexus."

Manilius was not alone in his contention. Aelius Gallus
also maintained that *nexum* was any act *per aes et libram*.[7]
This wide meaning of *nexum* need not detain us unduly.
Probably, though proof is not possible, the term was used
in this way in early times also. If this assumption is correct
then we have another instance where early legal vocabulary
was not technical, and where a word was not used in every
context with the same precise legal content.[8]

Varro alone attempts to describe the institution and his
text must be treated as fundamental. "A free person," he
says, "who gives his labor in service (*operas in servitutem*)
on account of money which he owed, until he should pay it,
is called *nexus*." Thus, according to Varro, the *nexus* had to
give his labor to the creditor until the debt was paid.
Whether payment had to be in bronze or whether the *nexus*
was meant to work off his debt is not made clear. But it
emerges—if we trust the text—that *nexi* were in a very different situation from *addicti* and *iudicati* (whom we shall
consider briefly later). There is no indication that the creditor had a legal right to put *addicti* and *iudicati* to work. Instead, they could be put in chains and if the debt was not
paid within sixty days the XII Tables allowed them to be put
to death or sold across the Tiber.[9] Seizure of the *iudicatus*
was by the "rough and ready" *manus iniectio*. There is no
sign that *manus iniectio* applied to *nexi*, though commonly
it is assumed that it did.[10] Geoffrey MacCormack[11] has already made us aware that in Livy a marked distinction is

---

[7] Festus, *s.v. Nexum*.

[8] See supra, pp. 47ff. Little can be made of Festus, *s.v. Nexum aes*:
"Nexum aes apud antiquos dicebatur pecunia quae per nexum obligatur." Certainly this text would not justify the alteration in Varro
Ling. 7.105 of *est* to *aes* with the consequent lack of sense in that
text: contra, e.g. Tomulescu, loc. cit.

[9] See infra, p. 122. [10] See infra, p. 116.

[11] "*Nexi, Iudicati* and *Addicti* in Livy," ZSS 84 (1967), 350ff.

observed between *nexi* on the one hand, and *iudicati* and *addicti* on the other.

The nature of *nexum* should not be obscured by Livy's account[12] of dissension between patricians and plebeians in 495 B.C. and his story of the distinguished veteran: indeed, that story reveals the true position. The dissension, we are told, was "maxime propter nexos ob aes alienum."[13] The veteran in filthy clothes and terrible physical condition—his back was covered with weals—had rushed into the forum and was there recognized as a man of military distinction. He explained that during the Sabine war, depredations had not only deprived him of his crops, but his farmhouse had been burned, his belongings plundered, and his flocks driven off. Taxes were demanded at an inconvenient time and he had contracted debt. Debt plus interest deprived him first of his ancestral farm, then of his remaining property, then like a disease had come to his body: he was taken by his creditor not into servitude, but to the prison and torture-chamber. It is this last clause which concerns us most at the moment: "ductum se ab creditore non in servitium, sed in ergastulum et carnificinam." The veteran's complaint is precisely that he was not taken "in servitium" which appears to have been expected and to be regarded as reasonable, but "in ergastulum et carnificinam" which, it appears, was regarded as improper and unreasonable. *Servitium* was right for a *nexus*, but not the *ergastulum* or *carnificina*. Thus, Livy on this point confirms Varro that a *nexus* was to give his services while the debt was outstanding, and he makes clear the difference in condition between a *nexus* and *iudicatus* for whom the *ergastulum* would have been appropriate.

But Livy also shows that *nexum* was open to abuse by the creditor: the difficulty of protecting the *nexus* is also made plain by the accounts of the events which led to the enacting of the *lex Poetilia*, namely, the attempted rape or seduc-

[12] 2.23-32.   [13] 2.23.1.

tion of the handsome young *nexus* by the creditor.[14] Often, too, chains were put on the *nexi* but whether this was an abuse or allowable so that *nexi* would be easily distinguishable from other people cannot be discovered. Thus, Livy tells us in 2.23.8 that *nexi*, both those in chains and those who were not, "vincti solutique," rushed into the streets from every side. The *vincti* were not shut up, *clausi*, or they could not have rushed into the streets. An inevitable result of this tumult would, of course, be that some creditors would seek to keep their *nexi* locked up, hence the consul's edict reported in 2.24.6: "ne quis civem Romanum vinctum aut clausum teneret, quo minus ei nominis edendi apud consules potestas fieret, neu quis militis, donec in castris esset, bona possideret aut venderet, liberos nepotesve eius moraretur." The edict would enable the *nexi* to fight in the war against the Volsci but it did not affect their basic status. When considered in its historical context the edict provides no evidence either that it was common or, indeed, legally permitted for creditors to keep *nexi* locked up.

Despite the possibility of abuse, *nexum* had advantages for the debtor as well as the creditor. It was a strong form of real security, a fact which could make it easier to borrow. If repayment became impossible, the life of a *nexus* was preferable to that of a *iudicatus* or *addictus* since the *nexus* could not be killed or sold across the Tiber. For the creditor, it was better to have a *nexus* than a slaughtered debtor, and to sell a debtor into foreign slavery might cause trouble. Interestingly, there is no evidence that debtors ever were in fact put to death or sold *trans Tiberim*. The greatest advantage of *nexum*, however, was that its nature made it flexible and its use might vary with the circumstances. Various possibilities can be envisaged.

First, a *paterfamilias* who needs money, borrows it and gives himself in *nexum* to the creditor. With the agreement of the creditor he remains in full *de facto* liberty, managing

[14] See Livy 8.28.

his own affairs, but to the creditor he represents a real security. If the *nexus* fails to repay the loan plus interest, the creditor can take him to work off the amount of the debt. Simply because the security is so strong, the creditor can be willing to allow the debtor full freedom of action until he defaults. Despite the authority of many scholars,[15] there is no reason or need to think that in early times the creditor had the right of *manus iniectio* without an action or judgment. Because of the publicity of the act of *nexum*—as in all acts *per aes et libram* five witnesses were required—the debtor usually could not deny that he was bound and would obey the creditor's command to follow him. If he did not, he ran the risk of the creditor's bringing an action and hence of falling into the much worse position of a *iudicatus*.

One may wonder how the *nexus* who was not working off his debt for the creditor could conduct his own affairs and enter contracts. The answer must be that the *nexum* did not prevent him from acting as *sui iuris*. One need not expect too rigorous an application of legal logic at an early period. It is certain at least that the *nexus* remained a full Roman citizen or he would not have been eligible for military service.[16]

Secondly, a *paterfamilias* who has previously borrowed from several creditors and is unable to repay, enters into *nexum* to one of them (or another person). The *aes* which is weighed out is used to pay the other creditors, and the *nexus* has to work off his debt since he has no capital. This arrangement has advantages all round. The debtor avoids being a *iudicatus* and the danger of being divided into pieces. The other creditors have got their *aes* back (or part of it) whereas cutting in pieces would give no financial sat-

---

[15] See e.g. Kaser, *Eigentum*, p. 149.

[16] As he certainly was: Livy 2.24.6. In classical law persons *in mancipio* could not incur an obligation; G.3.104. But the situation of *nexi* and those *in mancipio* could well have been different. According to Varro, *ling.* 7.105, Quintus Mucius would not regard the term "nexum" as including *mancipatio*.

isfaction, and selling *trans Tiberim* was probably socially unacceptable. The creditor who took the *nexum* would get the services of the debtor.

Thirdly, a *paterfamilias* who has previously borrowed from one creditor and has not been able to repay undergoes *nexum* to that creditor and presumably stays in his household until he works off the debt. If the formalities are strictly observed—perhaps they need not be—the *aes* will be weighed out and given to the *nexus* who will then return it to the creditor in payment of the previously existing debts.[17] That a person might give himself into *nexum* on account of outstanding debts is clear above all from Livy 8.28.2.

A problem, especially for the second and third practical situations which have just been described, is to know how the *nexus* secured his release once the debt had been worked off. If the *nexus* had been *sui iuris* then no one else could bring an action on his behalf. Perhaps one should see in this problem one of the difficulties for *nexi* which resulted in the institution being so hated that it had to be got rid of in the late fourth century. To some extent the problem would be mitigated by social pressures and social observances. The debtor's patron, above all, could bring pressure to bear on the creditor, and if it were the patron himself who was the creditor misbehavior on his part could make him liable to the provision of the XII Tables: "Patronus si clienti fraudem fecerit, sacer esto." Moreover, one cannot wholly exclude the possibility that the *nexus* could sue for his own release.

A fourth way in which *nexum* could be operated was that a *paterfamilias* who needed working capital might give in *nexum* a son or grandson. The descendant would then either work off the debt or remain in full *de facto* liberty until there was default in the repayment of the loan, which-

---

[17] The debts could be wiped out, I suggest, because the *nexus* was not regarded as ceasing to be *sui iuris*.

ever was arranged with the creditor. This latter case is alluded to in the consuls' edict cited in Livy 2.24.6: "neu quis ... liberos nepotesve eius moraretur."[18]

It is, I wish to argue, this delivery of descendants into *nexum* which is at the root of the provision (Tab. iv.2b) of the xii Tables: "Si pater filium ter venum duit, filius a patre liber esto." A *paterfamilias*, I suggest, retained *potestas* over his descendants given in *nexum*, but if the *nexum* were repeated for a third time the *potestas* ended. It has more than once been pointed out that the provision can scarcely have applied to three ordinary sales[19]—a father, in the nature of things, would scarcely have the opportunity to sell a descendant three times over. However, the provision did envisage three separate *mancipationes* of the *filius*; or at least so it was understood when the clause came to be used to permit the emancipation of a son from paternal power.[20] Any explanation of the provision must be able to account for the use of language appropriate to sale, show how the "sale" could occur three times and involve three *mancipationes*, and why the right of the father to repeat the "sale" an indefinite number of times was sharply curtailed. *Nexum*—

[18] See supra, pp. 103f.

[19] See e.g. H. Lévy-Bruhl, *Nouvelles études sur le très ancien droit romain* (Paris, Sirey, 1947), pp. 8off; R. Yaron, "Si pater filium ter venum duit," *T.v.R.* 36 (1968), 57ff; J. M. Kelly, "A Note on 'Threefold Mancipation,'" in *Daube noster*, ed. A. Watson (Edinburgh, London, Scottish Academic Press, 1974), pp. 183ff.

[20] This development (cf. G.1.132) and the further step that only one *mancipatio* was needed to emancipate other descendants seems early, and is usually thought to be due to the pontiffs. It is this which makes implausible Kelly's view—if I understand him properly —that the xii Tables' provision did not necessarily relate to *mancipatio*: "Threefold Mancipation," p. 185. But Kelly rightly emphasizes that "venum duit" need not refer to a situation which would fall within the later contract of sale. It is clear that in early Latin *venum*, *venire*, and *vendere* could be and were used even where the thing was to be only temporarily in the control of the recipient and in situations approximating to the scope of the contract of hire (as well as of sale) in classical law: Plautus *Mil.gl.* 1076; Cato *Agr.* 149.1, 150.1; Varro, *Rust.* 1.53.

and *nexum* alone[21]—really fits. A *paterfamilias* short of working capital gives his son in *nexum* in return for *aes*. When the debt has been worked off the son comes home and the father at some stage repeats the process. The practical realities are apparent. That the *nexum* could be regarded as an indignity for the son is clear, and the code's provision that if a father repeated the process three times the son was free from *potestas* is fully understandable.[22]

If the conclusion that the provision of the xii Tables concerned *nexum* is correct, then it provides support for a proposition which is often doubted, namely, that *nexum*, like, for instance, *coemptio* and the *testamentum per aes et libram*, is a variant form of *mancipatio*. Indeed, it is difficult to see what else it can have been: it was an act *per aes et libram*, it was regulated by the xii Tables in the same provision as *mancipatio*—"Cum nexum faciet mancipiumque, etc."—and later jurists debated whether *mancipatio* was covered by the term "nexum." The doubts which exist seem to be based on three separate objections. First, it is said *nexum* cannot be a *mancipatio* because the *nexus* does not fall into the *mancipium*-control of the creditor, but keeps his free personal rights.[23] This, I think, badly underestimates the flexibility of early law. A legal institution in a modified form does not inevitably have the identical effects

[21] Yaron has already shown that Lévy-Bruhl's theory that the provision concerned *noxae deditio* is untenable: "*Si pater filium*," pp. 57ff. Yaron himself tends to think the provision concerned a *mancipium*-relationship limited in time: pp. 71f. But such a relationship—apart from *nexum*—is otherwise completely unknown. H. Kaufmann regards the provision as relating to hiring: *Die altrömische Miete* (Cologne, Graz, Böhlau, 1964), pp. 243f. This view is untenable in its simple form since ordinary hiring would not involve *mancipatio* yet the provision must, as was argued above, have envisaged three separate acts of *mancipatio*.

[22] Though certainty is not possible, the wording of the provision indicates that during the first two *nexa* the *filius* remained in the *potestas* of his *paterfamilias*. If this is correct it lends support to the argument that a *pater* who gave himself in *nexum* remained *sui iuris* and could enter contracts.

[23] See e.g. Kaser, *RPR* i, p. 166, n. 5.

of the parent institution. For instance, *mancipatio* conveyed ownership, *coemptio* did not but gave *manus* to the husband of his *paterfamilias*, the *testamentum per aes et libram* in all probability gave the *familiae emptor* no real rights of any kind. Hence it would not be surprising if the *nexus* retained his personal rights.[24] Secondly, it is suggested that self-mancipation is entirely unknown to Roman law.[25] This, too, seems based on too pedantic a view of early law. Why should the early Romans not have allowed *nexum* as a self-mancipation if this seemed desirable? The *coemptio* of a woman *sui iuris* is, after all, not very remote from a self-mancipation. Thirdly, it is urged that if *nexum* is a *mancipatio* its release should be a *remancipatio* yet *nexi liberatio* must be identified with the *solutio per aes et libram* of G.3.173ff which was not a *remancipatio*.[26] This objection need not be taken seriously. There is nothing to suggest that Gaius was thinking of the long-obsolete *nexum* as one of the acts *per aes et libram*, and, moreover, nothing ties *nexi liberatio* to the *solutio per aes et libram*.[27]

[24] But it should be observed that it is merely a convenient supposition that he did. There is no direct evidence unless the suggestion, supra, p. 119, n. 22, is accepted.

[25] See e.g. de Zulueta, "Controversy," p. 141. It is also said that a conditional *mancipatio* is contrary to principle. Yes, but terms and reservations in a *mancipatio* were allowable: see infra, p. 145. In this respect *nexum* is similar to *fiducia*.

[26] See e.g. de Zulueta, loc. cit.

[27] It has recently been suggested on the basis of Livy 2.27.1, "Deinceps et qui ante nexi fuerant creditoribus tradebantur et nectebantur alii," that debtors might be compelled to enter *nexum*: MacCormack, "*Nexi*," p. 352; followed by Jolowicz-Nicholas, *Introduction*, p. 166, n. 1. But such a view is neither needed nor justified. The passage simply means that those who were *nexi* before were handed back to their creditors, and that other debtors entered *nexum*. The plebeians had hoped that the condition of *nexi* would be greatly alleviated, and even probably that the institution be abolished: Livy 2.24.11-25.5.

Numerous texts of Dionysius of Halicarnassus refer to the problem of debt and the plight of debtors in early Rome: 4.9,11; 5.53,64,69; 6.23,24,26,29,37,41,46,58,59,76,79,82,83; 16.5. But the references are mainly vague, the distinction between *nexi* and *iudicati* is not usually observed, and possibly one has to allow for Greek ideas;

Interestingly, it seems that this provision of the xII Tables was not innovating. Dionysius of Halicarnassus relates[28] that Romulus allowed a father to make a profit by selling his son three times: if the son were freed once and twice he was still his father's slave, but after a third sale he was freed from his father. Dionysius says[29] that he does not know whether this law was written or unwritten, but that in the early Republic it was recorded by the decemviri and was placed in the fourth of the xII Tables. It cannot be doubted that Dionysius here has in mind "Si pater filium ter venum duit, etc." That he should think it and the preceding royal law concerned actual sales is not surprising, even though he must be wrong.

As an appendix, we should look briefly at *iudicati*[30] and *addicti*.[31] The *iudicati* (and *confessi*) were much worse off than the *nexi* and their rights and liabilities were set out in the xII Tables in considerable detail. Aulus Gellius *NA* 20.1.45 reports what now appears in the editions as Tab. III. 1-4: "(1) Aeris confessi rebusque iure iudicatis triginta dies iusti sunto. (2) Post deinde manus iniectio esto, in ius ducito. (3) Ni iudicatum facit aut quis endo eo in iure vindicit, secum ducito, vincito aut nervo aut compedibus. Quindecim pondo ne minore aut si volet maiore vincito. (4) Si volet suo vivito. Ni suo vivit, qui eum vinctum habebit, libras farris, endo dies dato. Si volet plus dato."

Thus, a person who confesses his liability or a defendant who loses the action has thirty days' grace in which to pay

---

see e.g. de Zulueta, "Controversy," p. 152. But 4.9.7 shows that money might be lent on the security of free men, hence concerns *nexum* (*inter alia*). And in 6.83.4 the second category of debtors is certainly *iudicati*, the first probably *nexi*.

[28] 2.27.2.　　　　　　　　[29] 2.27.3.

[30] On this subject see now above all Kaser, *ZPR*, pp. 100ff and the references he gives. It is not appropriate here to discuss the topic in full.

[31] *Addictus* seems to be used as a synonym for *iudicatus*. For the special case of the *fur manifestus* see Aulus Gellius *NA* 11.18.8; 20.1.7; G.3.189.

the plaintiff or otherwise make amends. If he fails, he is to be led *in ius*, that is, before the praetor, for the *legis actio* known as *manus iniectio*. Gaius tells us[32] that the plaintiff says: "Quod tu mihi iudicatus" [sive "damnatus"] "es sestertium decem milia quandoc non solvisti, ob eam rem ego tibi sestertium x milium iudicati manu*m* inicio," and he takes hold of some part of the defendant's body. No doubt the magistrate has to see to it that the *legis actio* is legally justified and that everything is being properly carried out. The defendant cannot throw off the plaintiff's hand himself,[33] and if he does not satisfy the judgment and no one conducts the action on his behalf as a *vindex* the creditor leads him away. The creditor may bind him with sinew or fetters which may weigh fifteen pounds or less but not more.[34] The debtor can live on his own food but if he does not the creditor has to give him one pound of grain, *far*, each day, or more if he wishes to. Aulus Gellius further relates[35] that there was a *ius paciscendi*,[36] a right of reaching agreement, and that unless the parties made some agreement the debtor was held in bonds for sixty days. During these days the debtor was led before the praetor *in comitium* on three successive market days[37] and the amount of the judgment debt was proclaimed aloud. On the third market day he was put to death[38] or sold abroad ("peregre") across the Tiber.

[32] G.4.21.

[33] G.4.21.

[34] This is to reverse the readings "maiore" and "minore" in the text of Aulus Gellius: see e.g. Kaser, *ZPR*, p. 101, n. 67.

[35] *NA* 20.1.46,47.

[36] See now G. MacCormack, "The *ius paciscendi* of Twelve Tables 3.5," *Juridical Review* (1970), pp. 247ff, and the works he cites.

[37] There is something strange in Gellius' account. Markets were held each ninth day and the time relationship between the three market days and the sixty days of bondage is not clear. But we need not here consider the matter more fully.

[38] G. MacCormack expresses doubt as to whether the XII Tables prescribed the penalty of death: "*Partes secanto*," *T.v.R.* 36 (1968), 509ff, at 511f. But this is how Gellius understands the situation—as MacCormack freely admits—and on any other view it becomes impossible to take a straightforward approach to the "partes secanto" clause.

A further provision (Tab. III.6) regulated the situation where there was a plurality of creditors: "Tertiis nundinis partis secanto. Si plus minusve secuerunt, se fraude esto."[39] The creditors were to divide the body, and if they divided it unequally this was not to be counted a wrong.[40]

There is ample evidence, above all from Livy Book 6,[41] for the practice of imprisoning and fettering debtors. But there is no evidence whatever that any debtor was ever put to death, divided into pieces, or sold into foreign slavery. Gellius, indeed, relates that he never read or heard of a case of a debtor being divided.[42] Given the Roman awareness of the debtors' plight, we can be sure that if cases of killing, dissecting, or selling into slavery had occurred, they would have been recorded. In practice, the parties would avail themselves of the right of agreement or compromise, the *ius paciscendi*, and one may hazard the guess that the *iudicatus* would be allowed to work off his debt.

One may wonder, though, why the code gave legal rights which never were in operation. A further example is (Tab. VIII.2): "Si membrum rup⟨s⟩it, ni cum eo pacit, talio esto." There is no indication that *talio* was ever inflicted and the provision makes explicit the right of the parties to make a compromise. The most plausible solution to the general problem is that the provisions in question were framed as threats to force the debtor or defendant to pay up or work

---

[39] Aulus Gellius *NA* 20.1.49.

[40] Aulus Gellius *NA* 20.1.48f; Quintilian *Inst.* 3.6.84. See Kaser, *ZPR*, p. 102. There have been numerous, unsuccessful attempts to give the clause a different meaning: most recently MacCormack, "*Partes secanto*" (division at the end of the sixty days' period of the body of a debtor who died a natural death during that period); B. Collinder, "Shylock und das Zwölftafelgesetz" (Kungl. Humanistiska Vetenskaps-Samfundet i Uppsala, Årsbock 1967-68 [Uppsala, 1969]), pp. 5ff (castration); and Gjerstad, *Early Rome* 5, p. 327 (division of the debtor's property, a view held by several scholars, but rendered most implausible by "se fraude esto").

[41] 6.11.8; 6.14.3,7,10; 6.15.9; 6.20.6; 6.27.6,8; 6.35.4; 6.36.12.

[42] *NA* 20.1.51f. Of this provision Quintilian *Inst.* 3.6.84, says: "Quam legem mos publicus repudiavit." Tertullian *Apol.* 4.9 does not show that the clause was ever used.

off the appropriate sum. But they place him in an unconscionably weak position. Another possibility is that the fearsome sanctions could not operate because public opinion, very shortly after 450 at the latest, was so hostile.[43] It would be reasonable to suggest that these provisions[44] represent a failure by the decemviri. Certainty is not possible.[45]

[43] MacCormack finds explanations of this kind "highly unrealistic": *"Partes secanto,"* p. 514.

[44] Like that prohibiting intermarriage between patricians and plebeians.

[45] Early in 1975, too late for full treatment in this volume, appeared two works by O. Behrends which are relevant for this chapter: *Der Zwölftafelprozess, zur Geschichte des römischen Obligationenrechts* (Göttinger rechtswissenschaftliche Studien 92, Göttingen, Schwartz, 1974); "Das *nexum* im Manzipationsrecht oder die Ungeschichtlichkeit des Libraldarlehens," *RIDA* 21 (1974), pp. 137. Behrends' radical and ingenious conclusions in general do not seem sufficiently grounded on the evidence, legal, literary, or philological.

TEN

The *Legis Actio Sacramento in Rem*

The ancient proprietary action, the *legis actio sacramento in rem*, could be brought both where the object of the claim was a thing or a dependent member of the family. The basic case was, of course, the claim for a thing and that we will consider in the first instance. It is accepted that, whatever was the case in very early times, private property was legally recognized long before the XII Tables.[1] What is a matter of dispute is whether the law recognized ownership as a right distinct from other rights of property, and whether ownership was a mere relative right, that is, a reflection of the protection given by the proprietary action which settled only which of the parties had a better right to have the thing. To the *legis actio sacramento in rem* there are, I think, now three main approaches.[2]

The first and by far the most widely held is that both claimants of the thing were placed on equal terms, each swore an oath on the rightness of his claim, the action proceeded on the oaths, and the judge awarded the decision and the thing in question to the party with the better right whether or not he could be, in modern terms, considered as owner.[3] This theory, as I have argued elsewhere[4] does

[1] See e.g. Diósdi, *Ownership*, pp. 19ff.

[2] On the variety of opinions held see the survey in Diósdi, *Ownership*, pp. 94ff.

[3] This is above all the view propounded by Kaser in e.g. *ZPR*, pp. 37ff, but see also such authorities on procedure as M. A. Bethmann-Hollweg, *Der römische Zivilprozess*, 1 (Bonn, A. Marcus, 1864), p. 132; H. Lévy-Bruhl, *Recherches sur les actions de la loi* (Paris, Sirey, 1960), p. 71.

[4] "Towards a New Hypothesis of the *legis actio sacramento in rem*," *RIDA* 14 (1967), 455ff. The hypothesis in fact was not new, and

not fit the evidence, and we have a fairly full and reliable account of the procedure, not only in G.4.16 but also in Cicero's treatment of *manum conserere* in *Mur.* 12.26. The course of events before the praetor was in general as follows:

1st party:	Hunc ego hominem ex iure quiritium meum esse aio. secundum suam causam[5] sicut dixi, ecce tibi vindictam imposui. [*At this point he placed his festuca on the disputed object*]
2nd party:	Hunc ego hominem ex iure quiritium meum esse aio. secundum suam causam sicut dixi, ecce tibi vindictam imposui. [*Likewise he, too, placed his festuca on the object*]
Praetor:	Mittite ambo hominem.
1st party:	Postulo anne dicas qua ex causa vindicaveris.
2nd party:	Ius feci sicut vindictam imposui.
1st party:	Quando tu iniuria vindicavisti, quingenario [*or* quinquagenario] sacramento te provoco.
2nd party:	Et ego te
Both parties:	[*to the witnesses*]: Testes estote.

From Gaius' account it emerges that though both parties claim the thing in the same words, only the one who claims second is asked to justify his claim, and it is his claim which is challenged in the oath. Only his title to claim the thing is actively considered.[6] This lack of symmetry in the legal ap-

---

was to be found much earlier in E. d'Abgarowicz, *essai sur la Preuve dans la rei vindicatio* (Paris, A. Rousseau, 1912) and as, Diósdi points out, in E. Roth, "Beitrag zur Lehre von der *Legis actio sacramento in rem*," *ZSS* 3 (1882), 121ff. The failure to realize the antiquity of the hypothesis is a black mark against me, but not against the theory.

[5] In view of Valerius Probus 4.6 it is better to punctuate so that *secundum suam causam* goes with *sicut dixi &c.* and not with what precedes: see Diósdi, *Ownership*, p. 97: "In accordance with the position in which he finds himself as aforesaid, look I place my *vindicta* on him." There is no need to treat *causa* as referring to the title of acquisition. It is not intended here to discuss the precise meaning of *vindicta* and *festuca*.

[6] For this lack of symmetry see also Diósdi, *Ownership*, pp. 96ff.

proach to the parties is even more apparent in the modified form of the *legis actio sacramento in rem* which appears in Cicero's *Mur.* In that only one party expressly claims that the estate is his *ex iure quiritium.* Of course, if one discards the view that the parties are on a level and that the thing is awarded to the person with the better right, then a major prop of the theory of relative ownership disappears.

Both of the other major hypotheses start from the observation that the *legis actio sacramento in rem* is not symmetrical, that although both parties claim the thing, only one of them is asked to explain or justify his claim, and that the action proceeds on the correctness or otherwise of the oath sworn on the rightness of that claim. The title of the other party is not formally investigated. Here, the hypotheses part company: on one view, held by Diósdi and Pugsley,[7] the person who had control of the thing before litigation began is the one who has to prove he is owner; on the other, maintained in earlier days by Roth and Abgarowicz and now by myself, the person who has to prove his ownership is he who did not have the thing before the action began.

Diósdi's view is, I wish to maintain, untenable though both it and the one I favor are in harmony with the evidence for the procedure given in G.4.16. But Diósdi begins by blandly assuming that the party who claims first is the plaintiff and that the second claim in the same words is made by the defendant,[8] though he admits in a footnote that Gaius avoids using the expressions "plaintiff" and "defendant." "For the sake of convenience," he says, "I shall use, however, the familiar terms."[9] Once this assumption is made about the status of the parties, a close examination of the process inevitably leads him to the conclusion that the onus of proof of title is on the defendant. He correctly observes that this state of affairs contrasts sharply with contempo-

---

[7] *The Roman Law of Property and Obligations* (Cape Town, Juta, 1972), pp. 35ff.

[8] *Ownership*, p. 97. [9] *Ownership*, p. 97, n. 21.

rary legal ideas, and concludes that on that account modern legal historians have not dared to draw the inevitable conclusions.[10] But without the assumption that the plaintiff speaks first—an assumption made without argument or textual evidence—Gaius' account would be no support for the idea that the burden of proof of title was on the defendant, and, it should be observed, the idea has no other support in the texts. The question to be decided is which of two propositions—both of which can be argued from G.4.16 but both of which have a bizarre feature—is more reasonable and more in line with other evidence. One proposition is that the plaintiff spoke first in the *legis actio sacramento in rem* in front of the praetor and that he won the action unless the defendant could prove he was owner. The other is that the defendant first stated his claim and that he retained the thing unless the plaintiff could prove that *he* was owner.

For the correctness of the former proposition Diósdi urges that the proprietary remedy was originally connected with a suspicion of theft on the part of the person in possession.[11] This—to me startling[12]—idea is by no means new and has considerable support among contemporary scholars.[13] It is given an air of plausibility by three arguments. First, it is said the statement of the plaintiff in the action, "quando tu iniuria vindicavisti," is a charge of unlawful conduct.[14] But, of course, this argument rests on the assumption that the statement—whatever it may imply—is

[10] *Ownership*, pp. 102f: "The sudden fear of the inevitable conclusion is characteristically shown by Roth and Watson."

[11] *Ownership*, p. 103.

[12] What startles me, and what does not, should perhaps be made explicit. It does not startle me that when property which is known (or can be shown) to belong (or to have belonged) to one person is found in the hands of another the latter falls under suspicion of theft and is expected to show how he came by the property; see *Code of Hammurabi*, 9ff. It does startle me that when property in the hands of one person is claimed by another, that claim *ipso facto* creates a legally recognized suspicion of theft by the holder who then has to prove his title while the veracity of the claimant is not examined.

[13] Above all from Kaser: see now *ZPR*, p. 67; *RPR* 1, p. 127.

[14] Diósdi, loc. cit.

made by the plaintiff. If, as I maintain, the statement is the defendant's, it cannot support the idea that the defendant is under suspicion of theft. Secondly, it is said, "If the owner was informed that some goods of his were in another's possession, the first idea that came to his mind was that the possessor had stolen them from him. So it was the possessor's duty, nay his right, to clear himself from suspicion."[15] But this is to look at the situation exclusively from the angle of the plaintiff, of a thoroughly honest plaintiff at that, and even so there is some exaggeration of his attitude. Why should the law also see the situation only from this angle? Indeed, the abuses which would follow if it did are only too apparent. Thirdly, it is maintained that this attitude is confirmed by "the experience that undeveloped legal systems generally adopt this solution." But even if the instances adduced as parallelisms[16] were such—and they do not seem to be—this would not show as Diósdi claims that the solution was "the natural one" but merely that it was a possible solution.

More important than any supposed parallel with an unrelated system is the connection between the *legis actio sacramento in rem* and the *vindicatio rei*. The latter is the analogue in the later formulary system and in it the onus of proof is squarely on the plaintiff—unless he can show that he is the owner the disputed thing remains with the defendant. Such a reversal—on Diósdi's theory—is striking and demands an explanation which is not forthcoming. It would be no satisfactory explanation to say that the *legis*

---

[15] Diósdi, loc. cit.

[16] None of the instances adduced from Greek, Germanic, Babylonian and Egyptian law show the parallelism needed, namely, that in a proprietary action, the burden of proof of ownership was on the defendant, and that the plaintiff had no need to prove his own title. Mr. J. L. Barton and Professors G. Dilcher, P. Pestman, and R. Yaron have confirmed to me in carefully argued and documented letters that in the early English, Germanic, Egyptian, and Babylonian systems no rule existed like that supposed by Diósdi. It is not appropriate here to repeat their arguments but I should like to express my gratitude.

actio is primitive and the other is not. The law of the late Republic grows from that of the early Republic. The legal rules underlying the *vindicatio* stem from those behind the *legis actio sacramento in rem*. Again, the change suggested is so startling that it could scarcely leave Gaius unmoved, yet he is silent. Odder still, though we cannot date the introduction of the formulary *vindicatio* with precision, both it and the *legis actio sacramento in rem* were still in use side by side around 70 B.C.[17] How could this be tolerated, if both were actions for a thing but the burden of proof was as radically different as is alleged?

Fortunately, we do not have to rely on unaided reason. There is textual proof from Cicero *Mur.* 12.26—not discussed by Diósdi—that the person whose claim was examined was the plaintiff. From his account of *manum conserere*—the procedure used in Cicero's time in the *legis actio sacramento in rem* where the thing in dispute was land or could not easily be moved—we learn that only one party expressly claimed.[18] The other party is described as "ille unde petatur," hence the one who expressly claims is the plaintiff. The process eventually proceeds as in the normal *legis actio sacramento in rem* and the question is put: "Anne tu dicas, qua ex causa vindicaveris?" Since only one person had vindicated and that was the plaintiff, the party who is asked to justify his vindication must likewise be the plaintiff.[19]

For the hypothesis that the plaintiff fails unless he proves that he is owner, there is the difficulty that in front of the praetor it is the defendant who opens the proceedings. This

[17] Emerges from Cicero *Verr.* 11.2.12.31 and *Mur.* 12.26.

[18] See Kaser, *ZPR*, p. 74. For a further account of the argument see Watson, "Hypothesis," pp. 462ff.

[19] Pugsley develops the case that the burden of proof was on the defendant much less fully than does Diósdi. For him, however, the reason for reversing the normal burden of proof is that if the defendant was owner he would have no difficulty in proving it: *Property*, p. 36. He also fails to discuss Cicero *Mur.* 12.26. For *manum conserere* in general see R. Santoro "*Manu(m) conserere*," *Annali del Seminario Giuridico di Palermo* 32 (1971), 513ff.

is, of course, an unusual start to litigation, but it is appropriate here. "The defendant has been made to come before the praetor, the plaintiff's claim will certainly be forthcoming, and it is reasonable to begin by having the defendant's ownership expressly maintained against the forthcoming challenge to it. More important, this declaration helps to set the scene in that the defendant shows his position of power by placing his *festuca* on the slave and keeping it there. The purpose of the opening declaration and this behavior is to show the 'Machtlage.' In a formalized process for ownership in which both parties make identical declarations or claims—in itself a very unusual procedure—it would not be surprising if the first assertion is that of the defendant declaratory of the apparent state of affairs, the second the plaintiff's challenge to it. It would be much more surprising if the form were that the plaintiff made a formal claim that the slave was his, and the sole response of the defendant was weakly to declare in the same words that the slave was his."[20]

If this view of the procedure is accepted it follows that the defendant keeps the thing unless the plaintiff proves it is his. Moreover, the claim "meum esse ex iure quiritium" seems, as Diósdi stresses,[21] to be of an exclusive nature. Only by an unnatural interpretation can it be considered a claim to a relative title.

The XII Tables apparently contained a clause (Tab. VI.5a) beginning "Si qui in manum conserunt." According to Aulus Gellius,[22] who is our informant, this clause concerned the claim for land or a movable—that is, the ordinary *legis actio sacramento in rem*—and the proceedings took place in front of the praetor in the presence of the thing, even if it were land, which actually was grasped. Only later, as the result of the extended boundaries of jurisdiction, was it established that the parties could go to the land in dispute and bring some earth to the praetor's court.

---

[20] Watson, "Hypothesis," p. 457.
[21] *Ownership*, p. 105.   [22] *NA* 20.10,1,8,9,10.

It is occasionally suggested that originally and at the time of the xii Tables the *legis actio sacramento in rem* could not be used in respect of *res nec mancipi*.[23] It is unlikely, the argument goes, that the ritual procedure of this *legis actio* could be used both for important things and for less valuable objects.[24] But why is it unlikely, one must wonder? The procedure seems perfectly appropriate for claiming a pig, for instance, which is a *res nec mancipi*. Nor is it clear that the procedure is reasonably described as a ritual; but even if it is, why should this restrict it to *res mancipi*? But the real difficulty for this theory is to see what procedure could be used to claim *res nec mancipi*.[25] "Uber das Verfahren zur Verfolgung der *res nec mancipi* sind wir nur mangelhaft unterrichtet," says Kaser.[26] This is to exaggerate the extent of our information. There is no sign anywhere of any early action claiming ownership—other than the *legis actio sacramento in rem*—and hence, pace Kaser, no argument for the existence of such an action can be drawn from comparative law. The action in fact is a "trackless monster" and should not be presumed to exist. The need for such an action seems to be felt only if one claims that the *legis actio sacramento in rem* could not be used for *res nec mancipi*. That hypothesis should be rejected since it is not only based on weak arguments but creates further problems.

When it was disputed whether a woman was *in manu*, or a free person was subject to another's *potestas*, the remedy would also be the *legis actio sacramento in rem*.[27] There is no evidence as to whether the wording of the claim was the same as that in the claim for a thing or was varied to meet the circumstances. In the case where what was disputed was whether a person was a free man or a slave it is clear

[23] Kaser, *ZPR*, p. 68; *RPR* 1, p. 127; Pugsley, *Property*, pp. 36f.

[24] Kaser, loc. cit. for a further argument of his from *usus auctoritas* see infra, p. 151.

[25] This is no problem for Pugsley who thinks *res nec mancipi* were totally outside the law of property.

[26] *RPR* 1, p. 127.

[27] See e.g. Kaser, *ZPR*, p. 67.

that the wording of the claims differed.[28] Yet the *vindicatio in libertatem* or *vindicatio in servitutem* were forms of the *legis actio sacramento in rem*. This would imply that the action claming that a woman was *in manu* or a person was *in potestate* might well differ from an action claiming ownership of a thing.

It is often said that ancient Roman law knew only one unitary private form of control over all things subject to the legal power of the *paterfamilias*, over free members of the household, slaves, animals, and inanimate property.[29] The terminology, *potestas* or *manus*, might differ, and the content of the power for each object was determined in accordance with its function. Into this topic of conceptual jurisprudence I have no intention of going, except to express considerable skepticism. One argument produced for the proposition, however, is that the same institutions applied to both things and people—*mancipatio, legis actio sacramento, actio furti, noxae deditio, in iure cessio,* and *usus*—though later they tended to apply only to things. This argument fails to carry much weight. It is natural to give the small number of institutions available in early times as wide a usage as is convenient. Moreover, as we have seen in this book, the same institution (for instance, *mancipatio*) could come to have very different consequences when used in different spheres. It is enough here to remember that no *auctoritas* liability is known for *coemptio*.

[28] See Watson, *Persons*, pp. 220f.
[29] On this whole matter see e.g. Kaser, *Eigentum*; F. Gallo, "Potestas e *dominium* nell' esperienza giuridica romana," *Labeo* 16 (1970), 17ff; L. Capogrossi Colognesi, "Ancora sui poteri del *pater familias*," *BIDR* 73 (1970), 357ff.

ELEVEN

Mancipatio and the Transfer of Ownership

Mancipatio, the main mode of transferring certain kinds of important things, is the central institution of early Rome law. Many offshoots and variations of *mancipatio* were developed at an early date and it is impossible to form a satisfactory idea of family law and succession in the archaic period without an understanding of the institution which spawned them. Indeed, some scholars—of whom I am not one—believe that the power over a thing was a "mere manifestation of the comprehensive domestic power to which the head of the household was entitled, as much with regard to the persons belonging to the house community, i.e. the wife (*in manu*), the children, bondsmen and slaves, as with regard to property."[1]

In its basic form, the ceremony of *mancipatio* was primarily a conveyance[2] of those things designated as *res mancipi*, but it had also a contractual element. It required the presence of five witnesses and another party who held bronze scales, all of whom had to be Roman citizens of full age.[3] The ceremony did not involve the saying of anything by the transferor but the transferee grasped the *res mancipi* (for instance, a slave) and declared, "Hunc ego hominem

[1] M. Kaser, "The Concept of Roman Ownership," *Tydskrif vir Hedendaagse Romeins-Hollandse Reg* 27 (1964), pp. 5ff, at p. 6.

[2] The original nature of *mancipatio* is much disputed, but its basic character as a conveyance was undoubtedly established by the time of the XII Tables. On the early history I am in complete agreement with Diósdi, *Ownership*, pp. 62ff. Most recently A. M. Prichard suggests that *mancipatio* may have originated as an auction: "*Auctoritas* in early Roman Law," *LQR* 90 (1974), 378ff, at 392ff.

[3] A woman required the consent of her *tutor* for the transfer of a *res mancipi*; cf. infra, p. 155.

ex iure Quiritium meum esse aio isque mihi emptus esto[4] hoc aere aeneaque libra."[5] The appropriate weight of bronze was weighed out on the scales (perhaps before the declaration) and was given to the transferor. Only a Roman citizen—or, probably also, a foreigner who had *commercium* [6]—could acquire ownership by *mancipatio*.

The contractual aspects of *mancipatio* should not be obscured by either the fact that the ceremony involved no declaration from the transferor or because in classical law the *mancipatio* was regarded purely as a conveyance. The latter can be explained as the result of the emergence of *emptio venditio* as the contract. The former by itself has little weight.[7] *Mancipatio* as contract is revealed by the weighing of bronze and the reference to it in the transferee's declaration, both of which are integral parts of the ceremony. That the Romans (at least in the later Republic) were conscious of the contractual nature of *mancipatio* emerges from Quintus Mucius Scaevola's treatment of the contract of *emptio venditio* in his *Ius civile*, the first juristic attempt to arrange the civil law *generatim*.[8] Of the four consensual contracts, *mandatum* and *locatio conductio* do not appear at all in that work, *societas* and *emptio venditio* do appear, but at a distance from one another. Obviously, the four were not yet thought of together. *Mandatum* and *locatio* are omitted because they have no ancient roots,

[4] A. M. Prichard has convincingly shown that "emptus esto," is a past imperative: "Terminology in *mancipatio*," *LQR* 76 (1960), 412ff.

[5] This is the wording evidenced for later times: G.1.119-122.

[6] *Epit.Ulp.* 19.4,5 (which refers, though, to a much later period): see M. Kaser, "Vom Begriff des *commercium*," in *Studi in onore di Arangio-Ruiz* 2 (Naples, Jovene, n.d.), 131ff at 134ff.

[7] Though it has persuaded some distinguished scholars: contra, now Diósdi, *Ownership*, pp. 68f. I would not even accept, as he does, that the absence of any declaration by the transferor is evidence that *mancipatio* was unilateral. The transferor's involvement and agreement are adequately attested to the witnesses by his presence and silence.

[8] D.1.2.2.41 (Pomponius *sing. enchirid.*).

societas is dealt with because of its relationship with *ercto non cito*, *emptio* because of its connection with *mancipatio*. It is on that account that Quintus Mucius deals with servitudes after *emptio*.[9] But *emptio* is not genetically related to *mancipatio*; the connection is functional.

Res mancipi[10] were land,[11] rustic praedial servitudes,[12] slaves, oxen, horses, mules, and asses. The reason these kinds of animals are included and not others is that they are the animals which are broken in—"quae dorso collove domantur."[13] But whether they were *res mancipi* only when they were broken in (as the Proculians held in classical law) or from birth (as the Sabinians maintained)[14] cannot,

[9] For the argument see Watson, *Law Making*, pp. 143ff, especially p. 147.

[10] See G.1.120.

[11] At this early period we should probably specify land within Roman jurisdiction.

[12] G.2.14a, 17, 29; *Epit.Ulp.* 19.1; *Vat.Fr.* 45.

[13] We can be quite certain that this is the explanation, first because the Roman sources link these animals on that account and give no other reason: G.2.14a-16 (the reconstructions of Krüger seem acceptable); *Epit.Ulp.* 19.1; *Vat.Fr.* 259; secondly because none of the alternative hypotheses advanced by modern scholars fits all the facts. Against other hypotheses see now Diósdi, *Ownership*, pp. 56ff and the authors he cites. The prevailing opinion, which Diósdi finds acceptable, namely, that "the most important means of production of a peasant economy belonged to the *res mancipi*" must be rejected because horses were very little used as part of the workforce: see P. Vigneron, *Le cheval dans l'antiquité gréco-romaine*, 1 (Nancy, Faculté des lettres et des sciences humaines de l'Université, 1968), pp. 139ff; K. D. White, *Roman Farming* (London, Thames & Hudson, 1970), pp. 288ff (some use of horses was, however, made by agriculturalists: Cato *de agri cult.* 138).
Epit.Ulp. 19.1 says that although elephants and camels are broken in they are not *res mancipi* because they are wild animals (*bestiae*). One might add that such exotic creatures were not owned by Romans when the list of *res mancipi* became fixed.

[14] For the dispute see G.2.15. For the literature on the problem and views held see G. Nicosia, "*Animalia quae collo dorsove domantur*," *IURA* 18 (1967), 45ff; Watson, *Private Law*, p. 60, n. 5; Kaser, *RPR* 1, p. 123, n. 1. Evidence which is slightly in favor of the Proculian view being early is in Cicero *Top.* 8.36 from which it emerges that not all horses and mules had *postliminium*, but only those broken in.

I think, be discovered.[15] Whatever precisely may have been the criterion for inclusion in, or exclusion from, the category of *res mancipi*, it is apparent at least that stress was laid on what was useful, especially for farmers.

The business with bronze and scales involved an actual weighing out of the price and is not an indication of formalism in early Roman law. Not until around 280 B.C. did the Romans coin money. This date seems to apply not only to round coins (including *aes grave*) but also to the bronze ingots known as *aes signatum*.[16] Pliny the Elder's statement[17] that King Servius was the first to strike bronze coinage is unacceptable in view of the historical and archaeological evidence.[18] Crawford plausibly argues that this erroneous statement derives from a remark of Timaeus—Pliny's source—that the weighing out of bronze was an innovation due to Servius Tullius, and that before him the Romans were thought to accumulate bronze in heaps without measuring. This would mean that Servius Tullius was credited with laying down that a pound of bronze was a measure of value.[19] However this may be, the ceremony of *mancipatio* itself indicates unambiguously both that bronze had become the standard medium of exchange and that a fixed weight of bronze, such as a pound, had become a measure of value.

That bronze actually was weighed out for *mancipatio*

---

[15] Hence it seems pointless to speculate further on precisely why animals *quae dorso collove domantur* and only those animals were *res mancipi*.

[16] See now above all M. H. Crawford, *The Roman Republican Coinage* (Cambridge, Cambridge University Press, 1974), pp. 41ff, 131ff, 716ff.

[17] *HN* 33.13.42-44.

[18] Pliny *HN* 18.3.12 relates that Servius was the first to mark bronze with the effigy of sheep and oxen. If this were correct it would neatly tie in bronze with the known use of sheep and oxen as measures of value, but unfortunately it must be an *ex post facto* rationalization. In fact, we know of no bronze currency ingots which have the representation of a sheep, and other creatures besides oxen do appear: elephant, sow, chickens, dolphins, eagle.

[19] Crawford, *Coinage*, p. 37.

does not, of itself, mean that where there was no real weighing and no paying over of the appropriate weight of bronze there could be no valid *mancipatio*. The validity or otherwise of such a *mancipatio* would depend on the degree of abstraction which had been achieved, and upon policy. As we have seen, in the modified form of *mancipatio* known as *coemptio* there was no real weighing out and no payment of bronze (apart from a token), yet the ceremony had legal effect and the woman entered the *manus* of her husband.[20] Again, the variant for testamentary succession known as *testamentum per aes et libram* had legal effect though there was no weighing out and no payment by the apparent transferee, the *familiae emptor*. It does not seem in that case that the property actually passed to the *familiae emptor* at the time of the ceremony, but the legatees in the *testamentum per aes et libram* became owners automatically of the things bequeathed to them when the testator died.[21] In these circumstances it should be admitted that there was nothing in the nature of *mancipatio* as it was perceived at the time of the XII Tables which would have made the transaction inevitably void when there was no weighing and no real payment of bronze. But these special cases of *coemptio* and *testamentum per aes et libram* do not themselves reveal whether the Romans wished to relax the insistence on a weighing and real paying of bronze for the effectiveness of the normal *mancipatio*. Attention should be directed to three separate issues.

First, could the parties for their own private reasons—such as avoidance of liability for *auctoritas*[22]—state in the *mancipatio*, weigh, and deliver a very small amount, say one pound of bronze, though the price agreed on in reality was much greater? There seems no reason in theory why this should not have been, as later, a valid *mancipatio* which effectively conveyed ownership—since all the necessary ele-

---

[20] Cf. supra, pp. 14f.   [21] Cf. supra, pp. 62f.
[22] On *auctoritas* see infra, pp. 140ff.

ments are present—though whether it was used must remain an open question.

Secondly, in the absence of the declaration of a small fictitious sum where there was a real price, could the *mancipatio* omit the weighing and handing over of the bronze? It is much more difficult to accept that this would be a valid *mancipatio*. No doubt the law could have allowed such a *mancipatio* to be valid if there had been a compelling practical reason for the breach in theory, but where is the compelling reason? Moreover, even if the law had allowed a *mancipatio* of this kind to have effect, why ever would the parties have resorted to it? At times, presumably the seller would be willing to let the buyer have control and use of the *res mancipi* before the price was paid, but the practical, legitimate interests of the buyer would be served if the *res mancipi* were simply delivered to him without *mancipatio*, and the ceremony itself could be performed (and ownership transferred) when he paid the price.[23] This procedure would protect the seller since he would remain owner until he received the bronze.[24]

Thirdly, should the rule related in J.2.1.41 and said to be enacted by the xii Tables, that *traditio* in a sale does not transfer ownership unless the price is paid or security given, be made to refer to transfer of ownership by *mancipatio*? A positive answer cannot be absolutely excluded but seems very unlikely. To begin with, in view of what was said about the second issue, the rule is unnecessary for *mancipatio*. Where the buyer needed to use and control the *res mancipi* it could be delivered to him without *mancipatio* and that ceremony could be performed when the bronze

[23] It is possible to think of exceptions where the buyer's interest would not be served. A, who is short of ready bronze, has made B's slave pregnant and wishes to free her so that the child will not be born a slave. This he cannot do unless he is her owner.

[24] Otherwise, unless he took a separate *stipulatio* for payment it is impossible to see what remedy he would have against a defaulting buyer.

was paid. Indeed, only if it were both allowable and common for there to be a *mancipatio* without payment of the bronze—which, as has been argued, was not the case—would any need for the rule become apparent. Again, it is well recognized that *mancipatio* was in form and substance an immediate conveyance. Why ever should the law have wanted to alter the substance of *mancipatio* in the absence of a pressing need? It is worth remembering that in the exceptional variant, *testamentum per aes et libram*, where ownership was apparently not transferred (until the death of the testator and then to the legatees, not to the *familiae emptor*), the *familiae emptor* did *not* claim that the property was his.[25] Yet in the present instance, if the rule in question did apply to *mancipatio*, we should have to accept that where the *mancipatio* was upon a sale, ownership was not transferred, unless the price were paid or security given, even despite an express claim by the recipient that he was the owner.[26]

If the transferor by *mancipatio* were not the owner of the object, and the recipient were evicted from it, the latter had a remedy to recover from the transferor twice the price stated in the *mancipatio*.[27] The remedy was inherent in the

[25] For the general form of the declaration see supra, pp. 58f.

[26] The rule reported in J.2.1.41 is further discussed (and references to literature given), infra, pp. 145ff. The nature of *mancipatio* would, of course, change greatly when as a result of the introduction of coined money the business of the scales and the bronze became a mere fossilized relic and formality. Until that happened, the rule could not be interpreted in any way as applying to *auctoritas*.

[27] The literature on the subject is immense—for references see now Diósdi, *Ownership*, pp. 75ff; Jolowicz-Nicholas, *Introduction*, p. 146, n. 1; most recently, Prichard, "*Auctoritas*"—and the whole topic is one of great controversy. On the whole I follow the traditional view on the basis of the texts which are cited in nn. 28-31. None of the texts refers to the early period with which we are concerned.

That the relevant sum for the remedy was that mentioned in the *mancipatio* appears from the device of *mancipatio uno nummo*, where a ridiculously small and unreal amount was named in the *mancipatio*. (For *mancipatio uno nummo* see Kaser, *RPR* 1, p. 46 and the sources and authorities he cites.) That the relevant sum was doubled is seen in *P.S.* 2.17.1,3.

mancipatio and independent of any special agreement by the parties,[28] who indeed could not directly exclude the liability.[29] So much seems to be clear though the sources are too sparse to admit of absolute certainty, especially as to the details or the nature of the procedure involved.[30] The liability is spoken of as being "auctoritatis"[31] and the meaning of

[28] This emerges from Plautus *Persa* 524f.

> Ac suo periculo is emat qui eam mercabitur:
> mancupio neque promittet neque quisquam dabit.

There would be no reason for not transferring the girl by *mancipatio* —"mancupio . . . neque dabit"—unless the warranty was inherent in the conveyance itself. The same conclusion results from Cicero *Mur.* 2.3: "Quod si in eis rebus repetendis quae mancipi sunt is periculum iudici praestare debet qui se nexu obligavit, . . ." *Se nexu obligare* means to bind oneself by the *nexum*, that is, by the *mancipatio*, hence it is the ceremony which is regarded as creating the liability. A similar conclusion can be drawn from Cicero *Top.* 10.45. Moreover, unless the *mancipatio* contained its own warranty the device of *mancipatio uno nummo* would have no point.

[29] This also emerges from the very existence of the device of *mancipatio uno nummo*.

[30] In connection with this liability the *mancipio dans* is termed *auctor*: Plautus *Curc.* 498; Cicero *Mur.* 2.3 (in a pun); D.21.2.4pr. (Ulpian *32 ad ed.*). Valerius Probus 4.7, in his elucidation of abbreviations for *legis actiones*, has "Quando in iure te conspicio, postulo anne far auctor," and the substance of this clause is confirmed by Cicero *Caecin.* 19.54. The clause might suggest that the *mancipio accipiens* whose title was later challenged could, in the *in iure* stage of the procedure, call on his *mancipio dans* to provide evidence of his right to the thing: see e.g. Diósdi, *Ownership*, pp. 78ff and the authors he cites, p. 78, n. 104. But it does not imply that it was the seller who had to defend the buyer's title. It is improper to argue to this conclusion for early Roman law from the Germanic "Gewähren-zug": see Diósdi, *Ownership*, pp. 78ff.

[31] *P.S.* 2.17.1,3. The texts which call the *mancipio dans* the "auctor" are also relevant. The sources apart from D.21.2.76 (Venuleius *17 stip.*) do not seek to explain what *auctoritas* means. That text has: "Si alienam rem mihi tradideris et eandem pro derelicto habuero, amitti auctoritatem id est actionem pro evictione placet." A. Magdelain (who is rather unfairly treated by Diósdi, *Ownership*, p. 77, n. 98) observes that the words "id est actionem pro evictione placet" are universally regarded as interpolated (as is "tradideris" in place of "mancipaveris"), yet the definition of *auctoritas* which the words contain is accepted as giving classical law: "Auctoritas rerum," *RIDA*, *Mélanges F. de Visscher* 4 (1950), 127ff, at 136f. But if the

the word has given rise to enormous controversy. The same word also occurs in the context of *usucapio*,[32] and it would be reasonable to think that *auctoritas* means the same thing for both.[33] This, of course, is not to claim that *auctoritas* must necessarily have had a precise, technical meaning; like *potestas*[34] its substantive content could have varied from situation to situation. Nor is it to overlook that all in all the word *auctoritas* did have more than one meaning.[35] What is being suggested is that, since the word *auctoritas* appears with a sense which is far from clear in two distinct modes of acquisition of property, we should accept as a working hypothesis that it broadly means the same thing in both cases. Moreover, the meaning attributed to *auctoritas* in these cases must be explicable within the general history of the word.[36] Also, as Yaron emphasizes,[37] the interpretation must be simple, straightforward. Finally, among the very many texts which contain the word *auctoritas* there are four —two from Cicero,[38] one from Seneca the Elder[39] and one

---

definition is Byzantine and hence after the disappearance of *mancipatio* and *auctoritas*, its weight as evidence for the nature of *auctoritas* is greatly reduced. It should be stressed that no text speaks of an *actio auctoritatis*.

[32] The xii Tables has at vi.3: "Usus auctoritas fundi biennium est" (or "esto"); and at vi.4: "Adversus hostem aeterna auctoritas." The *lex Atinia* of the later Republic has: "Quod subruptum erit, eius rei aeterna auctoritas esto."

[33] This approach is apparently regarded by Diósdi, *Ownership*, pp. 85ff, as doubtful.

[34] Cf. supra, pp. 47ff.

[35] See *TLL* 2, 1213ff.

[36] It is on this account that I would ultimately reject Yaron's explanation: "We see then in *auctoritas* a reference to a claim, and if the claim is substantiated, to a power of recovering the object": "Reflections on *usucapio*" T.v.R. 35 (1967), 191ff, at 204: see Jolowicz-Nicholas, *Introduction*, p. 146, n. 1 (at p. 147).

[37] "Reflections," p. 197.

[38] *Caecin.* 26.74: "Fundus a patre relinqui potest, at usucapio fundi, hoc est finis sollicitudinis ac periculi litium, non a patre relinquitur, sed a legibus; aquae ductus, haustus, iter actus a patre, sed rata auctoritas harum rerum omnium ab iure civili sumitur"; *Har. Resp.*

from Papinian[40]—where the word occurs in a context relevant to us; any solution to the meaning of *auctoritas* for *mancipatio* and *usucapio* should explain it in these four sources. With some diffidence I suggest that a meaning which would meet all the necessary criteria, and which seems to be the sole meaning to meet the criteria, is "right of ownership" or "title of ownership."[41] Perhaps we can be rather more specific. The word *auctoritas* derives from *auctor*, and in this type of context the word *auctor* is best taken as "predecessor,"[42] hence *auctoritas* is the right or title of this predecessor.[43] Thus, it would seem that *auctoritas* is the right or title of ownership of a person who had control but has no longer.

A further action might arise on a *mancipatio* when land was transferred and its actual acreage was less than that stated in the *mancipatio*. The *actio de modo agri*, as it is

---

7.14: "Multae sunt domus in hac urbe, patres conscripti, atque haud scio an paene cunctae iure optimo, sed tamen iure privato, iure hereditario, iure auctoritatis, iure mancipi, iure nexi."

[39] *Con.Ex.* 7.26.23: "Triarius dixit: 'fugitivum, erronem non esse': ita si malum auctorem habemus, gener noster fugitivus est?" Blandus dixit: relegamus auctoritatis tabellas: 'furtis noxaque solutum.' haec generi nostri laudatio est."

[40] *Vat.Fr.* 10: "Iniquam sententiam evictae rei periculum venditoris non spectare placuit neque stipulationem auctoritatis committere."

[41] Indeed, this is the first meaning ascribed to *auctoritas* in the *Oxford Latin Dictionary* 1 (Oxford, Clarendon Press, 1968), p. 206. On this view there is no need to treat *P.S.* 2.17.1 as concerned exclusively with sales of *res mancipi* and a neater pattern for §1 to §3 emerges: §1 is concerned with liability on the sale, §2 with transfer on the sale by *traditio*, §3 with transfer on the sale by *mancipatio*. It is not intended to enlarge on the problem here partly because certainty and greater precision seem unobtainable, partly because I have little new of my own to offer. In very large measure and in all essentials I follow Magdelain, "*Auctoritas rerum*," who himself has his forerunners. On *usucapio* see infra, pp. 150ff. Magdelain says that in *Vat.Fr.* 10 "auctoritas" means "guarantee" (pp. 137f) but the change in meaning is easily explained; cf. the rubric to *P.S.* 5.10.

[42] See T. Mayer-Maly, "Studien zur Frühgeschichte der *usucapio* 11," *ZSS* 78 (1961), 221ff; Yaron, "Reflections," p. 207.

[43] "Auctoritas" is translated by Mayer-Maly as "Vormannschaft" and Yaron accepts "predecessorship."

called, lay for damages assessed on the difference between the area stated and the actual area. If the defendant denied liability the damages were doubled.[44] Probably the XII Tables contained a provision on the action.[45]

Finally, on *mancipatio* we must consider a strikingly clear yet strangely and intractably obscure clause (Tab. VI.1) of the XII Tables: "Cum nexum faciet mancipiumque, uti lingua nuncupassit, ita ius esto."[46] Questions immediately arise about the nature of *nexum* and the meaning of the word *mancipium* but both these matters can here safely be left aside.[47] But as regards *mancipatio* (and, indeed, *nexum*), what was the function of the clause? Was it merely affirming the legal validity of the *mancipatio*?[48] The ceremony was undoubtedly well established, and its confirmation by a clause of the code seems unnecessary and hence unlikely.[49] Was the clause simply reaffirming that in the case of a dispute the court would look to the words spoken, not to the intention of the parties? That such was the legal position is plain even centuries later, and a text of Cicero which is making that point has such verbal similarities[50] with our clause that he at least is connecting the clause in

---

[44] It is, indeed, this characteristic of the *actio de modo agri* (see *P.S.* 1.19.1) which enables us to identify it with the action mentioned by Cicero in *de off.* 3.16.65 as going back to the XII Tables: see e.g. Watson, *Obligations*, pp. 81f; Kaser, *RPR* 1, p. 133, and the authorities he cities, n. 11. Denial of liability did not result in a doubling of the (already doubled) sum in the *actio auctoritatis*. The existence of the *actio de modo agri* would also remove doubts, if there were any, that by this time land was *res mancipi* (if it was not so originally).

[45] This seems to emerge from Cicero *Off.* 3.16.65.

[46] Festus, *s.v. Numerata pecunia*. The text does not expressly relate that the clause was in the XII Tables but the provenance can scarcely be doubted: see e.g. Jolowicz-Nicholas, *Introduction*, p. 165, n. 1.

[47] For *nexum* see supra, pp. 111ff.

[48] For P. F. Girard, *Manuel élémentaire de droit romain*, 8th ed. by F. Senn (Paris, A. Rousseau, 1929), p. 310, the function of the clause was to make valid the *mancipatio* as soon as the right words were pronounced, even though there had been no weighing.

[49] For *Vat.Fr.* 50 see infra, pp. 148f.

[50] *Off.* 3.16.65: "Nam, cum ex duodecim tabulis satis esset ea praestari, quae essent lingua nuncupata, . . ."

question (or one like it relating particularly to the *actio de modo agri*)[51] with the stress on the words used in the *mancipatio*. But on this view, too, it is not easy to see why the clause was thought necessary. A third approach to the provision is that it was declaring valid *leges mancipio dictae*, reservations in the *mancipatio* such as would create servitudes, etc., in favor of the transferor.[52] The function of the provision would then be to make clear that such reservations were valid even although there could not be a conditional *mancipatio*.[53] If this third approach is correct—and it has considerable plausibility—then the clause would imply that the words spoken by the recipient in the *mancipatio* could give a right to the transferor.[54]

Things which were not *res mancipi* were *res nec mancipi* and the standard method of transferring ownership of corporeal *res nec mancipi* was by *traditio*, that is physical delivery. There was, we are told, a specific provision (Tab. VII.11) of the XII Tables on the subject which enacted that when the *traditio* was upon a sale, ownership was not transferred unless the price were paid to the seller or security was given to him.[55] It is often felt that this rule was inap-

---

[51] Greater precision is not possible. At one point Cicero certainly seems to have the *actio de modo agri* in mind, but perhaps he is confusing two clauses.

[52] See e.g. Buckland, *Textbook*, p. 238; Kaser, *RPR* I, p. 47; Jolowicz-Nicholas, *Introduction*, p. 145, n. 3.

[53] *Vat.Fr.* 329; D.50.17.77 (Papinian *28 quaest.*).

[54] Which would be important for the development of *fiducia*: see now Watson, *Private Law*, pp. 84ff, and the works cited.

[55] J.2.1.41. It is important to stress that this text claims the rule was expressly set out in the XII Tables: "quod cavetur quidem etiam lege duodecim tabularum." There can be no justification for an approach such as that of J.A.C. Thomas, "Institutes 2.1.41 and the Passage of Property on Sale," *South African Law Journal* 90 (1973), 150ff. He translates this part of the text properly (p. 150, n. 3) but otherwise treats it as telling us that the rule "goes back to the XII Tables" (p. 150). This eventually enables him to hold that the Institutes' rule as such was not the XII Tables: "It could well have *derived* from the XII Tables without being a provision of the Tables" (his italics; p. 158). Of course, it may be arguable that the Institutes' text does misstate the law of the XII Tables, but that proposition

propriate or impossible for the time of the xii Tables—to this we shall return—and the suggestion is made that originally it concerned *mancipatio* or the action on *auctoritas*.[56] But I have argued earlier in this chapter that any such rule was unnecessary for *mancipatio* and on that account most unlikely to have existed in such a context.[57] If the argument was correct then *a fortiori* the rule would not be created for the action concerning *auctoritas*. In actual fact, the rule is really needed in connection with the credit sale of *res nec mancipi*. When *res mancipi* were sold and the price was not paid, yet it was reasonable for the thing to be delivered to the buyer, the seller's rights and ownership could be preserved by the simple expedient of not making a *mancipatio* at the time of delivery. But in similar circumstances mere delivery of *res nec mancipi* would transfer ownership to the buyer,[58] and lose the seller his property rights unless some legal rule—like that attributed to the xii Tables—existed.[59]

---

would have to be argued on its merits (and an explanation of the misstatement given).

It should also be emphasized that a further qualification in J.2.1.41 to the rule (cf. D.18.1.19), namely, that if the seller followed the faith of the buyer, the thing becomes at once the property of the buyer, is not attributed to the xii Tables: for this qualification which effectively made the rule obsolete long before the time of Gaius see Watson, *Obligations*, pp. 62f.

[56] See the references given by Watson, *Obligations*, pp. 61ff. Most recently, Thomas holds that the rule originally concerned *auctoritas*: "Institutes 2.1.41."

[57] Supra, pp. 139f.

[58] Unless, perhaps, in each specific case the seller made it clear that he did not intend ownership to pass.

[59] Arguments for this understanding of the rule and its subsequent history are set out in Watson, loc. cit. Disagreement has recently been expressed by Thomas, loc. cit., but his arguments, if anything, strengthen my case. He is right to emphasize (p. 153) that one must explain the introduction of the third qualification (see supra, p. 145, n. 55) which nullified the rule in classical law but I submit that my previous explanation (*Obligations*, p. 63) is adequate. Thomas quotes part of that explanation out of context and interprets it to mean something which is both patently absurd and clearly contrary to my meaning. He correctly observes that there is a difficulty in

The widely held belief that the rule of the xii Tables did not in fact relate to *traditio* or at least not to *traditio* alone seems to be ultimately based on abstract conceptions of the law or economic practice of the time: for instance, it is maintained in the face of the evidence that *res nec mancipi* were at that time completely outside the scope of the law of property;[60] or that there would be no credit sales so early in Rome's history; or else it is claimed that the insistence on payment for an effective *traditio* is inconsistent with the care which the classical jurists showed in distinguishing between contract and conveyance.[61] But as to this last, one may wonder whether legal theory as to the separation of contract and conveyance would stand in the way of what was seen as a practical and useful reform. One may also question whether at this early period contract and conveyance were sharply distinguished. It has already been suggested in this chapter that *mancipatio* partook of both.

A question which must be left open is whether transfer of ownership of *res mancipi* and *res nec mancipi* could by this time be accomplished by *in iure cessio* which was a juristic device, a variation on the *vindicatio*, in which only the transferee claimed the property, the transferor (and own-

---

explaining why Justinian reports in full the rule which I believe was nullified in classical law, and he reasonably finds weak my explanation that the compilers failed to notice the effect of the third qualification (p. 153). But his own view is more implausible: the compilers themselves introduced the qualification which made the rule nugatory but it was not their desire to nullify the rule (p. 159). Presumably this view entails holding that the compilers were unaware that they had nullified the rule. Again, Thomas claims (p. 158): "Watson is himself open to challenge in accepting literally Justinian's assertion that the Institutes rule goes back to the xii Tables." But it is an advantage to a theory that it is in accordance with the textual evidence, unless the substance of the text can be shown to be implausible or impossible.

[60] See most recently, D. Pugsley, *The Roman Law of Property and Obligations* (Cape Town, Juta, 1972), p. 89.

[61] See F. Pringsheim, *Der Kauf mit fremdem Geld* (Leipzig, Romanistische Beiträge zur Rechtsgeschichte 1, 1916), pp. 50ff.

er) was silent, and the magistrate adjudged the thing to the transferee. Later at least, this could be used for a variety of purposes and was, indeed, the sole means of transferring incorporeal *res mancipi*. For its existence in the mid-fifth century we have the testimony of a text of Paul (*1 manual.*) *Vat.Fr.* 50, which gives as an argument "quia et mancipationem et in iure cessionem lex xii tabularum confirmat." But the text is suspect[62] and its import far from clear. The point at issue in the text[63] is whether there could be a reservation of, say, a usufruct in *mancipatio* or *in iure cessio* under a condition or from a particular time or to a particular time. The opinion of Pomponius, we are told, was that there could not be a reservation until a particular time in either *mancipatio* or *in iure cessio*. Paul then declares that he learned there could be such a reservation "quia et mancipationem et in iure cessionem lex xii tabularum confirmat." Unfortunately this argument of Paul's is not self-evident. Perhaps the most plausible view is that Paul is basing himself on the clause (Tab. vi.1) "Cum nexum faciet mancipiumque, uti lingua nuncupassit ita ius esto,"[64] whose purpose then would be, as some scholars have maintained, to make valid *leges mancipio dictae* including reservations.[65] If this approach is right then it should be stressed that the relevant clause of the xii Tables makes no mention of *in iure cessio*; and hence that by his use of the verb *confirmare* Paul is not implying that *in iure cessio* was mentioned in the xii Tables. That is, the rule for *in iure cessio* would be derived by interpretation from the xii Tables' clause which mentioned *mancipatio* and *nexum*. On this view then *Vat.Fr.* 50 would be no evidence for the

[62] For suggestions of interpolation in *Vat.Fr.* 50, see F. Wieacker, *Textstufen klassischer Juristen* (Göttingen, Vandenhoek & Ruprecht, 1960), p. 383; F. Schulz, *Geschichte der römischen Rechtswissenschaft* (Weimar, Böhlau, 1961), pp. 218f, and the authors they cite.

[63] See also *Vat.Fr.* 48, 49.

[64] See e.g. C. St. Tomulescu, "*Nexum* bei Cicero," *Iura* 17 (1966), 39ff, at 72f, who, however, rather exaggerates the closeness of the connection.

[65] See supra, pp. 144f.

existence of *in iure cessio* in the mid-fifth century,[66] and there is no other direct evidence. Moreover, no convincing *a priori* reason can be given either for holding that *in iure cessio* did exist or did not exist at the time of the xII Tables. For the latter it may be urged that it was a juristic dodge which required the active approval of the magistrate, and that logically it need never have come into existence at all. For the former one can argue that since the device of *manumissio vindicta* was in existence for some considerable time before the xII Tables, then so could *in iure cessio* have been since the imagination required for the dodges was the same in both cases. *Manumissio vindicta* is even best regarded as a case of *in iure cessio*, but it is a very special case and may be older than the form transferring ownership.

Since *in iure cessio* was in form an action it could be used only by parties who were competent to take part in *legis actiones*, that is to say, Roman citizens.

[66] See e.g. M. Kaser, *Eigentum*, p. 201. Most recently Kaser does take the text as showing that *in iure cessio* was known to the xII Tables: *RPR* 1, p. 48 and n. 4.

TWELVE

Usus and the Acquisition of Ownership

In the preceding chapter we were concerned with the modes of transferring ownership *inter vivos*. Here we shall consider ways in which ownership was acquired without being transferred. Pride of place must be given to prescription both because it was extensively treated in the XII Tables, and because of the ways of acquisition—as distinct from the modes of transfer—it alone, so far as our sources relate, was expressly dealt with in the XII Tables. Significantly, none of the original modes of acquisition was the subject of a clause of the Tables.

The main outline of usucapion, I venture to suggest, is now clear despite the immense literature on the subject.[1] The contents of the basic provision (Tab. VI.3) are to be reconstructed from Cicero as "Usus auctoritas fundi biennium est [or 'esto'], ceterarum rerum omnium annuus est usus."[2] The wording as far as "biennium" is reasonably secure. For the exact wording of the remainder there must be room for doubt, though G.2.54 appears to confirm that the provision spoke of *ceterae res*,[3] and there is ample evidence that the established period for the prescription of other things was one year.[4] The attractive, but unprovable, suggestion has been made that before the codification the period of prescription for all things was one year and that the

[1] For this see now, R. Yaron, "Reflections on *usucapio*," *T.v.R.* 35 (1967), 191ff; Diósdi, *Ownership*, pp. 85ff; Kaser, *RPR* 1, pp. 134ff.

[2] *Top.* 4.23; *Caecin.* 19.54; see G.2.42, 54, 204.

[3] See now Yaron, "Reflections," p. 196, n. 13. For "ceterarum rerum" in other contexts see also A. M. Honoré, "Linguistic and Social Context of the Lex Aquilia," *Irish Jurist* 7 (1972), 138ff.

[4] See e.g. Cicero *Top.* 4.23; G.2.42, 54, 204.

period of two years for land was an innovation. Such a suggestion would fit the apparent form of the provision.[5]

In the provision both "usus" and "auctoritas" are in the nominative case. *Auctoritas*, the subject of much dispute, should be taken as meaning "right of ownership" or "title of ownership,"[6] and its purpose in the provision is to emphasize that the right or title of the owner of the *fundus* remains for two years. *Usus* presents the other side of the situation and designates the nature of the control over the *fundus*, which will give ownership after two years. As to its meaning, the view of Yaron is persuasive,[7] that *usus* in this context has the literal meaning of *usus*, and that prescription follows not from possession but from the actual, reasonable, suitable use of the land.[8]

---

[5] See Yaron, loc. cit. and the works he cites.

[6] See supra, pp. 140ff. Certainty, it should be emphasized, is not possible. It remains here to observe that the unacceptable opinion of Kaser (now in *RPR* 1, pp. 135f) which he shares with many others that *auctoritas* means "Gewährschaft," "guaranteeing" leads him—because guaranteeing seems appropriate only for *mancipatio*—to hold that originally prescription was available for *res mancipi* alone. We need not follow him in this. Against that understanding of *auctoritas* see the convincing arguments of e.g. Yaron, "Reflections," pp. 197ff; Diósdi, *Ownership*, pp. 87f.

[7] "Reflections," pp. 209ff; see also Diósdi, *Ownership*, p. 89.

[8] Recently, A. M. Prichard has tried to go further; "Early *usucapio*," *LQR* 90 (1974), 234ff. He argues that it is difficult not to believe that the verb *capere* was used with *usu* in at least one provision, that with its clear Indo-European root its original meaning of physical taking is beyond dispute, and that the use of *capere* not just to mean "acquire" but to acquire without a taking would be very strange. "Indeed," he says, "the 'taking' will have occurred one or two years earlier and the acquisition will be a totally abstract occurrence." He then argues that if *capere* in the context did have its basic "taking" meaning, *usu* will have to be looked at again, and he suggests that it could be a dative, "with a view to use." The concentration would then be on *capere* as the act which begins the *usus*, rather than on the acquisition. He admits that at first sight the prohibiting provisions of the code pose a difficulty. It would, indeed, I believe, be difficult to hold that the provisions in question forbade taking with a view to use rather than that they forbade usucapion, and Prichard's view would be acceptable only if his arguments about *capere* were convincing. Prichard's case depends *inter alia* on two basic hypotheses which he does not attempt to demonstrate and of which the latter

The object of this two years' use was "fundus" which one might translate as "a piece of land." From Cicero *Top.* 4.23 we learn that the provision did not speak of "aedes," "a house," but that *usus auctoritas* here, too, was for two years on the basis that what holds good for one thing also holds good for its equivalent. This text of Cicero, along with G.2.42 which mentions both *aedes* and *fundus* in this connection, has led some modern scholars to hold that for the XII Tables the two-year period did not apply to houses which could be usucapted in one year. Only as a result of wide interpretation, it is said, was the two-year period extended to *aedes*.[9] One scholar,[10] indeed, wonders whether

---

at least is implausible. The first is that the verb *capere* had in Latin an original meaning restricted to "to take physically"; for this as the sole use of the verb, the Indo-European derivation by itself is not sufficient evidence. The second is that until the time of the XII Tables "to take physically" remained the sole meaning of *capere*. There is little evidence for the usages of *capere* before Plautus but that author uses *capere* frequently and with a wide variety of meanings such as "to perceive with the senses": *Pseud.* 596; "to understand, be aware of": *Aul.* 798; "to take or acquire something incorporeal" (such as appearance or satiety or good sense, or the occasion): *Amph.* 266, 472; *Trin.* 650; *Pseud.* 1022; *Stich.* 138; *Bacch.* 300; *Aul.* 488; *Poen.* 2; "to acquire": *Men.* 1161; "to take up" (one's hair): *Most.* 226; "to acquire" (a post or honor, etc.): *Bacch.* 438; *Stich.* 698; "to take a benefit or pleasure": *Amph.* 108, 114; *Stich.* 422; "to suffer an evil or disadvantage": *Amph.* 640, 722, 939; "to appoint": *Merc.* 736. Still other usages are to be found in Plautus and other early writers (cf. *TLL*, 3, 318ff) but enough has been said to make the point. On Prichard's view, all this expansion of meaning would have taken place after the XII Tables, which seems most unlikely. Since, if *usu capere* had occurred in the XII Tables, the meaning "to take physically with a view to use" would create more problems than it solves, it seems better to keep as its sense "to acquire by use."

[9] See M. David & H.L.W. Nelson, *Gai Institutionum Commentarii iv, Kommentar* (Leiden, E. J. Brill, 1960), p. 258. T. Mayer-Maly, "Studien zur Frühgeschichte der *usucapio* II," *ZSS* 78 (1961), 221ff at 223, 232f; Kaser, *RPR* 1, p. 135, n. 3. It cannot be suggested that at the time of the XII Tables *aedes* did not fall within the two-year period for usucapion because houses were not then attached to the land. The archaeological evidence shows that *aedes* were then very firmly built into the ground; see Gjerstad, *Early Rome* 4, pp. 401ff.

[10] Meyer-Maly, "Studien II," p. 223, n. 11.

the maxim *superficies solo cedit* is as old as is usually thought. The argument is not wholly persuasive in this form: Gaius certainly was of the opinion that the provision applied equally to land and houses from the start: "lex enim XII tabularum soli quidem res biennio usucapi iussit, ceteras vero anno."[11] Nonetheless we must account for the choice of the word "fundus" in the code. In early Rome, as elsewhere in Italy,[12] the farmer would not reside on his farm but in the city itself and would make daily journeys to the land on which he was working. Because many fields would lie fallow in alternate years,[13] and pastures would often be wholly seasonal and unoccupied and unprotected at other times, it would be relatively easy for an intruder to take control and continue in occupation for some time without the owner's knowledge. Hence a period longer than one year was desirable for the usucapion of farmland. The farmer's dwelling-house would not be on the *fundus*, hence would not be usucapted when the *fundus* was, and the *aedes* in the city was not so open to the same risks of prescription. Thus, it was natural for the XII Tables to speak expressly of the prescription of *fundus*. If the period of prescription for *fundus* and *aedes* differed, the dividing line would be between country property and town property, not between *solum* and *superficies*. In the absence of any clear

[11] G.2.54.

[12] There seems to be no direct evidence for Rome itself. But it seems reasonable to generalize from the evidence that around Veii there were remarkably few small villages or scattered farms: see J. B. Ward-Perkins, *Landscape and History of Central Italy* (The Second J. L. Myres Memorial Lecture, Oxford, 1964), p. 14; H. H. Scullard, *The Etruscan Cities and Rome* (London, Thames & Hudson, 1967), p. 63.

[13] There is no direct evidence for fallowing in early Rome, but one would not necessarily expect any. The practice was normal in Greece and if the Romans were not already familiar with it they would have learned about it from their contacts with Magna Graecia, etc. For fallowing in Rome in the period for which we have evidence see K. D. White, *Roman Farming* (London, Thames & Hudson, 1970), pp. 113ff.

indication that in other legal matters a distinction *was* drawn between country property and town property[14] it is probably best to think that though it is significant that *fundus* was the word chosen for the provision, it was used —as it can clearly be used—to mean *solum*;[15] hence buildings, too, would be usucapted only after two years. But it should be noted that the emphasis in the provision is on farmland.

It is within the context of acquisition of ownership by suitable use that we should understand the very practical clause of the xii Tables (Tab. vii.4) which Cicero tells us about in *de leg.* 1.21.55, forbidding usucapion of a five-foot strip along boundaries. A farmer, by encroaching on the edge of his neighbor's land was not to be allowed to extend his boundaries.

A further provision (Tab. iii.7) of the code provided "Adversus hostem aeterna auctoritas."[16] In early Latin the word *hostis* means simply *peregrinus*[17] or, as Varro explains,[18] a *peregrinus* "qui suis legibus uteretur."[19] The provision declares that the title of ownership remains permanently against a peregrine, that is that a peregrine is unable

---

[14] Only much later were the *actio finium regundorum* and the *actio aquae pluviae arcendae* restricted to the country: see Watson, *Property*, pp. 114f, 172f; *Law Making*, p. 115, n. 2. The distinction between urban and rustic praedial servitudes is not based on the situation of the property in town or country.

[15] See e.g. Ernout & Meillet, *Dictionnaire*, p. 261.

[16] Cicero *Off.* 1.12.37.

[17] Cicero *Off.* 1.12.37; Festus, *s.v. hostis*.

[18] *Ling.* 5.3.

[19] The view widely held by legal scholars that in this clause the word *hostis* means "that foreigner who shares with the Romans a legal community, even if a limited one" (see e.g. Kaser, *Eigentum*, p. 93) can be confidently rejected. No doubt there would be no need for a clause of this nature in respect to a foreigner who had no common legal rights with the Romans, and the clause would be aimed against those foreigners who did have some common rights with the Romans. But that is not to the point for the meaning of the word *hostis*. Most recently A. M. Prichard has conjectured that for *hostis* in this clause the meaning "enemy" is more likely; "*Auctoritas* in early Roman Law," *LQR* 90 (1974), 378ff, at 380ff.

to acquire ownership simply by lapse of time. It is sometimes suggested[20] that the rule applied originally only to
res mancipi but there seems no compelling reason to accept
this.[21] It is hard to believe that originally peregrines could
usucapt *res nec mancipi* but later lost the right.[22]

Yet another clause (Tab. v.2) declared that *res mancipi*
belonging to a woman under the *tutela* of her agnates could
not be usucapted unless they were transferred with the authority of her *tutor*.[23]

For ownership to be acquired by *usus* there was no need
—until much later times—either for a *iusta causa* or for *bona
fides*, for a transaction justifying the acquisition or for the
acquirer to begin his holding in good faith.[24] But a provision (Tab. viii.17) of the xii Tables provided either that
stolen property could not be usucapted or, less plausibly,
that the thief could not usucapt.[25]

Finally Cicero tells us[26] of one more provision (Tab.
x.10), that the xii Tables forbade the usucapion of the *bustum*—that is, the place where a body is burned and buried[27]
—and its *forum*, the entrance to the tomb. But that

[20] See e.g. Kaser, *RPR* i, p. 136.

[21] Unless one were to argue that there was no action to claim
ownership of *res nec mancipi*; but see supra, p. 132.

[22] The argument, if I understand it correctly, seems to be this.
The main purpose of *commercium* was to make *mancipatio* (and the
ownership of *res mancipi*) available to selected non-Romans, hence
the purpose of the present clause was to insist that, nonetheless, these
selected non-Romans could not become owners of *res mancipi* by
lapse of time.

[23] G.2.47; see Kaser, *RPR* i, p. 138 and the references he gives. That
the rule applied only where the woman was in the *tutela* of her agnates
appears from G.2.47 and Cicero *Flac.* 34.84.

[24] See e.g. Yaron, "Reflections," pp. 214f; Watson, *Property*, pp. 31f,
48ff.

[25] These seem to me the only two possible meanings of the provision; for the full argument see Watson, *Property*, pp. 24ff, and the
works cited. The former possibility now seems to me to be by far
the more likely especially since the provision was so understood by
Gaius: G.2.45; 2.49: cf. also D.41.3.33pr (Julian *44 dig.*); J.2.6.2; Theophilus *Paraph.* 2.6.2. Most recently Kaser favors the latter possibility;
RPR i, p. 137.

[26] *Leg.* 2.24.61.   [27] Festus, *s.v. bustum*.

res sacrae could not be usucapted was a rule of *ius gentium* and was not, according to Cicero,[28] expressly laid down by the *ius civile*.

In marked contrast to the information that the xii Tables contained several provisions on usucapion is the total silence about provisions on other ways of acquiring ownership; on the varieties of *occupatio, thesauri inventio, fructuum perceptio* or *separatio, specificatio* and *accessio* and its various forms.[29] We cannot suppose that these topics were extra-legal even though we may not with certainty reconstruct details. Nor yet can we presume that by some strange chance all the relevant clauses were lost to later generations and to us. The pattern of a total absence of information can only mean that the xii Tables contained not a single clause on any of these topics. This conclusion has importance beyond the confines of property. Once again we have evidence that a lack of information on clauses of the xii Tables is not due to a loss of the clauses, but to an original absence of any clauses. Thus it would appear, on the one hand, that the extent of loss of provisions is not so great as one might at first think; on the other, that we may be able to establish that we possess information on by far the greater part of the codification's contents.

Probably these topics were not dealt with because the law on them, where it was of practical importance, was well known and was not undergoing modifications.

[28] *Har. Resp.* 14.32.

[29] The provisions on *tignum iunctum* do not concern, or disclose anything for that period about, the ownership of the *tignum*: see infra, pp. 164f. Even if they did tell us something about ownership that fact would not invalidate the argument which is being constructed here, since it is clearly not the purpose of these clauses to relate the state of ownership.

THIRTEEN

Property

Land in the nature of things is usually bounded by other land, a fact which gives rise to rights and duties between neighbors, some of which are automatically imposed by law, others of which result from the acting of individuals. Rights and duties of both kinds existed as early as the XII Tables, and indeed feature prominently.

If we take first the rights and duties imposed by law the best starting point will be a text of the jurist Gaius[1] which says that in the *actio finium regundorum* we must remember to observe that provision which was in a way[2] drawn up on a model of that law which Solon is said to have passed at Athens: "If a man makes a rough wall close to another person's land, he must not go beyond the boundary; if it is a mortared wall, he must leave a foot clear; and if it is a house, two feet. If he digs a grave or a trench, he must leave a clear space as broad as the depth; if it is a well, space to the extent of a fathom. Olives and fig-trees he must plant nine feet from the adjoining property, all other trees five feet."[3] Though Gaius does not expressly mention the XII Tables in the text there is no doubt that that is the law he has in mind. Apart even from other considerations, the text comes from his commentary on the XII Tables. From the text we can deduce that the early Roman provisions restricting an owner's rights at the edge of his land in the interest of his neighbor were governed by the *actio finium regundorum*; that Gaius believed that the law of Solon was

---

[1] D.10.1.13 (*4 ad leg. xii tab.*)
[2] "In a way" is a translation of "quodammodo" which might possibly be taken as "to some extent."
[3] Monro's translation.

in some sense the model, though he does not claim that the Roman provisions were identical. Indeed, we cannot use this text either to reconstruct the details of the Roman rules (from the provisions of Solon) or to argue (because some of Solon's provisions seem inappropriate for Rome in the fifth century) that the law of Solon could not have been a model.[4]

This *actio finium regundorum*, then, governed the rule already mentioned[5] which forbade the usucapion of the five feet of land along boundaries.[6] It also covered the provision (Tab. VII.1) on *ambitus* which seems to have enacted that a "sestertius pes," that is, 2½ feet, should be left around a building, which means that a building could not be erected closer to the boundary than 2½ feet.[7] Such a rule is obviously excessively inconvenient in a town or city and not surprisingly never seems to have been observed in Rome. It was on this account, I believe, that much later the jurists restricted the application of the *actio finium regundorum* to the country.[8]

The XII Tables further established (Tab. VII.5) that the *actio finium regundorum* would be heard by three *arbitri*.[9]

[4] For the argument see Watson, *Property*, pp. 111ff; F. Wieacker, "Solon und die XII Tafeln," in *Studi Volterra* 3 (Milan, Giuffrè, 1973) 757ff, at 769f; Gjerstad, *Early Rome* 5, p. 323. That D.10.1.13 and a few other texts claim that individual provisions of the XII Tables were influenced by the laws of Solon is not necessarily significant for determining whether there was such a dependence, or a Roman embassy to study Greek law. Similarities are inevitable, and given the Roman tradition, so are such claims.

[5] Supra, p. 154.

[6] Cicero *Leg.* 1.21.55; ". . . controversia nata est de finibus; in qua quoniam usucapionem XII tabulae intra quinque pedes esse noluerunt, ... sed ex is tres arbitri fines regemus." Reasonably, editors emend to "sed e XII tres. . . ."

[7] Varro *Ling.* 5.22; Festus, *ss. vv. Ambitus*; Maecianus *assis distr.* 46.

[8] See for the argument Watson, *Property*, pp. 114ff; *Law Making*, pp. 114f and 115, n. 2.

[9] Cicero *Leg.* 1.21.55. This means that the action could not be a *legis actio per iudicis postulationem*; see for literature Watson, *Property*, p. 111, n. 4. The reference to Kaser should now be to *RPR* 1, p. 142, n. 7.

It seems likely, as the editors of the XII Tables generally suppose, that the apposite clause contained the words "Si iurgant."[10]

Another provision (Tab. VII.9) declared that where a tree overhung a neighbor's property, the neighbor was entitled to have the overhanging branches cut off up to a height of 15 feet,[11] though it is not clear whether the neighbor could himself lop off the offending branches or compel the owner to do so.[12] The main reason for the provision was no doubt to avoid too much shade falling on the neighbor's land, thus hindering its full productivity. It may also be relevant for the provision that 15 feet is about as high as can be pruned from the ground since a pruning hook longer than about 9 feet is unmanageable.

With this last provision is sometimes linked[13] a delictal one (Tab. VIII.11) which established a penalty of twenty-five pieces of bronze for each tree of another which a person wrongfully cut down.[14] Whether or not the main aim of this provision was to deal with a farmer who reacted over-vigorously to an overhanging tree, its scope was presumably wider and the texts make plain that it used the verb *succidere*, to cut down.

Acorns belonged to the owner of the tree, and the XII Tables provided (Tab. VII.10) that when they fell onto a neighbor's land the owner was to be permitted to gather them.[15] In this context it is appropriate to mention that the XII Tables (Tab. VIII.7) also gave a remedy where a man's animals caused damage by pasturing on a neighbor's land.[16]

[10] Cicero *Rep.* 4.8.
[11] D.43.27.1.8 (Ulpian *71 ad ed.*); 43.27.2 (Pomponius *34 ad Sab.*).
[12] See Watson, *Property*, pp. 117ff.
[13] See Kaser, *RPR* I, p. 126.
[14] Pliny *HN* 17.1.7; G.4.11; D.47.7.1 (Paul *9 ad Sab.*); 47.7.5pr (idem); 12.2.28.6 (Paul *18 ad ed.*).
[15] Pliny *HN* 16.5.15.
[16] *P.S.* 1.15.1; D.19.5.14.3 (Ulpian *41 ad Sab.*). It is sometimes said, with more or less assurance, that the *actio de pastu* lay only when the animals' owner had sent them onto the neighbor's land: e.g. Kaser, *RPR* I, p. 162 and n. 67; B. S. Jackson, "The Fence-Breaker

The code (Tab. VII.8) also contained a remedy in respect of dangerous rain water flowing from a neighbor's land. This has very obvious connections with—indeed, is creative of—the action well known in later times, the *actio aquae pluviae arcendae*, but it would be dangerous to argue back in time. Apart from other considerations, the XII Tables' provision read "Si aqua pluvia nocet" and though Pomponius tells us that the *veteres* interpreted this as "si nocere poterit"[17] we cannot be sure that this was the original intention of the draughtsmen.[18] Whether the XII Tables knew a remedy for threatened damage, *dammum infectum*, must remain undecided. On what seems to me the most likely explanation of D.43.8.5 (Paul *16 ad Sab.*) the code did provide an action, and a *cautio* was involved in the protective

---

and the *actio de pastu pecoris* in Early Jewish Law," *Journal of Jewish Studies* 25 (special issue, February 1974, *Studies in Jewish Legal History in Honour of David Daube*, ed. B. S. Jackson), 123ff, at 130. The view may or may not be correct, but there is no evidence to support it, and there is no sign of that requirement in the only text which is really relevant for the point, *P.S.* 1.15.1. Where my animals graze on your land and cause you loss, two possibilities exist for fixing liability on me; the law may make me liable simply because the animals are mine, or alternatively only in circumstances where I admitted my animals into your land. A very different situation arises where your acorns fall onto my land and are gobbled by my animals. No system would make me liable simply because my animals ate your acorns; at the most I would be liable if I sent in my animals to the field of mine to feed on your acorns. Thus, texts concerned with this second situation (such as D.19.5.14.3 and 10.4.9.1) which show a requirement, *immisso pecore*, are no evidence of any similar requirement for the *actio de pastu* which concerned animals grazing on another's land.

[17] D.40.7.21pr (7 *ex Plautio*).

[18] For a full account of the operation of the action in the later Republic see Watson, *Property*, pp. 155ff. It is a reasonable, but unprovable, hypothesis that the action of the early Republic, like that of the later, was given only where the damage would result from *opus factum*. The main danger would be from drainage channels on the higher land, whether these were surface channels or the *cuniculi* to be found in Latium and Southern Etruria: see H. H. Scullard, *The Etruscan Cities and Rome* (London, Thames & Hudson, 1967), pp. 68ff and the references he gives, p. 293, n. 56.

measures.[19] But there is no other direct evidence and, in view of the state of the text, certainty is not possible.

Rights in land which can result from the activities of neighbors rather than from operation of law are, of course, servitudes. There is ample evidence of servitudes relating to land—which have come to be called rustic praedial servitudes—but none of servitudes affecting buildings, now called urban praedial servitudes. The rustic praedial servitudes with which we are here concerned were *res mancipi*[20] and so could be acquired by *mancipatio* or *usus*.

Of what are regarded as the four basic rustic servitudes, *iter*, *actus*, *via*, and *aquae ductus*, only *via* was dealt with in the xii Tables so far as our information goes, though it is plausible to assert that the others also probably existed.[21]

One provision (Tab. vii.7) on *via* seems to have run: "Viam muniunto: ni sam delapidassint, qua volet iumento agito."[22] A reasonable translation would be: "Let them make a road. Unless they laid it with stones (or alternative-

[19] *Property*, pp. 131ff; not accepted by Kaser, *RPR* 1, pp. 126ff.

[20] That servitudes are *res mancipi* is not an argument for holding that they were originally considered to be corporeal or that the right to them was conceived in any way to be ownership: see Watson, *Property*, pp. 92ff; Diósdi, *Ownership*, pp. 109ff. Servitudes were obviously desirable, attempts must have been made to create them, inevitably *mancipatio* would be used for this purpose, hence they would be treated as *res mancipi*. Diósdi, pp. 114f, rightly uses both of the xii Tables' provisions to prove that *via* did not mean the ownership of a strip of land.

[21] A much later text, D.8.3.1.pr (Ulpian *2 inst.*) declares that *via* included *iter* and *actus*. It does not, however, logically follow (even if we accept this text as evidence for the scope of these rights) that the existence of the greatest right implies that the lesser rights could exist as separate entities. On some interpretations D.43.8.5 might be thought evidence of *aquae ductus*. In view of the slight uncertainty and the absence of any evidence for the recognition of these other servitudes as legal rights they will not be discussed here.

[22] Festus, *s.v. viae*. The text is by no means in perfect form but this, a widely accepted reconstruction, seems plausible. Other reconstructions would have "delapidassunt," "iumentum" or "iumenta," "ageto." The various possibilities do not affect our understanding.

ly, 'set curbstones'), let him drive his beast where he wishes."[23] "Sam" is an early form for "eam."[24]

The plural form in two of the verbs, the singular in the third, show that the personages involved are different. Since "agito" must be used of the owner of the dominant land, the subject of "muniunto" and "delapidassint" must be the owners of the servient land. With respect to the owners of the servient land the *lex* uses language appropriate to the imposition of a legal obligation: "Viam muniunto." And at first sight this servitude of the xii Tables seems to conflict with the principle of later times, "servitus in faciendo consistere non potest."[25] But can we determine with any precision the nature of this "obligation"? If we look first at the sanction we see that this is not an action by the owner of the dominant land to compel compliance or to pay damages. Nor is there a right to a fixed sum, or, indeed, so far as we can tell any direct recourse to the courts on this point. The sole sanction seems to be that the owner of the dominant land need not keep to the *via* when driving his beasts across the servient land.[26] Thus, once the servitude has come into existence, the owner of the servient land could treat this "obligation" stated in the *lex* as being limited to the case where it was more in his interest to perform it. Then *delapidare* cannot mean that the owner of the servient tenement was to provide a paved road or a properly made up road. Such an understanding would be completely anachronistic for the fifth century.[27] Possibly it should be taken as meaning

[23] This sense is confirmed by Cicero *Caecin.* 19.54, where in a context relating to the xii Tables he has "Si via sit immunita, iubet qua velit agere iumentum." See G. Franciosi, *Studi sulla servitù prediali* (Naples, Jovene, 1967), pp. 30ff; Diósdi, *Ownership*, p. 114.

[24] See Festus, *s.v. Sam.*

[25] The difficulty involved in accepting this was one factor which induced L. Aru to take the view that *munire* meant "to fortify" and "dilapidare" "to pull down a wall": "Nota minima sulla origine storica della *servitus viae*," *Studi Calgiari* 24 (1936), 409ff, at 414.

[26] The suggested interpretation in Cicero *Caecin.* 19.54 is not to be taken seriously.

[27] See the references given in Franciosi, *Servitù*, p. 32, n. 103.

that enough stones had to be strewn or set in the *via* to make it reasonably passable. Perhaps a more likely meaning is that curbstones should be set to mark the edge of the road.[28] Do *munire* and *delapidare* mean the same thing? On *a priori* grounds it is plausible to maintain that there was some difference in sense but it is not easy to be more precise. Franciosi would exclude as the meaning of *munire viam*, "to trace for the first time,"[29] and he suggests that *munire* could already have included the placing of boundary stones.[30]

A further provision (Tab. vii.6) provided that the breadth of the *via* should be 8 feet on the straight, 16 feet at the bends (*anfractus*).[31] Diósdi rightly argues that this provision would have been superfluous if *via* had meant ownership of a strip of land (as some scholars hold) since the territory would have been defined when land was bought.[32] But more than that, the implication is that the servitudes of *via* under consideration are acquired by *usus*, not by agreement followed by a *mancipatio*. When a servitude is created by agreement, the parties will normally fix its extent, hence a provision of the xii Tables establishing the latitude would not have been necessary. But when *via* is acquired by use, its boundaries will not be clearly defined, and it becomes sensible for statute to set out the width.

There is no direct evidence for the nature of the action claiming a servitude. The common view is that it would be the *vindicatio* and it is easy to imagine that the *legis actio sacramento in rem* could be used, perhaps in a variant

[28] See Wieacker, "xii Tafeln," p. 306; Gjerstad, *Early Rome 5*, pp. 323f.

[29] *Servitù*, pp. 32f.

[30] *Servitù*, p. 34, with a reference to the *Tabulae Heracleenses*, 60ff.

[31] D.8.3.8. (Gaius 7 *ad ed. prov.*); "Viae latitudo ex lege duodecim tabularum in porrectum octo pedes habet, in anfractum, id est ubi flexum est, sedecim"; Varro *Ling.* 7.15: ". . . leges iubent in directo pedum viii esse viam, in anfracto xvi, id est in flexu."

[32] See supra, p. 161, n. 20.

form.[33] There is no indication that the claim would be "meum esse ex iure quiritium."[34]

Rights between neighbors are, of course, by no means the only real rights, but we are even less informed about others. Thus, it is very widely accepted that the forms of real security, *fiducia* and *pignus*, existed by the time of the XII Tables,[35] but there is no evidence.[36]

A clause (Tab. VI.7) of the XII Tables did, however, cover the incorporation of things belonging to one person into another's immovable property. Festus[37] gives the provision as: "Tignum iunctum aedibus vineave et concapit ne solvito." The text is obviously corrupt at "et concapit" and numerous emendations have been suggested. I propose "concaput" which is an otherwise unknown word meaning "something attached to the top, a support," and the clause would then be: "Do not take away a beam built into a house or a support from a vine." This enables one for the first time to give a proper meaning to *tignum*, "a beam."[38] The eco-

[33] Diósdi's view of the *legis actio sacramento in rem* would make that action unsuitable for claiming a servitude, and he concludes that the legal protection of servitudes in ancient times remains a riddle: *Ownership*, p. 115.

[34] Hence no arguments can be drawn from the action for a servitude to support the idea of relative ownership; see Watson, *Property*, p. 92, n. 4.

[35] See Diósdi, *Ownership*, p. 116.

[36] I believe that the element of trust and good faith which is essential to *fiducia* resulted from the wording adopted in the appropriate *mancipatio*, and that the resultant action was governed by the XII Tables' clause "Cum nexum faciet mancipiumque, uti lingua nuncupassit, ita ius esto": *Obligations*, pp. 172ff. But this is no argument for dating the creation of *fiducia* to before or after the XII Tables. In the former alternative, the clause would confirm what was already the case; in the latter, the clause would be understood as applying to the innovation.

[37] *S.v. tignum.*

[38] For all this see A. Watson, "*Tignum iunctum*, the XII Tables and a Lost Word," *RIDA* 21 (1974), 337ff. On the whole, the choice of emendation makes little difference to the understanding of the clause. Even those who believe "et concapit" somehow refers to theft could not think that only where the property was stolen was it irremovable.

nomic function of the clause is apparent but the clause does not allow us to determine who is the owner of the beam or support.

A further provision (Tab. vi.9) also concerned vines. Of it we have, "quandoque sarpta, donec dempta erunt,"[39] "from the time of pruning until the fruit has been gathered." But we cannot recover the context.[40]

We also know that a clause (Tab. vii.3) contained the word *tuguria*, "cottages,"[41] and that *hortus* had the meaning later given to *villa*, while for *hortus* the word used was *heredium*.[42]

Finally, it should be noted that the overwhelming stress in the property provisions is on farming. Nothing in the code reveals the existence of any industry.[43]

[39] Festus, *s.v. sarpuntur*.

[40] Possibly this is part of, or is connected with, the provision just mentioned.

[41] Festus, *s.v. tuguria*.

[42] Pliny the Elder *HN* 19.4.50; see K. D. White, "Roman Agricultural Writers I: Varro and His Predecessors," in *Aufstieg und Niedergang der römischen Welt* I, iv, ed. H. Temporini (Berlin, New York, de Gruyter, 1973), 439ff and 441. According to Varro *Rust.* 1.10.2 two *iugera* formed a *haeredium* because this was the amount first allotted by Romulus to each man, which would go to the heir.

[43] Yet Plutarch *Num.* 17.3 plausibly states that eight guilds were created in the regal period: flute players, goldsmiths, carpenters, dyers, leather-workers, tanners, bronze-smiths and potters. If he is correct then industry was well developed; see H. H. Scullard, *A History of the Roman World, 753 to 146 B.C.*, 3rd ed. (London, Methuen, 1961), pp. 341ff. The xii Tables' viii.27 concerns guilds.

FOURTEEN

Private Law and Legend in Livy 1-3

In the first three books of Livy there are five, possibly six, tales or legends which have some private legal content;[1] the five certain instances have direct relevance for this book and have already been discussed in greater or less detail. But it is valuable to look at all six together, even though no common origin or history can be claimed.

The first tale is that of the "Maid of Ardea," the plebeian girl faced with two suitors of whom one was a patrician.[2] R. M. Ogilvie argues that "the case was a paradigm of certain provisions of the XII Tables as emended by the Lex Canuleia."[3] But David Daube has already pointed out the weakness: if the case was a paradigm of the pro-plebeian *lex Canuleia*, "the girl would have to be a patrician and her tutors against her stooping to a union with a plebeian; or alternatively she could be a plebeian, but in that case the resistance to the union ought to come from the patrician suitor's people."[4] In this book we have used the case to elucidate the consents required for the marriage of a fatherless girl, and the case can also be taken as indicating that father-

[1] Here we are leaving aside the whole account of the formation of the XII Tables. Nor need we consider the criminal law instance of *perduellio* (or *parricidium*) in Livy 1.26, nor the *vadimonium* set on Quinctius on a criminal charge in Livy 3.11ff.

[2] See supra, pp. 26ff.

[3] "The Maid of Ardea," *Latomus* 21 (1962), 477ff. Professor Ogilvie kindly tells me that he would now reject "paradigm" as a correct description of this case and that of Vindicius. He would prefer something more like "unhistorical stories invented as a result of a point of law."

[4] *Roman Law, Linguistic, Social and Philosophical Aspects* (Edinburgh, Edinburgh University Press, 1969), pp. 112ff.

less girls of marriageable age could have tutors.[5] But the case cannot be seen as a paradigm of any legal rule or provision, and it is certainly not a legal aetiological myth. It should not be suggested that the tale—assuming it is not historical—was invented to explain points of private law. The legal points are not stressed apart from the question of the right of the tutors or mother to choose the husband and even there the legal issues are not clarified. Yet all the points of law inherent in the tale are accurate—or at least very plausible—for Rome around 443. Too much cannot be made of this, however, since in the matters in question the law was still the same in Livy's time. No guide to the date of origin of the legend can be provided by its legal aspects.

The second case, the rape and suicide of Lucretia,[6] is rather different. The legal detail—that Lucretia is acting as if her father and husband with two friends comprised a *iudicium domesticum* and that she kills herself because death is the appropriate punishment for unchastity—is obscured in Livy's account, and it seems likely, indeed, that Livy was totally unaware of the legal detail. It seems plausible to assert that Livy's source itself passed over this legal point in silence though it had once been more prominent in still earlier accounts. The story of Lucretia could never have been created as a paradigm for the *iudicium domesticum* and still less could it ever have been a legal aetiological myth. But again the legal point is accurately used even to the emphasis being laid on the father rather than the husband: we are told first that Lucretia sent a message to her father at Rome, only secondly that she sent the same message to her husband at Ardea.[7] This time, too, there is no way of estimating the age of the legal point in the tale of Lucretia. The law had not undergone any great develop-

---

[5] See e.g. Ogilvie, "Maid," p. 479; E. Volterra "Sul diritto familiare di Ardea nel v secolo a.c.," in *Studi Segni* (Milan, Giuffrè, 1966), pp. 3ff, at p. 10. In this chapter the important question whether the law of Ardea was regarded by Livy as the same as that of Rome is left aside; see infra, pp. 175f.

[6] See supra, pp. 35f.   [7] Livy 1.58.5.

ment between the kings and Livy. If the arguments given above are accurate and the point was more prominent in earlier accounts we still have no evidence that it was of great antiquity or an integral part of the original story.[8]

The third instance, the manumission of Vindicius, has the appearance of an aetiological myth.[9] As such it cannot have been the creation of Livy who, in fact, does not overly stress the legal issues. The tale seems to be accurate in dating *manumissio vindicta* with the effect of granting citizenship to a considerable time before the XII Tables, but not in thinking that from its very beginning *manumissio vindicta* also gave citizenship.[10] This accuracy in dating *manumissio vindicta* with full effect is either an inspired guess or an indication of the early origin of the myth.

The fourth instance, the *vindicatio in servitutem* for Verginia, is again of a different nature. Modern historians[11] have good reason for rejecting the tale as historical: the fall of the decemvirate because of the lust of Appius Claudius appears to be an invention to parallel the downfall of the monarchy through the lust of Sextus Tarquinius; the name Verginia is just too fitting to command belief; and her plebeian status in most of the sources can only be the result of the later political struggles between the orders. Yet despite a widely held view to the contrary,[12] it does not seem credible that Livy's sources presented the tale as a paradigm of the *causa liberalis* as defined by the XII Tables. One would not choose as a paradigm a story where, as in this case, the wrong decision was given on the legal issues (apart altogether from the accuracy of the facts), and where Appius Claudius' legal argument for his absurd decision to give

---

[8] Some scholars, it should be noted, seem almost willing to believe in the historicity of Lucretia; e.g. Ogilvie, *Commentary*, pp. 218f, 477.

[9] See supra, pp. 88f.   [10] See supra, pp. 89f.

[11] See supra, p. 97, n. 76.

[12] E.g. E. Täubler, *Untersuchungen zur Geschichte des Dezemvirats und der Zwölftafeln* (Berlin, Historische Studien, 148, 1921), p. 32; J. Bayet, *Tite-Live: histoire romaine* 3 (Paris, Belles Lettres, 1954), p. 145; Ogilvie, *Commentary*, p. 478.

vindiciae secundum servitutem at the first hearing could be thought plausible.[13] The point of a paradigm is to instruct, not deceive the reader. That the story is not an aeitological myth scarcely needs saying.

Yet in this tale, more than in any other in the early books of Livy, the legal details are stressed and lingered over. Most prominent of all are the arguments used by Appius Claudius to justify his grant of *vindiciae secundum servitutem*[14] though it was he, we are told, who was responsible for a clause in the XII Tables that *vindiciae* should always be given *secundum libertatem*.[15] The legal twists are used to heighten the drama of the situation and it is perhaps not fanciful to think that they may have a rhetorical origin. Certainly they are exploited in a plausible and sophisticated manner. A relatively late date for the introduction of the legal details cannot be excluded.[16] On the points in issue the law had not undergone any significant change between the decemvirate and Livy.[17]

The fifth instance is of *nexum* and the "Distinguished Veteran." The legal points are not at all stressed but it would seem that the position is accurately described.[18] The emphasis in this tale and elsewhere in Livy is on the social problem of debt and the political implications of *nexum*, and if the story is an invention it was not conceived to illustrate law. But *nexum* had disappeared as a result of the *lex Poetilia* of the late fourth century B.C., and it is apparent that long before Livy even jurists had ceased to have any secure knowledge of its nature. Since it is unlikely that awareness of the difference in treatment legally appropriate

---

[13] That its plausibility can still mislead is shown by its acceptance in Ogilvie, *Commentary*, p. 483.

[14] 3.45.

[15] 3.44.12-45.1; cf. D.1.2.2.24 (Pomponius *sing. enchirid.*).

[16] It was for this reason that so little use was made of the tale in the account of *vindicatio in servitutem*; supra, pp. 00.

[17] The procedure could have changed from the *legis actio* to the formulary *vindicatio*. Important as this change is, it would not affect the matter for us.

[18] See supra, pp. 114f.

to *nexi* and *iudicati* would long survive the passing of the *lex Poetilia*, we have evidence here—though not conclusive evidence—that the ultimate source for this story is very old.

The final case, the "Corpse in the House of Sestius,"[19] is the one which was not discussed in earlier chapters since it is not concerned with family structure or even property. It is also the one which is doubtfully relevant for private law. Livy relates the tale as proof of the moderation of the decemviri. A corpse was found in the house of a patrician, Publius Sestius, and was produced before the assembly. Sestius' guilt, we are told, was as obvious as it was atrocious, yet the decemvir Gaius Julius summoned him to court and appeared as prosecutor. Thus the decemvir who was the lawful judge surrendered his right "so that he might add to the liberty of the people what he took from the power of the magistrate." Though the fact is not mentioned in this context, it should be recalled that when the decemvirate was established the normal constitutional workings were suspended, that there was no right of appeal from a decemvir, and that no other magistrates were appointed.[20]

Ogilvie sees in the tale a paradigm of the XII Tables X.I: "Hominem mortuum in urbe ne sepelito neve urito."[21] This surely is to be excluded. The *res atrox* of which Sestius was accused was certainly not burying a body inside the city, but murder. Ogilvie elsewhere[22] considers the case was also designed to exemplify another provision of the XII Tables, IX.1-2: "De capite civis nisi per maximum comitiatum . . . ne ferunto." But as with Tab. X.1, there is the problem that the episode is supposed to have occurred before the promulgation of the law which it is thought to illustrate. It is perhaps

[19] Livy 3.33.9f; see also Cicero *Rep.* 2.36.61.
[20] Livy 3.32.6: "Placet creari decemviros sine provocatione, et ne quis eo anno alius magistratus esset."
[21] "Maid," p. 478. I believe Professor Ogilvie would now abandon this position.
[22] *Commentary*, p. 458.

more reasonable to think that the story had no legal purpose but was intended to show the reasonableness of the decemviri. It does, of course, also illustrate the extent of the legal powers of the decemviri. If the view proposed here of the "Corpse in the House of Sestius" is accurate, then that tale has no connection with private law and need not be further considered.

These then are the five or six tales with some private legal content. None of them, I have argued, was intended as a legal paradigm though one is an aetiological myth. In another, the legal twists seem emphasized for dramatic purposes, but in the others the legal issues are not stressed. What is remarkable is the high degree of accuracy and understanding in the legal details. This is the more surprising in that it is plain that Livy himself had little knowledge or comprehension of law. He misuses even the simplest technical terms—for instance, *manus*[23]—and makes fundamental blunders—thus, in 39.9.2 he appears to think a woman could be a *tutor*. The legal understanding in the five (or six) tales must reflect the quality of Livy's sources, direct or indirect. It would be reasonable to suppose that some of the stories at least were polished up at a relatively late date[24] by a source who had particular legal knowledge. The name which springs to mind is Q. Aelius Tubero, the jurist and annalist, who, we know, was one of the main sources of Livy's first decade.[25] Yet too much credit must not be given to Tubero. The main stories had certainly been fixed by 70 B.C., and probably much earlier. Thus, we know that the case of Lucretia was discussed by Fabius Pictor,[26] and her summoning of kinsmen is recorded by Diodorus Siculus.[27]

---

[23] See supra, pp. 51f.

[24] Livy expressly excludes the old accounts at 3.47.5.

[25] Livy lists Tubero as one of his sources at 4.23.1 and 10.9.10; cf. P. G. Walsh, *Livy: His Historical Aims and Methods* (Cambridge, Cambridge University Press, 1961), pp. 115ff. On Tubero, see Klebs *RE*, 1, 537f.

[26] Dionysius of Halicarnassus, 4.64.3.

[27] 10.20.3.

That latter author also reports the *vindicatio in servitutem* of Verginia in front of Appius Claudius.[28] The source of Plutarch and Dionysius for the story of Vindicius must have been Valerius Antius[29] who *floruit* 80-60 B.C.[30]

[28] 12.24.

[29] For the argument see Ogilvie, *Commentary*, p. 242.

[30] Cf. Ogilvie, *Commentary*, pp. 12f. I am grateful to Professors Ogilvie and Walsh for much helpful criticism with this chapter.

FIFTEEN

The Law of Rome and the Law of the Latins

In the phrase of A. N. Sherwin-White, "the term *Latini* is comparable in origin to 'the Peloponnesians' rather than to 'the Dorians,'" and in early days *Latinus* was simply "a dweller in the plain."[1] The *Latini* were of mixed origin,[2] and one of their dwelling places was Rome. It is certain that the inhabitants of early Rome were Latin-speaking[3] and they can fairly be called *Latini*, though there is considerable evidence of a Sabine element in the population. The common tie between the early Latin villages would be partly racial and cultural, partly the language bond, and partly the contiguity of many villages in the plain of Latium, some of which might be as little as two miles distant from the next. Sherwin-White plausibly suggests that *conubium* and *commercium* were rights which were enjoyed originally because of a person's status as a Latin, before the concept of local citizenship had hardened.[4]

When for the present book we look at the problem of private law in the Latin settlements we do not have to consider the unreal question of an original identity of law in early Latium. There are two facts which we can regard as certain. First, given the cultural, linguistic, and geographical links, legal rules in some villages would very often be the same on many points, whether this was the result of bor-

---

[1] *The Roman Citizenship*, 2nd ed. (Oxford, Clarendon Press, 1973), p. 30.

[2] See Gjerstad, *Early Rome* 5, pp. 35ff; 6, pp. 14f.

[3] See e.g. H. H. Scullard in *Oxford Classical Dictionary*, 2nd ed. (Oxford, Clarendon Press, 1970), *s.v.* Rome, p. 926.

[4] *Citizenship*, pp. 30f.

rowing from one another[5] or in some cases owing to a common origin in a homeland outside Latium. Secondly, given the different economic, political, social, and even ethnic factors which would come into play at different times in the various villages, legal rules on many points would differ between one place and another.

What does concern us is whether, on the matters for which information is available, the law of the Romans was the same as, or was different from, the law of other Latins. Two points should be noted. When we have evidence for one other Latin town, say Ardea, this does not indicate that the law was the same in all other Latin settlements. Again our information for the law of the Latins comes from the Romans: we have no independent evidence. Hence, whether we like it or not, what we are investigating in each case is whether on that matter the Romans thought Roman law and the law of the Latins was the same or was different.

Aulus Gellius reports Servius Sulpicius' view of betrothal "in that part of Italy which is called Latium." From that practice of mutual promises, both on account of the girl and by the future husband, Servius derives the word "sponsalia" for the contract, "sponsa" for the woman who was promised, and "sponsus" for the man who promised to take in marriage. These words are, of course, the standard Roman terms, and the derivation of them from the early legal practice and law in Latium indicates Servius' belief that on this point Roman law had been no different from that operating in the rest of Latium.[6] But at some time Roman law changed; as early as Plautus, it seems, a promise of marriage had ceased to be actionable, and the promise by the bridegroom had disappeared.[7] In Latium, however, accord-

---

[5] On the phenomenon of legal borrowing see A. Watson, *Legal Transplants: an Approach to Comparative Law* (Edinburgh, Scottish Academic Press, and Charlottesville, University Press of Virginia, 1974).

[6] See Watson, *Persons*, pp. 11f; and supra, pp. 29f.

[7] See Watson, *Persons*, pp. 14ff.

ing to Servius, the early practice and law were unchanged until citizenship was given to all Latium by the *lex Iulia* of 90 B.C.

Aulus Gellius[8] is also the source for a second detail. According to tradition, he says, for almost five hundred years after the foundation of Rome there were no *actiones rei uxoriae* and no *cautiones rei uxoriae* in the city of Rome or in Latium, since they were not needed because there were no divorces. Servius Sulpicius, he goes on, wrote that *cautiones rei uxoriae* were first regarded as necessary when Spurius Carvilius Ruga divorced his wife. Elsewhere I have argued[9] that this account is basically accurate for Rome, that only following upon this divorce of around 230 B.C.— which, however, cannot be the first in Rome—were *cautiones* taken for the return of the dowry, and the *actio rei uxoriae* were introduced. For the situation in the rest of Latium we have only the tradition reported by Aulus Gellius.

But the most interesting information is that provided by Livy 4.9 about Ardea in 443 B.C. From the story of the Maid of Ardea we learn that the population of that place was divided into two groups as at Rome, into plebeians and *nobiles*;[10] that intermarriage between members of these two groups was possible[11] as it also was at Rome except between the date of the xii Tables and the *lex Canuleia* of 445 B.C.; that a fatherless girl even of marriageable age would be under tutelage, and that there could be more than one *tutor*,[12] all as at Rome. Earlier in this book we have consid-

[8] *NA* 4.3.1f.

[9] "The Divorce of Carvilius Ruga," *T.v.R.* 33 (1965), 38ff.

[10] 4.9.4ff: see E. Volterra, "Sul diritto familiare di Ardea nel V secolo a.c.," in *Studi in onore di Antonio Segni* (Milan, Giuffrè, 1966), pp. 3ff, at p. 9.

[11] 4.9.4ff.

[12] 4.9.5ff. Since nothing indicates how the *tutores* were appointed— though we are told they were plebeian like the girl—it seems pointless to speculate on the existence of *patria potestas*. G.1.55 would not be against the idea of *patria potestas* at Ardea since Gaius is con-

ered the conflict between the *tutores* and the mother as to who the girl should marry, and concluded that the dispute and the legal response to it were explicable in Roman terms.[13] Rightly or wrongly, Livy seems to have been representing the law of Ardea as if it were the same as that of Rome.

These very few texts provide all the information we have on early Latin law. It will be observed that so far as the sources go, either the law of the Latins and the law of the Romans was the same (or at least very similar) or that it was so envisaged by the later Romans. But it will also be noticed that all the texts concern family law. The significance of this cannot be determined. The fact may reflect nothing more than mere chance—the number of texts is so small—or the interest of later Romans.[14] It may, however, also be that it was in the law of persons in particular that the Romans felt there was an affinity between the rules prevailing in the various Latin communities.[15]

---

cerned with his own day; by that time the inhabitants of the old Latin settlements would long have been Romans.

[13] Supra, pp. 26ff. Volterra claims that the Livy passage pictures the law of marriage at Ardea as very different from that of Rome: "Diritto familiare," pp. 14ff; accepted by D. Daube, *Roman Law, Linguistic Social and Philosophical Aspects* (Edinburgh, Edinburgh University Press, 1969), p. 113, n. 3. But this is due to a failure to disentangle the strands of the situation.

[14] See supra, pp. 4ff.

[15] For similarities of moral outlook see Aulus Gellius *NA* 10.23, who claims that in early times the women of Rome and of Latium had been abstemious. Nothing in the passage indicates, however, that the serious penalties for wine-drinking existed also outside Rome

SIXTEEN

The XII Tables in the Light of Family Law

According to Roman tradition the XII Tables were a product of the class struggle between the plebeians and the patricians. Livy's version is that in 462 B.C. a tribune of the plebs, C. Terentilius Harsa demanded a law appointing five men to write down the consuls' *imperium* because, he claimed, it was almost crueler to have two consuls who had uncontrolled and infinite power than one king.[1] The *patres*, alarmed by this proposal, were able to prevent anything being done for eight years despite repeated action from subsequent tribunes.[2] The tribunes eventually laid aside their proposal which had come to lose its vigor and suggested a more moderate scheme. Framers of laws should be appointed jointly from the plebeians and patricians to bring forward rules which would be advantageous to both groups and secure equal liberty.[3] The patricians did not reject the idea but said that only patricians should propose the laws. Because both sides were in agreement over the laws and only differed over the proposers, an embassy was sent to Athens to copy out the laws of Solon (which had been promulgated about a century and a half earlier) and to acquire knowledge of the institutions, customs, and rules of other states of Greece.[4] In 451, ten men, the decemviri, all of whom were patrician, were appointed, to compile the new laws, and the ordinary constitution was suspended.[5] The decemviri, whose justice and impartiality is stressed, set up ten tables, and urged the people to consider each point and

[1] 3.9.
[2] E.g. 3.10.5; 3.14; 3.15.1; 3.16.5,6; 3.17.2; 3.19.1; 3.21.2; 3.24.1; 3.25.2; 3.29.8; 3.30.1.
[3] 3.31.7. [4] 3.31.8. [5] 3.33.

determine amendments and improvements. When this had taken place, the *comitia centuriata* adopted the Law of the Ten Tables. It came to be generally felt that two further tables were needed and it was decided to appoint another decemvirate.[6] This second body—again all patricians according to Livy, but containing three plebeians according to Dionysius[7]—became tyrannous, but did produce the two further tables.[8] They held onto power until they were overthrown in 449 as a result of the uproar over the lust of Appius Claudius.

The tradition in other writers is not so very different. Dionysius of Halicarnassus makes C. Terentius responsible for the first attempt to establish equality of rights,[9] and he states that in the following year the tribunes claimed that the best political institutions for free men are an equality of rights, and that all business, private and public, should be carried on in accordance with law. Dionysius adds that at that time there was no equality of rights for the Romans, that only a very few laws were written down, and only the patricians had knowledge even of these.[10] As early as 459 in Dionysius' version, the tribunes promised the *concilium plebis* that they would bring forward a law that ten men should be chosen in assembly who were to draw up laws on all matters, public and private, and that the code should be exposed in the forum for the benefit of both magistrates and private citizens.[11] The patricians again were able to hold things up, but eventually ambassadors were sent both to Athens and the Greek cities in Italy and they returned in 450.[12] A proposal of Appius Claudius was accepted to the effect that ten men be appointed to form a body of laws from both Roman usage and the Greek laws brought back by the ambassadors, and that all other magistracies be abolished so long as the decemviri held office.[13]

Only Livy and Dionysius report an embassy to Athens.

[6] 3.34.   [7] 11.23.   [8] 3.36,37.   [9] 10.1.5.
[10] 10.1.2-4.   [11] 10.3.3f.   [12] 10.54.3.
[13] 10.55.4f.

Other sources at most speak in general of travels to Greek cities which in some cases may mean only to the cities of Magna Graecia.[14]

It cannot be to the purpose of this book to investigate in full the accuracy of the tradition of the genesis and aims of the xii Tables, but it is appropriate to consider what light is thrown on that code by its provisions on family structure. Not much help can be provided by property law since we have so little background information.

At the outset, one can say that there is no evidence of Greek influence, whether from Athens or from nearer home, on the relevant provisions. But no one would wish to attribute any significance to this fact.[15] Again, though it is not really relevant to this book, it may be mentioned that the

[14] Cicero *Verr.* II.5.72.187; D.1.2.2.4 (Pomponius *sing. enchirid.*); Pliny the Younger *epist.* 5.24.4; Florus *Ep.* 1.24.1; D.1.2.2.24 (Pomponius *sing. enchirid.*). For a different tradition of Greek influence (from Hermodorus) see Pliny the Elder *HN* 34.2 and again D.1.2.2.4.

[15] For the literature on the question of Greek influence on the xii Tables see F. Wieacker, "Solon und die xii Tafeln," in *Studi Volterra* 3 (Milan, Giuffrè, 1971), 757ff, at 757, n. 1 and add Ogilvie, *Commentary*, pp. 449f. On the whole I am not persuaded that there was much Greek influence on the form or substance of the code: see *Legal Transplants: an Approach to Comparative Law* (Edinburgh, Scottish Academic Press, and Charlottesville, University Press of Virginia, 1974), pp. 25ff. The strongest arguments for direct influence seem to come from the similarities between two provisions on mourning restrictions in the laws of Solon and two similar ones in the xii Tables: see Wieacker, "Solon," pp. 772ff. But against too great a resemblance in the provisions imposing limits on the garments which might be buried with the corpse see Watson, *Transplants*, p. 25, n. 23. (Restrictions of this kind are also to be found in other societies, for instance among Jews: see D. Daube, *Roman Law, Linguistic, Social and Philosophical Aspects* [Edinburgh, Edinburgh University Press, 1969], p. 128). The other provisions relied on seem even more dissimilar. Solon forbade laceration of the flesh by mourners, the use of set lamentations, etc. at the funeral ceremonies of another (Plutarch *Solon* 21.4) while the xii Tables forbade women to tear their cheeks at funerals. Solon's provision, but not the Roman, was against *commercialized* mourning: see Wieacker, "Solon," pp. 776f. Even if it should be conceded that the mourning provisions of the xii Tables owe something to the laws of Solon, it is inconceivable that burial and mourning practices previously unknown to the Romans were accepted by them once they were observed to

code is not at all concerned with the *imperium* of the consuls or other magistrates, or indeed with public law at all. Likewise, the provisions which contain a sacral element are not concerned with the organization of the state religion or with the offices of religious dignitaries.

The first major matter which we should consider is whether the XII Tables enshrines in private law class distinctions between persons who are freeborn citizens. The answer must be that it does, but to a surprisingly small degree. The most important instance is the prohibition of intermarriage between patrician and plebeian. But this is an exceptional case, and appears in the Roman tradition itself as the work of the second, tyrannous, set of decemviri.[16] It also appears to have been an innovation and caused so much resentment among the plebs that the *lex Canuleia* of 445 once again allowed intermarriage. Yet, however insulting the provision might have seemed to the mass of the plebs, in practical terms it would have affected only the upmost ranks of the plebeians who would be as different from the mass of the plebs as the patricians were.[17] Nonetheless, the clause was written in what was conceived to be the interest of the patricians.

A further instance is the provision on patron and client, "Patronus si clienti fraudem fecerit, sacer esto." This is concerned to regulate matters between individuals who have a particular relationship with one another, not the relationship of any patrician to any plebeian. Yet it is of general importance since *clientela* was so common, and at least earlier all plebeians were *clientes* to some patrician. The provision imposes a (negative) obligation on the patron, and

---

exist in far away Athens. One would have to postulate that the practices were already known to the Romans, presumably as a result of contact with Magna Graecia.

[16] A second decemvirate is sometimes denied, e.g. by Gjerstad, *Early Rome* 5, p. 98.

[17] See supra, pp. 20ff.

there is no corresponding provision dealing with the obligations of a *cliens*. To that extent the XII Tables should be regarded as favoring and protecting the *clientes*. Whether or not it was the case—as it seems to have been in the regal period—that *patroni* were always patricians and *clientes* always plebeians, we can be sure that in general the *clientes* were the humbler free members of society. The positive *legal* duties which were imposed on both *patroni* and *clientes* by laws of the kings seem to have disappeared, though on both sides the social duties remained strong.[18]

The remaining instance of a social distinction being enshrined in private law is rather obscure: "Assiduo vindex assiduus esto; proletario iam civi quis volet vindex esto."[19] The text concerns the giving of a surety on behalf of a defendant who has just been summoned *in ius*.[20] A defendant who is an *assiduus*—which probably means "landowner" though certainty is not possible[21]—can only have another *assiduus* as *vindex*, though anyone can be *vindex* for a *proletarius*, which must here mean a person of lesser stature. The provision can scarcely be regarded as discriminating against the lower classes, and it rests on economic desirability. But two things stand out. In the first place, the distinction is based on the social standing of the defendant, not on the amount at issue in the lawsuit. One might see class soli-

---

[18] See supra, pp. 101f.

[19] Aulus Gellius *NA* 16.10.5. The manuscript tradition of Gellius is not secure at this point, and it may be, for instance, that *iam* should be deleted: see P. K. Marshall, *A. Gellii Noctes Atticae* 2 (Oxford, Clarendon Press, 1968), 489. F. Wieacker prefers ". . . proletario iam civis qui volet"; "Zwölftafelprobleme," *RIDA* 3 (1956), 459ff, at 464: but Gellius at §6 shows that he takes *proletarius* and *civis* together. (This may allow us to decide what Gellius wrote in §5, but not that his version of the XII Tables' provision was accurate.)

[20] We are not well informed on this topic; see e.g. L. Wenger, *Institutionen des römischen Zivilprozessrechts* (Munich, M. Hueber, 1925), pp. 92f; Kaser, *ZPR*, p. 49 and the works cited by these authors.

[21] Nor is it needed in the present context; but see Gjerstad, *Early Rome* 5, p. 311. For texts which may throw light on the meaning of *assiduus* and *proletarius* see Bruns, p. 18.

darity in this, but the provision would rather tend to help a *proletarius* who was sued for a sizable amount since he might find it very difficult if the only person who could be a *vindex* for him was an *assiduus*. In the second place, the distinction is not between the two groups supposedly at odds, the patricians and plebeians, but is a much more practical one between those who are seemingly economically reliable and those who are not.

Thus, legal distinctions between groups or classes of freeborn persons are not at all prominent in the xii Tables. For instance, there is nothing akin to the rules in some ancient Near Eastern codes where the status of the free victim might determine the penalty for assault or theft. This conclusion gives rise to a second question: Are there provisions in the xii Tables which would apply only to patricians or at least to the very rich? The answer is a heavily qualified affirmative.

Thus, it would seem that a clause mentioned the acquisition of *manus* by *confarreatio*,[22] and *confarreatio* was presumably restricted to patricians.[23] But *confarreatio* appears in the provision only as one of a list of the ways of creating *manus* and it is not stressed. Interestingly, it is the second of three—the least obvious—in the list, which itself does not talk of *manus* being acquired by *confarreatio* but uses the neutral word *far*.[24] Again one might suspect that adoption by *adrogatio* or the making of a *testamentum calatis comitiis* would in practice be restricted to the wealthy and socially prominent, since both were legislative acts before the *comitia calata*. Both institutions existed, it seems, though neither is mentioned in the xii Tables. Lastly in this connection should be mentioned succession on intestacy by the *gentiles* as ultimate heirs. It has been suggested in this book that succession by *gentiles* would very much favor the

[22] For the argument see supra, pp. 9ff.

[23] Supra, p. 14.

[24] Not too much should be made of this point since the word *confarreatio* may be a later coinage.

upper classes,[25] and if this is correct then it becomes worth noting that the fact does not appear on the face of the provision. Much more important, then, become the signs that the rule that the nearest agnate should take the inheritance if there was no *suus heres* was an innovation. The rights of the *gentiles* and hence of the upper classes were being diminished.

These, then, are the provisions of the XII Tables which either give legal backing to social distinction or whose application would be restricted to the rich and powerful. They are neither numerous nor prominent. The effect of considering them together is to emphasize just how much out of harmony with the other provisions is the prohibition on intermarriage between patrician and plebeian.

The tradition of the background to the XII Tables points another question, namely, to what extent was the code innovating or restating existing law? No straightforward answer can be given, either for the code as a whole or for the provisions more closely concerned with family structure. If one believes that an embassy was sent either to the Greek mainland or to Magna Graecia then one would also believe that considerable law reform was at least envisaged. If one thinks that the laws which are reported for the regal period were neither repealed by later legislation nor fell into desuetude, then one would think that the XII Tables were responsible for much reform. The real problem is the absence of sufficient background information. Of the provisions which concern this book, pride of place must again be given to the prohibition of intermarriage between pleb and patrician. Once more, it must be emphasized what a special case this is. It was not part of the Ten Tables, hence not part of any original scheme, but was the work of the tyrannous second decemviri. A special case in a different way is a second instance, "Uti legassit super pecunia tutelave suae rei." It was argued above[26] that the purpose of the clause was to give legal recognition of what had become the prac-

---

[25] Supra, pp. 67f.　　　　[26] p. 61.

tice of making bequests and appointing *tutores* by means of a modified *mancipatio*. Hence, what is new is solely the statutory approval which provides the theoretical justification for what was being done in any event.

A straightforward case of innovation, however, seems to exist in the provision which opened up intestate succession to the nearest agnate. One may say that this reduced the possibility of the upper classes taking as *gentiles*, and one may even claim that there had been resentment at the rights of the *gentiles*; nonetheless, the basic reason for opening succession to the *agnatus proximus* must have been the feeling that in the absence of a *suus heres* it was wrong that agnates should be excluded from inheriting.

If the preceding paragraph is correct, and succession by the *agnatus proximus* is an innovation, then by necessary implication we must find that other provisions are also innovatory! That a connection exists between the right to be *tutor* or *curator* and the right to be heir on intestacy is well established. Yet there seems to have been a clause of the code calling agnates to the *tutela* of an *impubes* when no *tutor* had been appointed by the will of the *pater*.[27] Another clause gave agnates (followed by *gentiles*) *potestas* over the person and property of a lunatic,[28] and yet another provided that the property of a prodigal should be in the *curatio* of his agnates. All these must be saying something new if previously agnates had had no rights of intestate succession. If this is so, it is difficult to resist the conclusion that other clauses must contain innovations which are hidden from us.[29]

Three provisions seem to repeat earlier legislation. This is said to be so of the rule that *vindiciae* should always be given *secundum libertatem*,[30] which for the XII Tables is said to be the work of Appius Claudius who was a member

[27] See supra, pp. 71ff.   [28] See supra, pp. 76ff.
[29] The suggestion should be remembered that prescription of land in two years is an innovation: see supra, pp. 150f.
[30] D.1.2.2.24 (Pomponius *sing. enchirid.*).

of both decemvirates.[31] If Dionysius of Halicarnassus is to be trusted, the provision, "Si pater filium ter venum duit, etc." repeats legislation of Romulus.[32] Gaius relates that a provision of the XII Tables gave Vestals freedom from *tutela*, while Numa is given the credit for that rule by Plutarch.[33] Then the interdiction of prodigals is said to have existed as a result of custom before it was enshrined in the XII Tables.[34]

The XII Tables is, of course, not a code in the modern sense: there was no intention of setting out the whole of the law. But the question must be asked whether there was any intention of setting out the rules on everyday matters, perhaps where the law might be considered doubtful? Are there provisions regulating unusual or uncommon situations? To this latter question—which clarifies the former— the answer is an emphatic yes. Divorce, as we have seen, must have been exceedingly rare, yet there was a clause on the subject.[35] Nor can the interdiction and *curatio* of prodigals have been common but both were covered by the code.[36] It should perhaps be noted, however, that both *interdictio* and divorce existed before the XII Tables.[37]

Finally, would the XII Tables have enabled the plebeians to know what the law was, and to exercise their private law rights? No! Law remained a mystery. Though the code is explicit on how to summon a defendant to court, on appropriate sureties and so on, there is not a word on the forms of action. One would not learn from the code how to frame the appropriate *legis actio*. It is in this fact that we should see the importance attached by tradition to the *Ius civile Flavianum* which was issued, if at all, in 304 B.C. or slightly earlier. In this, Gn. Flavius, scribe to Appius Claudius Cae-

---

[31] See supra, pp. 95f. [32] See supra, p. 131.
[33] See supra, p. 76. [34] See supra, p. 79.
[35] See supra, pp. 33ff. [36] See supra, pp. 78ff.

[37] A different situation which need not be discussed here is involved in the provisions containing a savage sanction on debtor or wrong-doer if a compromise is not reached, and where there is no evidence that the savage sanction was ever inflicted in fact: see supra, pp. 121ff.

cus, first published the forms of action[38] which had previously been knowledge jealously guarded by the pontiffs.[39] Hence also the practical importance of Sextus Aelius Paetus' *tripertita* of around 200 B.C. which set out not only each clause of the XII Tables and its interpretation, but also the appropriate *legis actio*.[40] Again, there was nothing in the code on the form and main effects of *mancipatio*, nothing on the modes of acquisition of ownership apart from *usus*, nothing on minimum age, prohibited degrees of relationship, and the necessary consents for marriage, no provision dealt with the manumission of slaves, and so the list could go on. David Daube has recently emphasized one reason for omissions, namely, that a basic rule can be so taken for granted that it is not referred to: only the really needful is set out, the settlement of doubts and reforms.[41] On this basis he explains the omission from the XII Tables of, *inter alia*, the grounds of enslavement. The acuteness of the general observation cannot be denied, but how far this provides a full or satisfactory explanation for what is omitted and for what is contained in the XII Tables cannot be determined in the state of our present knowledge.

[38] D.1.2.2.7 (Pomponius *sing. enchirid.*).

[39] Livy 9.46.5. We need not enquire too closely into the accuracy of the tradition.

[40] See Watson, *Law Making*, pp. 112f.

[41] "The Self-Understood in Legal History," *Juridical Review* 18 (1973), 126ff. Other omissions are to be explained, he says, by the fact that law keeps out.

Index of Texts

I. Legal Sources

Library of Congress Cataloging in Publication Data

Watson, Alan.
 Rome of the XII Tables.

 Includes bibliographical references and index.
  1. Leges XII tabularum. 2. Persons (Roman law)
3. Inheritance and succession (Roman law) 4. Property
(Roman law) I. Title.
Law   346'.37'01   75-3481
ISBN 0-691-03548-2